WOLFHOUNDS
AND
POLAR BEARS

WOLFHOUNDS AND POLAR BEARS

THE AMERICAN EXPEDITIONARY FORCE IN SIBERIA, 1918–1920

Col. JOHN M. HOUSE, US Army (Retired)

THE UNIVERSITY OF ALABAMA PRESS
Tuscaloosa

The University of Alabama Press
Tuscaloosa, Alabama 35487-0380
uapress.ua.edu

Hardcover edition published 2016.
Paperback edition published 2019.
eBook edition published 2016.

Typeface: Garamond and Helvetica

Cover image: General Graves and staff and Ataman Seminoff and aides; courtesy of National Archives and Records Administration
Cover design: Michele Myatt Quinn

Paperback ISBN: 0-8173-5949-2

A previous edition of this book has been catalogued by the Library of Congress as follows:
Library of Congress Cataloging-in-Publication Data
Names: House, John M., author.
Title: Wolfhounds and polar bears : the American Expeditionary Force in Siberia, 1918–1920 / Col. John M. House, US Army (Retired).
Description: Tuscaloosa : The University of Alabama Press, 2016. | Includes bibliographical references and index.
Identifiers: LCCN 2015039996| ISBN 9780817318895 (cloth : alk. paper) | ISBN 9780817388980 (ebook)
Subjects: LCSH: Soviet Union—History—Allied intervention, 1918–1920. | Soviet Union—History—Revolution, 1917–1921—Participation, American. | United States. Army. American Expeditionary Forces.
Classification: LCC DK265.42.U5 H68 2016 | DDC 947.084/1—dc23
LC record available at http://lccn.loc.gov/2015039996

Contents

Acknowledgments

No endeavor such as this is the work of one person. My study of the intervention in Siberia began when I decided to undertake a masters in history from the University of Kansas while assigned to the Combined Arms Operations Research Activity (CAORA) at Fort Leavenworth, Kansas, in 1984 (CAORA eventually became the Training and Doctrine Command Analysis Command—Fort Leavenworth or TRAC-FLVN). Fortunately I was able to take some courses through the US Army Command and General Staff College at Fort Leavenworth. I also took a few courses at the University of Kansas main campus. My previous tour in Germany had sparked an intense interest in history. Dr. Ted Wilson from the University of Kansas served as the chair of my committee. His understanding of the dual pressures I faced in a full-time duty position at Fort Leavenworth combined with his astute mentorship kept me on track regardless of the challenges I faced. After taking a few courses I began to look for a topic. Dr. Larry Yates of the Combat Studies Institute at Fort Leavenworth suggested the Siberian intervention as a topic, served on my committee, and was one of my professors through the Command and General Staff College. Dr. Lloyd Sponholtz of the University of Kansas rounded out my committee and provided an important reminder that business interests affect history including this intervention. My other professor in this degree effort was Dr. George Gawrych from the Combat Studies Institute whose specialty was Middle East history. While this was not directly related to this research, his enthusiasm for history provided me continual inspiration to learn more regardless of the region of the world concerned.

Of course, I have to thank the staff of the University of Alabama Press and in particular Mr. Dan Waterman. Without their help, this manuscript might never have reached publication. Preserving the story of the people who served in such a cold and faraway place has been a goal of mine for years that came to fruition thanks to the University of Alabama Press. Susan Harris also warrants special mention for her willingness to work with me to edit the manuscript into the form you see. I very much appreciate her patience and attention to detail.

The staffs of several libraries were of immense assistance in this effort that began in 1984 in Kansas. The staff of the Combined Arms Research Library of the US Army Command and General Staff School provided me assistance in using the records of the American Expeditionary Force–Siberia on microfilm and in finding several student papers regarding the operations in Siberia. The librarians at the Donovan Research Library of the US Army Infantry School (now part of the Maneuver Center of Excellence) at Fort Benning, Georgia, helped me find several student research papers written by members of the American Expeditionary Force (AEF) when later assigned to Fort Benning for school. The staff of the Kautz Family YMCA Archives at the University of Minnesota Library provided valuable information regarding YMCA activities and experiences in Siberia. The librarians at Duke University helped me locate a microfilm copy of Gen. Robert L. Eichelberger's papers from the expedition. Librarians from the University of Georgia and from the Columbus Public Library, Columbus, Georgia, helped me unravel the mystery behind the name of one officer in the AEF who was awarded the Distinguished Service Cross for heroism. Mr. Ron Basich acted as my research assistant with the papers of Maj. Gen. William S. Graves held by the Hoover Institution Archives at Stanford University.

I would also be remiss if I did not acknowledge the staff of the Columbus State University Library, which honored numerous interlibrary loan requests for materials not held locally. The staff of the National Archives worked very hard to help me identify photographs to include in this book. Without the assistance of these wonderful people, who were always energetic in their willingness to help, writing this book would have become very frustrating and ultimately a failure.

I must also thank the Association of the US Army, specifically Lt. Col. (retired) Roger Cirillo. Roger encouraged me to keep pushing ahead when I was about to give up. His counsel and encouragement were much appreciated. Mr. Tim Frank was of invaluable assistance in tracking down many of the maps and photographs you see enclosed.

Of course, my family always deserves thanks for their willingness to put up with my musings and the periodic gleam in my eye when I would announce "I'm going to Siberia" or some such thing. Shannon and Amanda, my oldest children, who now are adults and married, suffered through my absences in their youth while I pored over old documents and made countless notes. Mary and Carole, my youngest daughters and also now all grown up, were blessed with missing most of this mania except when they came home from college after I took up the Siberia quest once again. My best friend and spouse of many years, Marilyn, actually typed my original draft on our first computer, while using a shareware word processing program. Then when I decided to tackle the subject and expand it into a book twenty years later, Marilyn agreed to retype it because we no longer had an electronic copy that our more modern computer system could process. This gave me a point of departure for the book. The current book is greatly expanded from the original manuscript. Marilyn will always hold a special place in my heart because she has always done so much for me in this and so many other endeavors. She knows more than anyone what I meant when I had to go to Siberia.

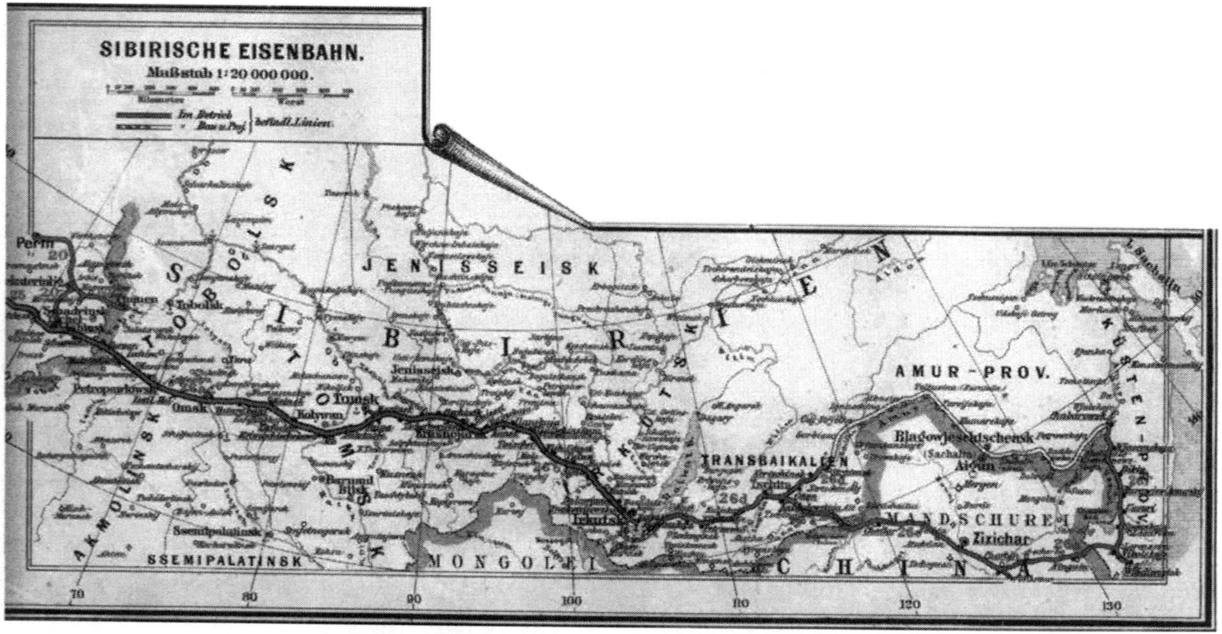

Map 1. Trans-Siberian Railroad, 1897

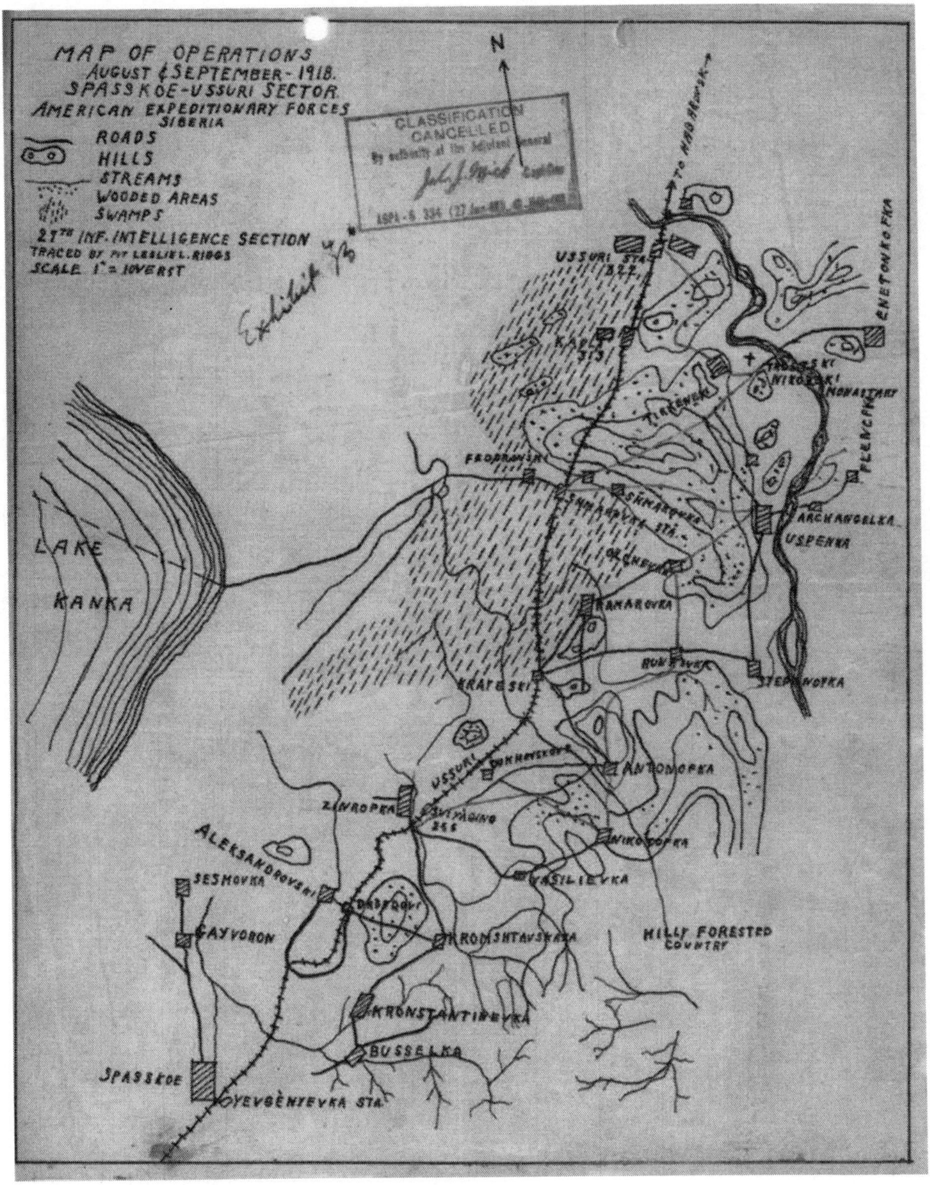

Map 2. Map of Operations, August and September 1918, Spasskoe-Ussuri Sector. National Archives and Records Administration.

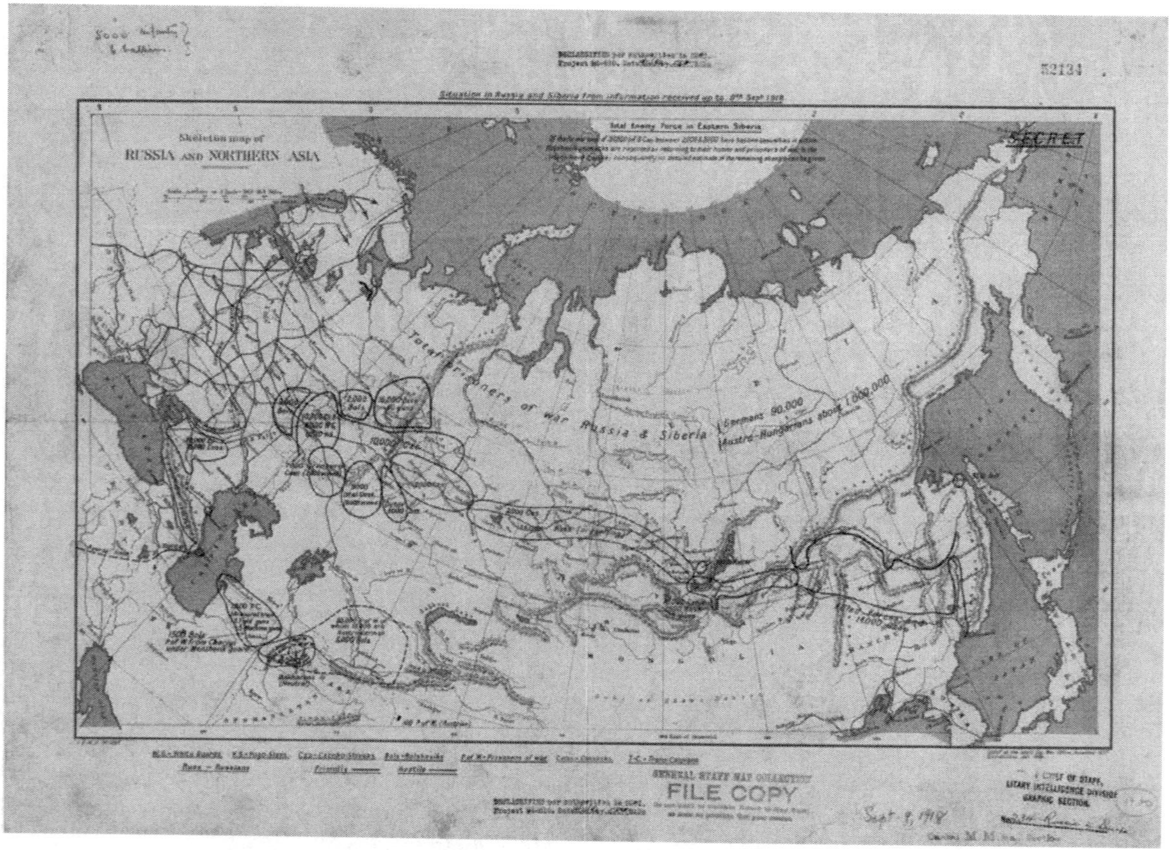

Map 3. Situation in Russia and Siberia from information received up to September 9, 1918. National Archives and Records Administration.

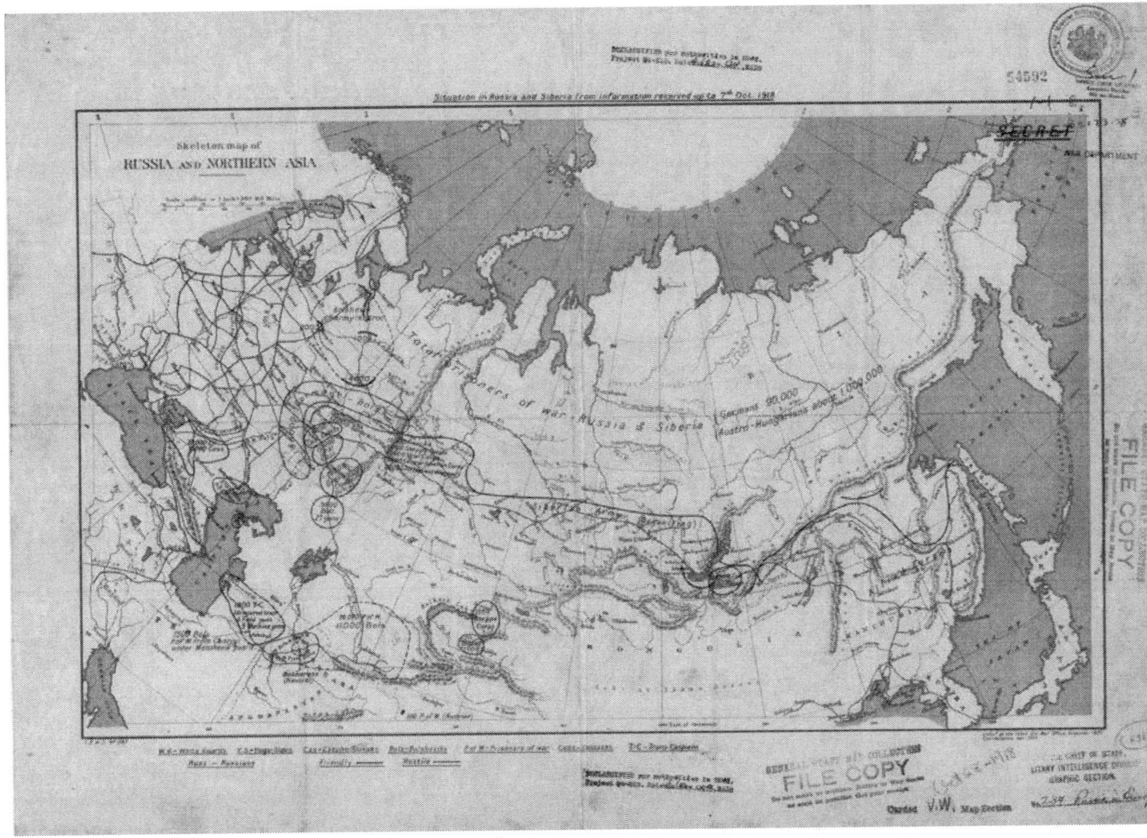

Map 4. Situation in Russia and Siberia from information received up to October 7, 1918. National Archives and Records Administration.

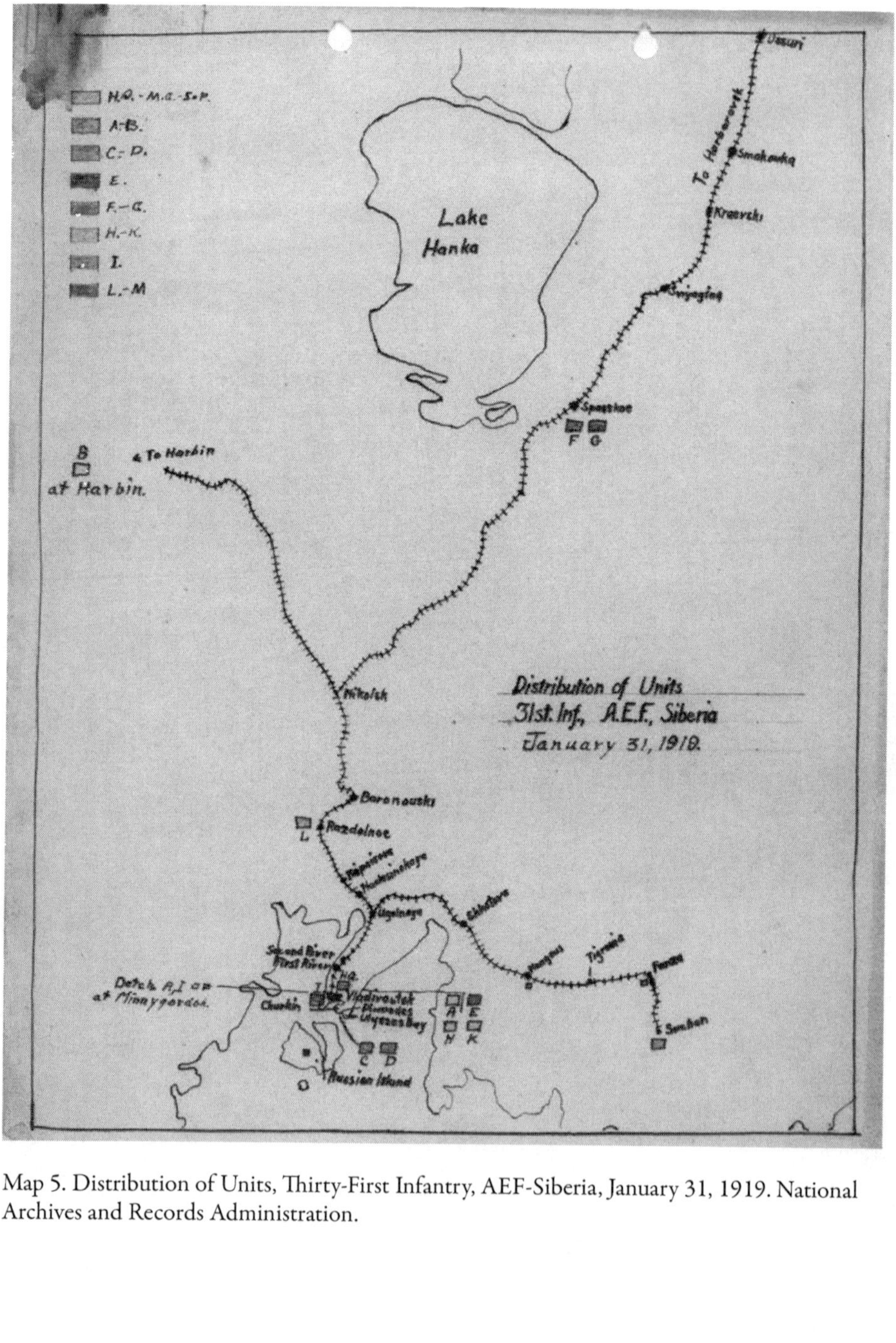

Map 5. Distribution of Units, Thirty-First Infantry, AEF-Siberia, January 31, 1919. National Archives and Records Administration.

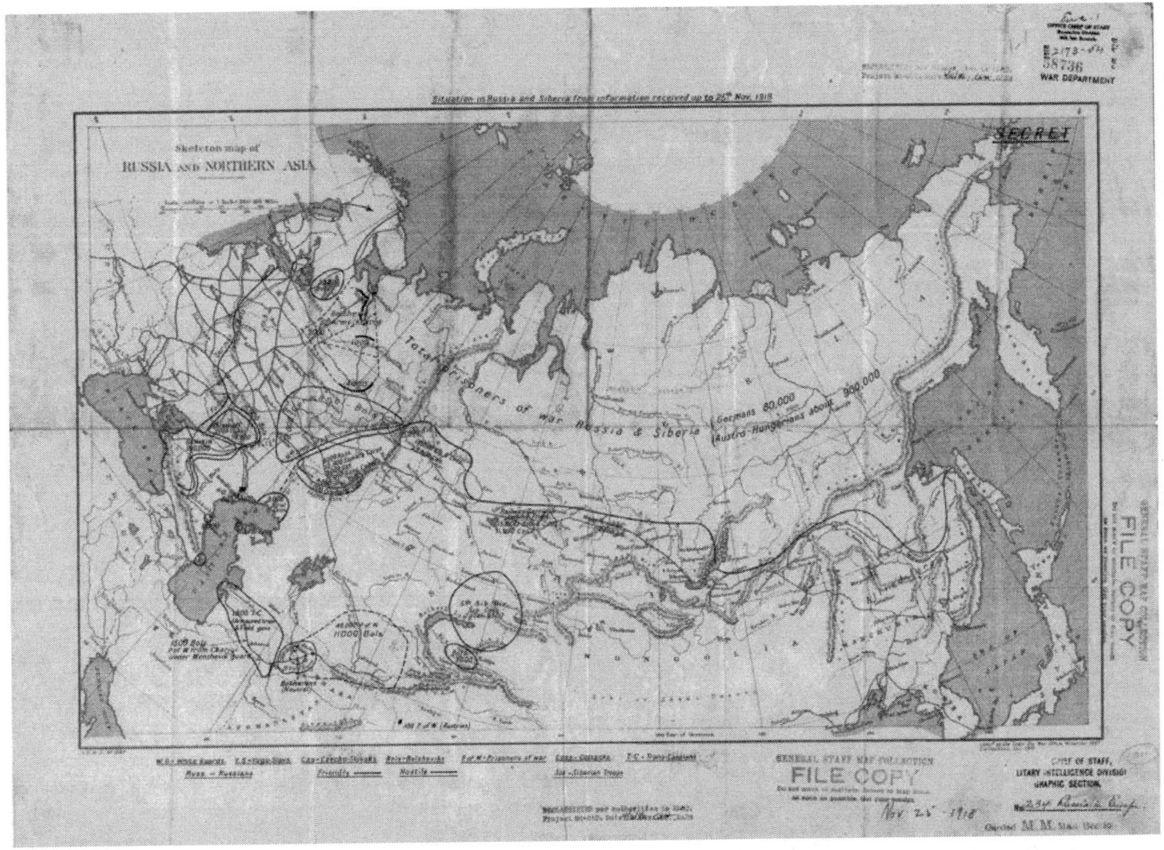

Map 6. Situation in Russia and Siberia from information received up to November 25, 1918. National Archives and Records Administration.

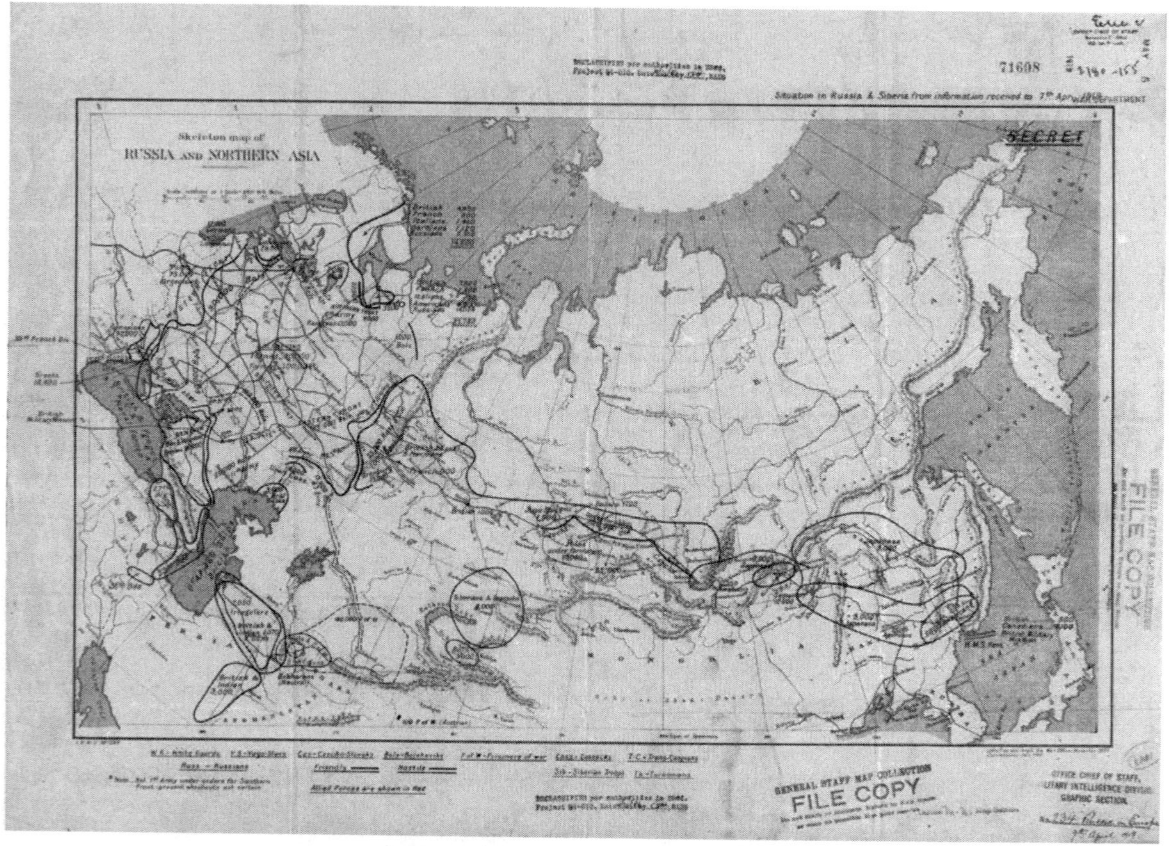

Map 7. Situation in Russia and Siberia from information received up to April 7, 1919. National Archives and Records Administration.

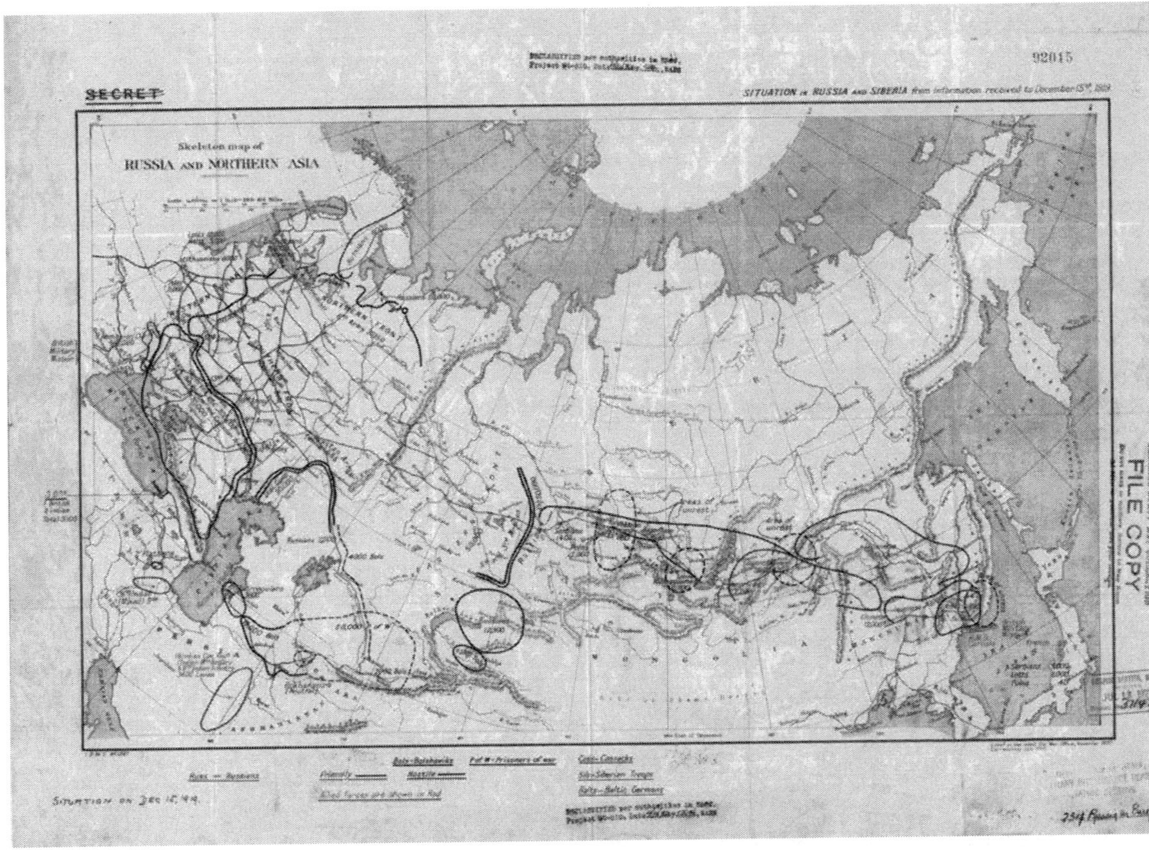

Map 8. Situation in Russia and Siberia from information received up to December 15, 1919. National Archives and Records Administration.

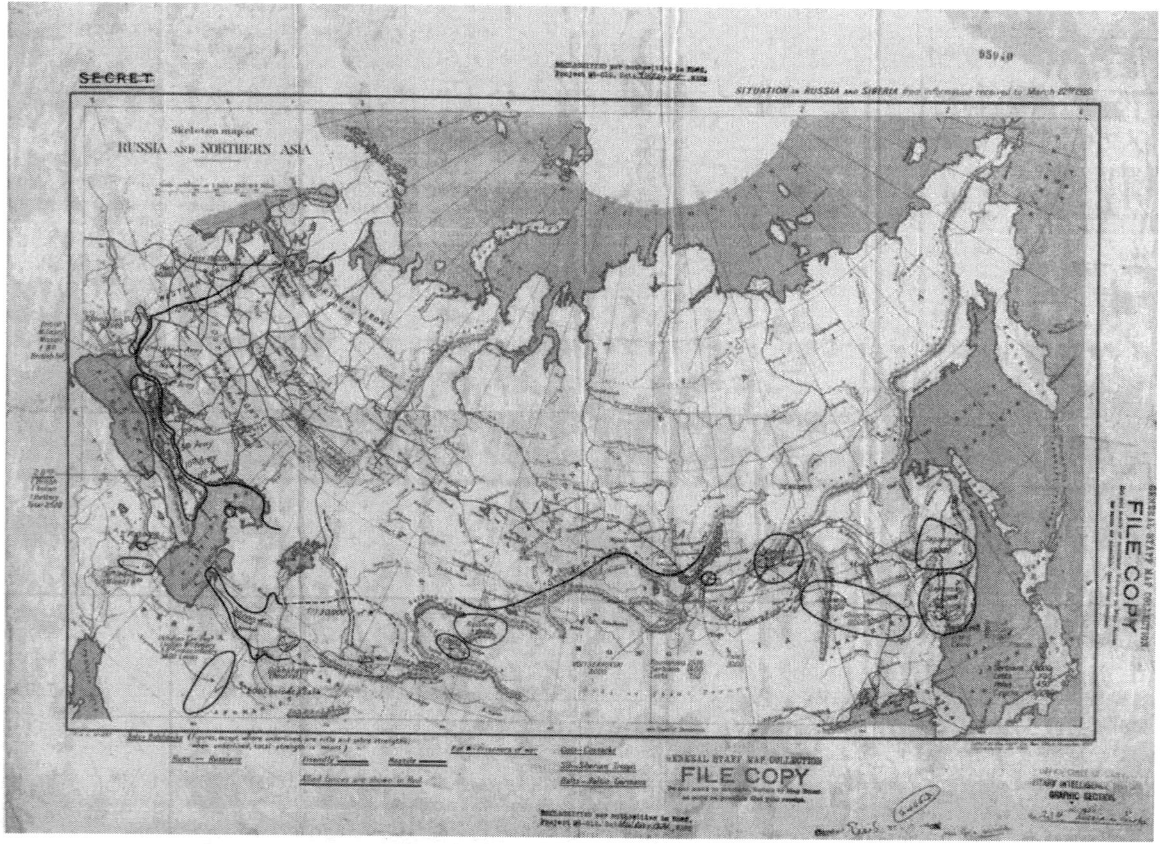

Map 9. Situation in Russia and Siberia from information received up to March 22, 1920. National Archives and Records Administration.

WOLFHOUNDS AND POLAR BEARS

1
The Beginning

World War I was in its final months though no one knew that was the case. One of the Allies was caught in the death throes of a civil war. American doughboys were fighting alongside French and British soldiers in the trenches on the Western Front. America's families were learning the pain of loss and worry over loved ones far away. The Great War was ending its fourth year. The date was August 6, 1918.

A late evening meeting at a train station in the Midwest marked the start of a remarkable adventure that few Americans today know anything about. The details seem almost to come from a spy novel in which two men meet quietly in an out-of-the-way location to launch thousands of young men on an invasion of a foreign nation halfway around the world. The situation is murky. The threat is unclear. Intelligence is limited. Strong-willed military and civilian leaders from the United States and its allies argued for and against the invasion. Insufficient numbers of American or Allied soldiers were available for occupying the entire country.

Imagine the thoughts rolling through the mind of Maj. Gen. William S. Graves —an 1889 graduate of the US Military Academy and commander of the US Army's Eighth Division headquartered at Camp Fremont, California—when he was summoned to a meeting in Kansas City, Missouri, by the US Secretary of War Newton Baker.[1] Graves arrived at the Kansas City train station at 10:00 P.M. after a two-day train ride from his duty station. Time was short so rather than meet at the Baltimore Hotel as planned, the two men discussed a fateful decision at the train station. Baker told Graves he would lead the American Expeditionary Force (AEF) that was deploying to Siberia. Baker also said, "If in the future you want to cuss anybody for sending you to Siberia I am the man." Graves received a sealed envelope with a seven-page letter titled "Aide Memoire" dated July 17, 1918. This document provides an outline of American policy in Russia. Baker's last instructions to Graves were, "Watch your step; you will be walking on eggs loaded with dynamite. God bless you and good-bye."[2] Such words would make anyone wonder just what they had been told to do. Graves would discover just how much dynamite was in those eggs in the months ahead. The American soldiers with him would also discover the truth in Baker's warning.

Earlier in 1918, Graves had been the executive assistant to the US Army Chief of Staff, Gen. Peyton C. March, who had handpicked him for the Siberia assignment with the personal approval of the secretary of war. One of Graves's assistants was Capt. Robert L. Eichelberger, who would later rise to be a general officer himself. When Graves learned that he was to take command of a division to deploy overseas, he had Eichelberger select a division for the two of them to join. Therefore, Graves and Eichelberger found themselves reassigned to the Eighth Division at Camp Fremont, near Palo Alto, California, in July 1918. Graves expected the division to deploy to Europe in late August. During their trip to California, Graves told Eichelberger that the government was considering sending soldiers to Siberia with him as the commander even though March had assured Graves that he would go to Europe and not Siberia. Eichelberger, who would stay with Graves and accompany him to Siberia serving as chief of staff and intelligence officer at different times during the deployment as the AEF-Siberia experienced the typical rotation in personnel, would rise to the rank of lieutenant colonel. Maj. Sidney Graves, the general's son, also would deploy to Siberia. Obviously, General Graves's plans to command in Europe changed. While Graves did not show his staff the complete "Aide Memoire" at any time, the document served as their guide to American policy throughout their stay in Siberia.[3]

Graves's new mission would take him thousands of miles away to a land where few Americans had been and even fewer wanted to visit. He would have to balance the demands of the Allies and American officials with the needs of his soldiers and the human suffering of the people who lived in the region. Orders and morality would sometimes conflict. Throughout this mission the instructions in the "Aide Memoire" would serve as a guide. Graves worked hard to achieve this balance so he could follow his orders and protect the innocent civilians in Siberia. The soldiers of the Twenty-Seventh Infantry Regiment Wolfhounds and the Thirty-First Infantry Regiment Polar Bears[4] provided the muscle when he needed it whether in combat or humanitarian support. Their sacrifices are not well known, but they are worth remembering.

The following story will cover the reasons the US leadership decided to land soldiers in Siberia during the Russian civil war and while World War I still raged in Western Europe. Understanding the events on the Western Front and within revolution-torn Russia is necessary to begin to understand why American soldiers found themselves in Siberia. The poor road network made railway operations critical. The people controlling the railroad controlled the movement of people and supplies in the region. The discussion of AEF-Siberia operations will demonstrate the soldiers' efforts to cope with combat and humanitarian missions in a strange and very challenging environment, where even erstwhile allies could be enemies.

Even though few people know much about this intervention, it was one of the United States' first efforts in the twentieth century to use military power overseas to protect its interests without a formal declaration of war. The intervention in Siberia was part counterinsurgency, part combat, and part stability operation. The American soldiers persevered under trying circumstances and always tried to accomplish the assigned mission, even when the situation was unclear and the means to do so not always available. Shifting alliances and weak allies are not new experiences, though such lessons are not always easily learned.

Our history also can influence our present. Nations can have very different understandings of the same events. These differing views can then influence how national leaders relate to one another. The story of the intervention in Siberia includes the fear of Bolshevism that influenced the decision by the World War I Allies to send troops to northern Russia and Siberia. Time did little to reduce that tension between the Communist Soviet Union and the capitalist Western democracies. During World War II, in order to combat a common foe in Nazi Germany, Western democracies joined forces with the Communist Soviet Union. This alliance resulted in victory but did not develop into friendly relations for very long. The Cold War and division of Europe after World War II made these conflicts in objectives and policies very clear. The differences in political and economic systems ensured some level of disagreement, and the Soviet leaders also remembered that the Western powers had invaded their land once before.

The premier of the Soviet Union, Nikita Khrushchev, visited Los Angeles, California, on September 19, 1959. In his speech, he noted the thanks of the Russian people for American humanitarian support in 1922. However, he also remarked, "We also remember the grim days when immediately after the great October Revolution American soldiers went to our soil headed by their generals to help our White Guard combat the revolution." Khrushchev went on to blame Great Britain, Germany, Japan, Poland, and all other capitalist countries in Europe for the devastating civil war that closed factories and ruined farms, which caused famine. However, American relief saved children from starving.[5] Clearly Khrushchev remembered the Siberian intervention and blamed the West for the deprivations and loss of lives that followed. With such thoughts on his mind, it is no small wonder that some level of distrust of Western motivations or possible actions might have colored any decision he made.

Contrast this with President Richard Nixon's televised speech in the Soviet Union in May 1972. Nixon remarked that the United States and Soviet Union "have never fought one another in war." Nixon recalled the meeting of American and Soviet soldiers at the Elbe River during World War II including that both countries were allies fighting a common enemy. He saw the United States and Soviet Union as having had common interests at least once in our histories.[6] Nixon did not know or did not acknowledge that Americans and Soviet soldiers had at one time fought one another. President Ronald Reagan made similar comments in his 1984 State of the Union address. Reagan called for the people of the Soviet Union to support the United States in ridding the world of nuclear weapons. As a preface to these comments he emphasized that the two countries had never fought each other in a war.[7] A *New York Times* survey conducted in 1985 found only 14 percent of Americans knew that the United States had sent soldiers to Siberia in 1918.[8] Given that it has now been over ninety-five years since American soldiers deployed to Siberia and northern Russia, this history is most likely receding from the consciousness of most Americans. This lack of understanding of the conflict in American and Soviet history could not help but add to the mistrust accompanying interactions between two nations or groups of nations. There is no common understanding of our pasts upon which to base future interactions.

As our nation interacts with other nations in government and business, it is important for us to understand our corresponding views of our joint history. These memories may affect our willingness to cooperate or assist each other. Understanding the history of our allies and our enemies is important so that we also understand our resulting attitudes toward our futures. This then should help two countries find a common ground to meet other than a battlefield. At least such a goal is better than ignoring our past and finding that a relationship that might have been repaired was not.

The following chapters will afford an opportunity to review the situation in World War I, when conditions in Russia argued for intervention, as well as the varied reasons for that decision. A description of the military forces and the geographic difficulties faced by those forces operating in Siberia provide the baseline necessary to understand the AEF-Siberia's actions. A short discussion of the Russian Railway Service Corps explains their essential and sometimes overlooked role in this story. Several chapters provide a description of the actual operations by the AEF. These chapters typically end with a discussion of military operations elsewhere in Russia in order to provide a context for the actions occurring in Siberia that are the focus of this book. However, chapter 12 differs from the others in that it focuses on the typical sights along the railway by that stage in the intervention. The experiences of Americans who traveled great distances on the railroad rather than guarded specific facilities or patrolled areas around cities, railroad infrastructure, or other fixed sites provide a different perspective regarding events in Siberia. The final days of the AEF in the country are described next and followed by conclusions that can be drawn from the intervention. Throughout this operation, the lack of a clear mission supported by all elements of the US government and our Allies would interfere with America's soldiers surviving and accomplishing anything of value. Sit back now and get ready for a journey to a land far away during a period of time few people remember.

2
A World at War

An assassin's bullet began the twentieth century's bloody conflict now known as World War I. Gavrilo Princip was a member of a Slav revolutionary group known as the Black Hand Society that was determined to form a Greater Serbia through the merger of several Slav-dominated provinces in Bosnia-Herzegovina with Serbia. Princip's heritage was Serbian, but he was an Austrian citizen. On June 28, 1914, he murdered Archduke Franz Ferdinand and the archduke's wife, Sophie, while they rode in an open car on the streets of Sarajevo on the way to visit an officer wounded in a previous assassination attempt that day from a hand-thrown bomb. Ferdinand was the heir to the throne of the Austro-Hungarian Empire. This assassination provided the justification for Austria-Hungary to attempt to crush Serbia. Unfortunately for Austria-Hungary, Russia was allied with Serbia. Nations chose sides based on powerful interests so that two basic groups resulted. Germany, Austria-Hungary, and Italy formed the Triple Alliance, though Italy would desert the Alliance in 1915. Great Britain, France, and Russia composed the Triple Entente, later known as the Allies or Allied Powers as the group enlarged. Czar Nicholas II of Russia ordered mobilization on July 31, 1914. Germany then had to mobilize to support its ally, Austria-Hungary, but now faced the possibility of a two-front war.[1]

Germany's Schlieffen Plan called for an opening attack against France if faced with a two-front war. This was part of the German plan because the German military command believed that France could mobilize faster than Russia. Defeating France before she mobilized would then allow Germany to concentrate is military power against first one front and then the other. However, to initiate this attack against France, German army forces would have to advance through neutral Belgium and Luxembourg. Even though this risked war with more countries, Germany executed its plan. Germany's military mobilized on August 1 and the government demanded free passage through Belgium on August 2. After the Belgium government refused the demand on August 3, Germany then attacked on August 5. Great Britain had a treaty obligation since 1839 to protect Belgian neutrality. Germany also was a party to this treaty but clearly chose to ignore that. Germany ignored Britain's protest of this violation and did not stop its attack, so Great Britain declared war. Patriotic fervor inspired people to celebrate war as a great adventure.[2]

The Western Front

The war evolved relatively quickly to a murderous stalemate on the Western Front. British, French, and German soldiers faced one another across a no-man's-land of torn earth, tangled debris, and shattered dreams of a quick victory and glory. Losses were appalling and robbed both sides of any chance of a rapid advance and quick end to the war. Massive artillery barrages pulverized towns into nothingness. Rotting bodies dotted the landscape until the continuous shelling obliterated any resemblance to humanity. Soldiers learned to ignore the bodies of the dead swallowed by shell craters and trenches. Farms and villages no longer covered the French countryside, which now more closely resembled the moon. Eventually airplanes, machine guns, and chlorine gas debuted during World War I and added to the carnage of the trenches. Death callously roamed Europe seeking victims on both sides. Great Britain incurred at least fifty-seven thousand casualties on a single day of battle in July 1916.[3] Europe remorselessly destroyed its manhood while the Atlantic Ocean protected the United States from the bloodlust of the Western Front. However, events in February 1917 began to unravel this feeling of safety derived from distance and a large body of water.

The German kaiser ordered unrestricted submarine warfare on February 1, 1917, in an effort to apply pressure on the Triple Entente powers. American president Woodrow Wilson severed diplomatic relations with Germany. Great Britain increased American hard feelings toward Germany by providing a January 17, 1917, telegram from Germany to Mexico. This telegram advocated an attack by Germany and Mexico against the United States if American neutrality ended.[4] A few weeks after these events, German U-boats sank several unarmed American ships, killing American citizens in an apparent direct provocation. The United States declared war on Germany on April 6, 1917.[5]

US entry into World War I came none too soon for the beleaguered Allies. Massive casualties wrecked French morale and resulted in a French army mutiny during the Nivelle Offensive of April 1917.[6] Exhaustion hindered any attempt to regain the ability to maneuver and win the war. The mobilization of the United States and the formation of the American Expeditionary Force (AEF) that then deployed to Europe was a welcomed relief. Gen. John J. Pershing commanded the AEF.

The American entry into the war did not end the struggle, of course. American soldiers needed training for war in the trenches. American troops also had to reach France. While the Allies prepared to use this new resource, weapons development continued unabated. On November 20, 1917, the first large-scale use of tanks in combat occurred near Cambrai. British tanks forged a ten thousand–yard penetration in the German line. Even though this initial success was promising, the failure to adequately reinforce this success allowed the Germans time to coordinate counterattacks that recaptured most of the lost territory.[7]

Fresh American troops on the battlefield posed a significant problem for Germany. No new allies were set to join her. Germany needed to win and to do it soon before the weight of men and materiel became unbeatable. Operation Michael was designed to hit the Cambrai to Saint Quentin portion of the Allied front near the juncture of British and French armies. Germany massed resources between November 1917 and March 1918 in order to strike a hard blow.[8] By March, six American divisions reached France and were deployed in quiet sectors. These American divisions were large compared to Allied and German divisions. An American division in 1918 was authorized a total strength of 28,059 soldiers in two brigades of two regiments each. US casualties had reached 1,722 by this point; however, only 162 American soldiers had died due to battlefield action.[9] Germany planned a great offensive before American manpower fully deployed to the front. Operation Michael began on March 21 with 6,100 German guns pounding the British lines.[10] Germany continued to attack and advance step by step until June when the Allies managed to halt the offensive. American troops continued to arrive in France throughout this period. French and US forces counterattacked on July 18, 1918, to cut off the Marne River salient.[11] The Allies had finally stopped Germany's great offensive.

The Eastern Front

Russia surprised Germany with the speed of her mobilization and then the invasion of East Prussia on August 17, 1914. While the initial Russian advance was successful, this changed when the German army concentrated against the Russian Second Army at Tannenberg. The Germans achieved this massing of forces by using only a cavalry division to slow the attacking Russian First Army to the north. Germany destroyed the Russian Second Army and captured 120,000 prisoners. Austrian forces to the south also managed to check the Russian advance.[12] Offensives and counteroffensives continued as the lines rolled back and forth with casualties mounting on both sides. Russia's lack of success and growing casualty list exacerbated problems within the country that had begun before the first shot was fired.

Russia created industrial capacity in order to produce weapons and ammunition to support a strong military; however, this also led to severe economic and social strain. Industrial modernization meant a large urban society that needed food. Unfortunately, Russian farmers were unable to produce the food required. Poor military administration, inadequate rations for soldiers, and the massive losses caused the soldiers to lose faith in the country's ability to win and to question the czar's right to rule.[13] Peasants banded together in a cooperative effort to help one another economically.[14] By March 1917, the Russian people reached a breaking point and took to the streets to protest conditions.

Food riots erupted in Petrograd, later known as Leningrad, on March 8, 1917. By March 12, the riots had exploded into revolution. Even the czar's Imperial Guard revolted against the government.[15] Civilians, police, and soldiers battled in the streets. Roving bands of armed civilians attacked police and military officers.[16] Chaos engulfed parts of the country. Czar Nicholas realized that his time as ruler was over and abdicated on March 15 in favor of his brother Michael, who never wore the crown. The Duma, or Russian parliament, formed a provisional government.[17]

Woodrow Wilson initially welcomed the revolution because he thought that this would free the Russian people from tyranny. This then would put the war in its proper place as a struggle of the forces of democracy against the evil of militarism. Corruption in the czar's government was the real problem with the Russian army. Their soldiers lacked a fighting spirit because the government's misconduct had crippled their fighting spirit. A democratic Russia would take its rightful place in this war and stabilize the Eastern Front. The leaders of the Russian Provisional Government argued that they were devoted to democracy in Russia and were a stable, middle-class group who would continue the war effort.[18] The US ambassador to Russia, David R. Francis, also welcomed the revolution and removal of the czar as the best hope for democratic reform in Russia.[19]

Socialist and non-Socialist elements of the revolution then tried to rule the country after the revolution. The non-Socialists had the political and administrative skills necessary to form and run the government. The Socialists had the organized manpower that existed in soviets composed of soldiers and industrial workers.[20] Events soon to follow would doom this initial attempt to cooperate and share power.

Officers did not fare well in the initial stages of the revolution. Sailors at Kronstadt and Helsingfors murdered their officers. The Executive Committee of the Soviet in Petrograd issued an order for all army and naval forces to elect their own committees, or soviets, and then send delegates to Petrograd after the Provisional Government formed. Actions such as these undercut the authority of military leaders and made cooperation difficult among the competing interests of the groups that established the Provisional Government. Copies of this order spread throughout Russia beginning on March 14. The order made it clear to anyone who did not support the Bolsheviks that the Bolsheviks intended to run the government eventually.[21]

The United States recognized the new Provisional Government on March 22. This provided strong moral encouragement to the Russians and encouraged American entry into the war against Germany. With the czar no longer in power, America would enter into the war without having to be an ally of an absolutist monarchy. US allies would be democracies in opposition to Germany in Europe.[22] Germany initially attempted to make peace with the Russian Provisional Government and treated it carefully. Negotiating Russia out of the war would allow Germany to realize one of its primary goals of not fighting a two-front war in Europe. The German government allowed Nicholai Lenin (born Vladimir Ilyich Ulyanov) to cross from Switzerland through Germany to Russia because he promised to overthrow the Provisional Government and make peace. Lenin arrived in Petrograd on April 16, 1917, with no interference from the Provisional Government. The leaders mistakenly believed that Lenin's negotiations with the Germans would so damage his reputation that he would not be a threat. Leon Trotsky, another important Bolshevik leader, also faced no interference when he traveled from his home in New York to Petrograd. Trotsky arrived on May 17, 1917.[23]

Alexander Kerensky, a Social Revolutionary, initially was the Provisional Government's minister of justice, then minister of war, and finally the prime minister.[24] Kerensky supported the war against Germany, which resulted in a Russian forty-five division attack toward Lemberg on July 5, 1917. The Russian soldiers advanced over twenty miles before stopping, which was remarkable given past performance and the unrest in Russia. Unfortunately the Germans counterattacked and regained all of the ground lost. Later in July, Russia's Fourth Army attacked along a sixty-mile front in the Carpathians, but the attempt failed. At this point, both sides settled into a relatively passive defense mode.[25] In the months after the czar abdicated, the Provisional Government and revolutionary groups argued over continuing the war effort. The Provisional Government was determined to prove itself a good ally of Great Britain and France. The revolutionaries wanted to make peace with Germany and end the war quickly. The All-Russian Convention of Delegates from Councils of Workmen's and Soldiers' Deputies adopted a resolution on June 25, 1917, which blamed the war on "the imperialistic tendencies of the ruling classes of all countries." The group did not call for a separate Russian peace accord with Germany. Instead, the convention demanded an "international socialist conference to reestablish the international solidarity of the working class" as a means of forcing the peace process on all of the war's belligerents.[26]

When Kerensky's offensive effort failed, the Bolsheviks attempted to overthrow the Provisional Government, but their coup failed. Lenin then fled to Finland to avoid being imprisoned. Kerensky tried to make peace with all factions in order to preserve the government.[27] He failed ultimately, and civil war resulted. The Russia he hoped to save would change its character into the Communist nation of the twentieth century.

The pitiful condition of the Russian army was evident to anyone who cared to look. An estimated 120,000 soldiers roamed the streets of Petrograd during July 1917, refusing any orders to return to the front lines.[28] After Raymond Robins, the chief of the American Red Cross mission to Russia, visited a Russian unit near Stalna in October 1917, he recorded in his diary that "the war is dead in the heart of the Russian soldier." Shortly after this visit, Robins had a revealing discussion with British general Alfred Knox with respect to the Bolsheviks. On November 2, in the Hotel Europe in Petrograd, Knox remarked, "I'll tell you what we do with such people. We shoot them." Clearly Knox did not have a high opinion of the Bolsheviks and felt comfortable letting other people know it. This attitude would cause major problems for the AEF later when it was in Siberia. Robins's reply to Knox disclosed his astute perception of reality with respect to conditions in Russia. He said, "You do if you catch them. But you will have to do some catching. General, I am not a military man. But you are not up against a military situation. You are up against a folks' situation."[29] On November 6, 1917, Ambassador Francis proposed to the American secretary of state that two or more US divisions deploy to aid Russian forces. He recommended that the divisions enter Russia via Sweden or Vladivostok and felt the moral effect of such a decision would be more important than any material assistance provided.[30]

Unfortunately for Kerensky, the Bolsheviks did not plan to allow anyone to rule Russia other than themselves. In early November 1917, the Congress of Soviets met in Petrograd with Bolshevik delegates representing organizations spread across the entire country. This convention concluded that the Provisional Government was not looking after their interests. Consequently, Lenin ordered a revolt against the Provisional Government.[31] Rebellious soldiers from the Petrograd soviet surrounded the Winter Palace that housed the Provisional Government on the night of November 7.[32] The Bolshevik crew from the cruiser *Aurora* fired the cruiser's guns in support of the revolt. Kerensky had no choice but to step down and flee to save his life.[33]

On November 8, Lenin called for an international conference to end the war, and he warned Russia's allies that Russia might leave the war effort whether they agreed or not.[34] Trotsky notified the Allied diplomatic mission on November 21 that the Bolsheviks were in power.[35] The Allies were not pleased with this turn of events. The United States refused to recognize the Bolshevik government.[36] A genuine concern was that Lenin would carry out his threat to sue for peace alone. Ambassador Francis felt that Russia's agreements with her allies allowed

Russia to conclude a separate peace with Germany if forced to do so due to internal revoluntion.[37]

On November 23, 1917, Trotsky began publication of secret treaties between Russia and the Allies concerning territorial divisions. The Allies had not consented to this before Trotsky acted and were not pleased that these secret agreements were no longer secret.[38] Secret treaties were negotiated between Great Britain, France, and Russia beginning in March 1915. These agreements divided Thrace, Turkey, Syria, and other Middle Eastern areas into possessions, "zones of interest," and "federations" of Russia, France, and Great Britain. Palestine was to be internationalized.[39]

The Bolshevik coup did not end the power conflict in Russia. Various groups of non-Socialists and monarchists arose to dispute Lenin's right to rule. The Entente nations, or the Allies, referred to these groups as White Russians because they were not determined to change the social order of the world. While this opposition continued to solidify, Lenin proceeded to negotiate peace with the Germans. A Russian-German armistice was implemented December 17.[40] Negotiations culminated in the Brest-Litovsk Treaty on March 3, 1918.[41]

War would occur within Russia before this treaty agreement. Many commissioned and noncommissioned officers in the Imperial Army remained loyal to the former government. Bolshevik propaganda did not sway them to join the Red Army in nearly the numbers associated with the enlisted men of the old army. The Russian army noncommissioned officers were much better trained that the average enlisted man; however, the number of noncommissioned officers was small compared to that of enlisted men in the Russian army and even the number of noncommissioned officers in the German army. The quality of the Russian noncommissioned officer had not been helped during the war by the shortages of ammunition and other supplies necessary to enable effective combat. While the Russian artillery had a reputation for expertise, once again the shortage of ammunition crippled the ability of the artillery arm to change the terms of battle. The shortage of ammunition had been a significant problem in 1915, but Russian senior officers also used it as an excuse to hide the growing unrest in the army and their own inability to solve the tactical problems they faced.[42] The nation often had sufficient ammunition, but ammunition is only useful if the right units have the resources they need at the time and place required.

The Russian army had another classic arm that was strong. Cossacks formed the heart of the Russian cavalry. When the revolution occurred, the Cossacks with their cultural affinity for mobile warfare on horseback tended to support the White Russian forces. For the previous four hundred years, the Cossacks had defended the borders of Russian lands from invaders such as the Ottoman Empire.

The czar had afforded the Cossacks more autonomy than other ethnic groups. The Cossacks' special lifestyle and ethnic loyalty to their units encouraged them to stay dedicated to the remnants of the former Russian army. Many Cossacks owned land and lived with a degree of independence that the average Russian inducted into the infantry did not enjoy. Clearly some Cossacks did join the Bolsheviks; however, most remained true to the White Russians. Their gray or green uniforms, sabers, and silver-decorated ammunition bandoliers would strike fear in many opponents.[43]

One Cossack defect was that if a leader threatened the Cossack way of life or independence, a mutiny was likely. Cossacks were reliable troops when rough action was needed whether to break up a mob or assault a retreating enemy. Their warlike spirit served them and their masters well as long as those masters respected their customs and lifestyle. They were also generally uneducated and unaware of larger issues that might be affecting the situation in which they found themselves. Even most of the commissioned officers had little formal training.[44]

One example of the impact of a threat to their lifestyle was the Bolshevik decision to confiscate Cossack lands in December 1917. This decision drove the Don Cossacks to join forces under the leadership of General Lavr Kornilov and General A. M. Kaledin. This force then attacked north through Kuban and Don Basin. The Cossacks and Bolsheviks engaged in several battles that did not result in decisive action for either side. Both sides, White and Red, worked to mold their respective bands into true armies. April and May 1918 would later see Georgia, Armenia, and Azerbaijan declare independence as revolution continued to result in widespread unrest and the inability of any central government to form and rule Russia in its entirety.[45] Throughout these months in mid- to late 1918 the civil war simmered and at times broke out into open warfare between White and Red Russian groups all across Russia. No single group seemed able to bring stability or was willing to compromise its ideals. A test of arms would be the only way to resolve who would lead Russia in the twentieth century.

Against the direct backdrop of the war was the concern that Bolshevism could spread from Russia to elsewhere in Europe. Karl Marx had concentrated on Germany as the location of a proletarian revolution in line with his teachings during the 1870s. He saw war as a potential catalyst for revolution. Marx had originally thought that the opportunity for revolution in Russia to be unlikely. He initially believed that the czar's hold on power was too strong and that the conditions had not been set for the people to revolt. However, as conditions changed in Russia with a move toward capitalism, Marx felt that the conditions were developing to support the revolution. He even felt that Russia might leap past capitalism and progress directly to a revolution. His internationalist outlook encouraged a view that revolution in Great Britain and France remained possible. Marx threatened the ruling classes by encouraging workers to revolt against the abuses by their rulers. There was nothing to lose by revolution except their domination by others.[46]

The Allies were in a difficult situation. The virtual stalemate on the Western Front did not assure victory. Russia's leaving the war removed an ally with great potential power and greatly eased Germany's task because Germany no longer had to fight in two directions simultaneously. Reestablishing the second front was one way to pressure the Central Powers and prevent the transfer of their soldiers to face the Allies on the Western Front. However, reopening the Eastern Front meant soldiers were desperately needed to backfill the casualties in the West. The war was bleeding the Allies of more than one generation of young men. Technological improvements promised to add mechanization to the Allies' armies, but they still needed manpower. The Allies could not yet see just how close Germany itself was to collapse and surrender. The German army still seemed to be capable of winning this war and making all of the sacrifices seem meaningless. Something had to be done to prevent defeat. The Central Powers also had taken massive casualties; however, if the Eastern Front was no longer a concern, Germany could concentrate all of her forces against France and Great Britain. The Allies required American soldiers on the Western Front to replace their manpower to hold the line and fight the Germans. The Allies also needed Russia back in the war because an active Eastern Front would prevent Germany from concentrating in the West.

This dilemma of how to deal with a Germany able to shift troops on interior lines if Russia truly was out of the war as well as a number of other factors led the Allies to intervene in Russia using military forces. Reluctant allies in this endeavor would eventually become enemies, even though rarely openly, in the morass of civil war amid the grab for power, influence, and economic resources in a cold, forbidding place that few Americans ever expected to visit and whose sacrifices largely remain unacknowledged. The reasons for the intervention were varied and added to the difficulty in coordinating the actions of the different national contingents.

3
The Reasons and the Decision

Before the Allies would intervene, of course, they had to struggle with a variety of reasons for making such a decision. Given the commitment to the war in Europe, any diversion of troops to another front had to bring some benefit. The situation in Russia was also unclear with the Allies arguing over the viability as well as the benefit of deploying troops. Competing visions of the purpose for sending military forces would plague the Allies throughout the intervention. A variety of factors would affect the final decision to intervene.

The Reasons to Intervene

Several reasons encouraged the Allies to intervene in Russia. Historians disagree about the importance of each. The record is at times confusing because the Allies did not agree regarding the importance of these factors or the objectives of the intervention. Agencies within the US government did not agree on the objectives of the operation. This lack of consensus led to confusion and even animosity among the Allied forces in Russia. British, French, American, Canadian, and other elements landed at Murmansk in northern Russia; French units landed at Odessa[1]; and British, French, American, Chinese, Japanese, and other forces moved into Siberia. Although Siberia is, of course, the focus here, many factors affecting Allied actions in Siberia also affected operations in the other areas. Reasons for intervening included survival on the Western Front, saving an ally, previous military and nonmilitary support to Russia, restraining Japanese intervention, and supporting the Czechoslovakian Legion then fighting on the Eastern Front. Overlaying these reasons was the need to maintain the Trans-Siberian Railroad in order to support any intervention, whether for combat or humanitarian support. The rail line was the critical transportation infrastructure system that allowed the consistent movement of people and goods year-round. The Allies also applied pressure to intervene for a variety of these reasons.

Survival on the Western Front

The peace moves by Nicolai Lenin's government relieved Germany from fighting a two-front war in Europe. Germany could concentrate its military resources on the Western Front. Understandably, a German concentrated effort in the west caused the Allies great concern. They had hoped a strong, democratic government supporting the war would be formed after the revolution.[2] With the Alexander Kerensky Provisional Government downfall it did not appear that a strong, democratic ally would emerge from the massive unrest and confusing situation in Russia, unless the Allies forced it to happen. If a means could be found to reestablish the Eastern Front, Germany would be forced once again to fight in two directions simultaneously. However, the Bolsheviks wanted peace with Germany, not war.

Besides the opportunity to remove troops from Eastern Front positions to shift to the West, another potential source of enemy manpower existed for the Central Powers with the collapse of the Eastern Front—prisoners of war. Article 8 of the Brest-Litovsk Treaty called for repatriation of prisoners of war.[3] Estimates went as high as two million prisoners of war being held by Russia. However, even with these numbers, several US officials contradicted the reports that massive numbers of armed prisoners existed and downplayed the threat.[4] Regardless of the reports warning of the existence of armed prisoners and the reports indicating the threat was not real, given time, a large number of repatriated soldiers could have helped the Central Powers.

Another aspect of the German problem included a fear that Germany would take advantage of Russia's weak condition and establish control over it.[5] One concern that prompted the north Russian intervention was the fear that Germany might be able to establish submarine bases at Murmansk and Archangel.[6] Additional submarine bases would threaten Allied shipping and the war effort. As noted earlier, unrestricted submarine warfare had already forced the United States to join the war.

Saving an Ally

Western leaders feared the turmoil caused by the Russian Revolution. Russia was unable to fulfill its role on the Eastern Front and the revolution risked the destruction of an ally. This new order challenged the old. The ideology that motivated many Russians to revolt was Bolshevism and was a threat to international and internal stability wherever its supporters found dissatisfied people willing to listen to their message. The Bolsheviks preached state, not private, ownership. They relied on Karl Marx's *Communist Manifesto* as an ideological base. Marx argued for the abolition of inheritance rights, the centralization of communications and transportation in the state's hands, a heavy progressive or graduated income tax, and the abolition of private land property. French marshal Ferdinand Foch believed that French security relied on a weakened Germany and the destruction of Bolshevism. David Lloyd George worried that the Bolsheviks might ally with Germany and attack the West. He feared that Germany would fall under the influence of Bolshevism, rearm, and retrain before renewing its attack on the Western democracies. The concern that Germany would turn to Bolshevism affected the Allied ideas on peace terms because an onerous peace might push Germany and even Eastern Europe into Bolshevism, whereas a just peace, possibly even allowing Germany to join the League of Nations, would encourage Germany not to fall under the influence of the Bolsheviks.[7] Clearly Bolshevik aims did not endear them to the capitalist Allies.

After the November revolution, many Americans continued to believe that the Russian people supported the war effort to defeat Germany. Some people believed that the Bolshevik rise to power was due to German influence.[8] If this was true, the Red tide had to be stopped and reversed in order to save the world from the evils the Bolsheviks represented. Failure to eliminate Bolshevism in Russia might lead to its spread all over Europe. Allied leaders were concerned that Bolshevism would spread to the Central Powers nations when they lost the war.[9] Leaders in Great Britain feared that Bolshevism would spread to India and threaten the empire.[10] Some historians have concluded that concern over the spread of Bolshevism influenced the decision by Great Britain, France, and Canada to intervene in Siberia, while others have insisted that some of our Allies wanted to negotiate with the Bolsheviks because Germany was clearly the larger threat.[11]

It is important to note that fighting the Bolsheviks was not an objective of the US government even though selected Americans, such as Ambassador David R. Francis,[12] advocated such an objective. Even with the ideological differences between the Bolsheviks and capitalist nations, the primary concern had to be survival on the Western Front. However, this desire to help the Russian people find their way out of the turmoil of revolution and back into the world of nations would influence the missions provided to the AEF-Siberia.

Military and Nonmilitary Support to Russia

The Allies had provided large quantities of military supplies to the czar's government to support its participation in the war. Without a strong, pro-Allied government, these supplies would not be used to help defeat the Central Powers. In fact, there was concern the Bolsheviks might allow the Germans to seize the supplies and use them against the Allies.[13] Foreign-supplied materials in Vladivostok included rubber, cotton, harvesting machinery, barbed wire, ammunition, leathers, aircraft parts,[14] thirty-seven thousand railway truck wheels, steel rails, field guns, automobiles, shoes, copper and lead ingots, and a submarine.[15] Disposition of these supplies was an unknown. The lack of stability in Russia forced the Allies to consider protecting their investments. Russian debt to Allied nations totaled in the billions of rubles. Russia owed Great Britain $7.5 billion and France $5.5 billion.[16] On May 16, 1917, the United States had extended $100 million credit to Russia. By July 6, 1917, $35 million in loans were made.[17] The totals rose to $325 million credit with $187,729,750 actually loaned by January 1918.[18] The Allies adopted a "no fight, no loans" approach to coerce the Provisional Government to support the war effort. This policy hastened the fall of Kerensky's government because the Russian people were tired of fighting.[19] Bolshevik peace promises brought them support. In addition to the credits noted above, other loans were made to Russia. On August 8, 1919, the Russian Provisional Government still owed the United States $406,092 for war materials sold earlier. Food provided through the American Relief Association totaled $4,465,465.07. Several private loans totaled another $96 million. Russia owed over $302 million to the United States.[20]

In addition to military aid provided to Russia, nonmilitary economic support was a consideration. International business enterprises had factories and supervisory personnel in Russia. The Singer Sewing Machine Company had three factories in the country. The International Harvester Company had factories in Russia. Overseas business operations were crucial to International Harvester as evidenced by one estimate that 40 percent of its business was the result of foreign sales.[21] In addition to Singer and International Harvester, J. M. Coates (producing thread) and Westinghouse had factories in Russia.[22] Diplomatic relations existed between those nations because Russia was a member of the Allied coalition. This resulted in many foreigners being in Russia in support of diplomatic and economic activities. America had to protect its citizens overseas.

Restraining Japan

Japan posed a significant problem for the other Allies in Siberia. Though Japan was ostensibly allied with Great Britain, France, and the United States against Germany, all were competitors for trade and influence in Asia. Great Britain was established in Hong Kong and the Yangtze River valley. France controlled parts of southern China. Japan controlled Formosa and Korea. Russia had its railroad concession in Manchuria. Germany controlled part of China's Shantung Province and Mongolia. The United States under its Open Door Policy was dedicated to equal trade opportunities for all in Asia.[23] Regardless of the sides chosen in World War I, competition in Asia among all these nations existed.

The 1904–5 Russo-Japanese war established Japan as a first-rate power in the Pacific. This power forced the United States to view Japan as a trade rival. World War I provided Japan an opportunity to seize Germany's possessions in the area and expand into China.[24] The 1917 revolution gave Japan a chance to grab the Sakhalin Islands as a potential oil resource. The mainland also possessed attractive coal and timber resources.[25] In addition to the raw materials available, Japan needed territory for its excess population. One author has suggested that the Japanese military wanted more people to put in uniform.[26] Mainland Asia could provide such a resource. The US Army chief of staff, Gen. Peyton C. March, believed Japan wanted land based on his experiences as a military attaché and observer in Manchuria with the Japanese army during the Russo-Japanese War.[27]

The Bolshevik revolution gave Japan the pretense to deploy forces to Siberia and Manchuria against little organized resistance. This then made possible a direct attack into China if Japan chose to do so.[28] Great Britain feared Japan would assume leadership of the "dark races" and institute problems in India.[29] The United States feared that giving Japan a free hand would mean recognition of Japan's supremacy in the Far East and force the abandonment of future trade and business in the area.[30] On the other hand, Japan did not want to intervene unless the United States did also. Japan did not want to dissipate its forces while allowing the United States to conserve military power.[31] After the Allied forces intervened, the American military attaché in Tokyo sent a cable to the AEF-Siberia Intelligence Office warning them that the embassy staff had received information indicating Japan was using junior officers, disguised as medical personnel and even soap peddlers, so that they could infiltrate Siberia and Manchuria with the express purpose of mapping the region.[32]

Initially, the Japanese government also had to wrestle with its long-term plans to dominate Asia and prevent Western countries from interfering with its plans. Japan was focused on China and had resisted calls from its European allies to send forces to the Western Front. The Allies' apparent confusion over the reasoning for an intervention into Russia further disrupted the Japanese government's ability to plan a response to the Bolshevik revolution and the Allies' calls for intervention. However, as the power of the Bolshevik message spread eastward and Bolshevik forces grew in size, the Japanese government began to see cause for alarm in a complete Red takeover of Russia. Revolution in European Russia was very different from revolution in the Asian part of Russia as far as the Japanese were concerned. This dilemma forced the Japanese to consider whether some form of acceptance of the Bolsheviks would enhance their position in Asia or if they should support the opponents of the Bolsheviks in order to take advantage of the chaos of the civil war. The economic resources in Siberia were too great to allow the Western countries a free hand to do as they liked.[33]

The Czechoslovakian Legion

Another reason for the United States and its allies to intervene was to support the Czechoslovakian Legion, which was composed of deserters from the Austro-Hungarian army and formed into units under Russian officers beginning in 1914.

Word of the existence of this organization spread through Austria-Hungary's units prompting more desertions. The Czechoslovakians felt little loyalty to Austria-Hungary and wanted their own country.[34] The Allies supported the aims of many nationalities under the domination of the Austro-Hungarian Empire as a way to generate problems in the empire's army.[35] Besides the Czech units formed in Russia, several also organized in France beginning in 1914 and later in Italy.[36] Volunteers included steelworkers of Slavic descent from the United States.[37]

When the czar abdicated, the Czech units continued to support the war effort as part of Russian general Brusiloff's army. They took part in the unsuccessful July 1917 offensive and formed the rearguard for the retreating Russian army. When Kerensky's government failed, the Czech legion was an army corps of approximately forty thousand soldiers after successful recruiting efforts in prisoner of war camps and Russian munitions factories.[38]

Declaration of a Czechoslovakian nation in January 1918, with the decision by the Czechs that they would continue to fight Austria-Hungary, laid the groundwork for future conflict with the Bolsheviks.[39] As a result of this, Lenin was faced with the prospect of having a force on Russian soil that was determined to continue a war he hoped to end. The Czech Legion declared its neutrality toward all political groups in Russia on March 3, 1918, and started moving toward Vladivostok for subsequent transfer to the Western Front. As the legion departed the general area of Kiev, it was forced to hold off advancing German units. German and Czech units battled for railway stations near Bachmach as the Czechs attempted to entrain. After losing approximately one hundred dead and two hundred wounded while inflicting losses three times that on the Germans, the Czechs defeated the Germans and began their long journey to the east.[40]

On March 26, the Bolshevik government agreed to allow the Czechs to cross Russia, providing all weapons except one rifle for each ten men were surrendered. By this time, the legion had grown to approximately forty-five thousand and required sixty-five trains to move eastward. On May 5, the two lead infantry regiments under the command of the legion's chief of staff, Gen. Milo K. Dietrichs, reached Vladivostok. The remainder were scattered over 4,500 miles of railroad, as far west as the Volga River, due to minor bickering with numerous Bolshevik officials, railway system inefficiency, and a lack of locomotives.[41]

The peace with the Bolsheviks was only temporary. On May 14, 1918, at Chelyabinsk in the Ural foothills, an incident occurred that dramatically altered the situation. A German prisoner of war train entered the station and stopped. The station was filled with Czechs moving eastward, repatriating German and Austro-Hungarian prisoners moving westward, and Bolshevik officials and guards. As the prisoner of war train stopped, this mixture of people mingled around it. Conversations broke out among many small groups. Suddenly, shouts exploded, and

Czechs charged a German car. Using a piece of metal, a prisoner of war had hit and killed a passing Czech soldier. Pandemonium filled the station yard as the Czechs dragged the suspect out of the train and beat him to death. Bolshevik guards moved into the melee to restore order. The Bolsheviks carried off Czechs and prisoners of war for questioning. The prisoner of war train pulled out but the Czechs refused to leave without their countrymen.[42]

The matter could have been settled at this point, but when a delegation of Czechs went to the police station to ascertain when their comrades would be released, the Bolsheviks jailed the delegation. As might be imagined, a cohesive group of well-disciplined soldiers like the Czechs was not prepared to accept such injustice even though they were only lightly armed. The Czechs stormed the police station and freed their fellow soldiers. This story rapidly spread all along the Trans-Siberian Railroad so that free passage could no longer be expected. Lenin's government ordered that all Czech movement be stopped. The Czechs, of course, were not willing to abide by Lenin's orders and continued eastward fighting their way through Bolshevik ambushes and repairing destroyed tracks. Czechs fought with rifles, clubs, and stones seizing additional arms as they marched eastward.[43]

Allied governments realized the Czech Legion was a potent force that could be used to bring stability to Russia and assist Allied intervention. On June 22, France informed the legion that it was the advanced guard for a massive Allied intervention. The Czechs were told to hold the Volga River. They accepted the order.[44]

On June 29, open fighting broke out between Dietrich's Czechs and the Reds in Vladivostok. The Reds lost and a White Russian government was installed. On July 29, Lenin declared a state of war existed between Soviet Russia and the Allies.[45] By the end of August the Czech Legion controlled the Trans-Siberian Railroad from the Volga River to Vladivostok. They established friendly governments in the cities along the railway.[46] In September and October 1918, the United States, France, Great Britain, Italy, and Japan recognized the Czechoslovakian National Council as the government of a cobelligerent nation fighting the Central Powers with its army in Russia an Allied army.[47] By July, it should have been clear that the Czechs did not need rescue.

Trans-Siberian Railroad

The Trans-Siberian Railroad linked European Russia to Siberia (see map 1). The railroad's economic importance was unsurpassed by other infrastructure as it provided a means of crossing several thousand miles of inhospitable country much more quickly than by road. However, in many places it was only a single track that restricted two-way traffic. Extensive use of sidings prevailed in order to allow trains to pass one another.[48] Railroad transportation also allowed refugees to escape war or persecution. Two such trains carrying 1,057 Serbians from Odessa were in Harbin, Manchuria, during the winter of 1918–19. These refugees lived for seven months in boxcars and coaches, with standing room only in many of the railroad cars.[49]

The railway line left Russian soil east of China and entered Manchuria. Passage through Manchuria was originally sought to save construction and freight costs because it was a shorter route to Vladivostok. Additionally, it provided Russia an opportunity to exert influence over Manchuria and Korea without overt military action. China agreed to the pact settling the issue in 1896 as a means of paying back Russia for forcing Japan to abandon the Liaotung Peninsula containing the year-round ports of Port Arthur and Talienwan. Russia joined forces with Germany and France to accomplish this after Japan had obtained the land by defeating China in 1894. The European countries feared Japan's competition as they were attempting to expand their power in the Pacific area. This section of the line was technically known as the Chinese Eastern Railway. In order to disguise the actual Russian government domination of the line, China granted the railway concession to the Russo-Chinese Bank, a private business created by Russia's finance minister and supported by French bankers. The Russo-Chinese Bank then transferred the concession to the Chinese Eastern Railway Company, whose shares were principally owned by the Russian Treasury.[50]

In February 1903, the Chinese Eastern Railway opened. European Russia was then connected to the Pacific Ocean by railroad except at Lake Baikal, where ferries were used to cross the lake until the 162-mile line around the southern rim of the lake was completed. After Russia lost its war with Japan in 1905, Russian authorities saw the need for an alternate route to the one through Manchuria. Consequently, they built a rail line on Russian territory north of the Amur River and the Manchuria border. When the bridge at Khabarovsk was completed in 1916, the Amur line opened.[51] Even though the Amur line was now a reality, the Chinese Eastern line continued to see more use than the Amur line because the Chinese Eastern was the least expensive and shortest route.[52]

The Siberian population depended on the railroad for commerce; however, the railroad did not operate smoothly.[53] The Provisional Government asked for American assistance. John F. Stevens with five railway experts traveled to Vladivostok in May 1917. He concluded American aid was required because the Trans-Siberian Railroad was incapable of distributing the supplies needed to support the people there. Russia agreed to the offer in August 1917. Stevens's plan called for twelve units of American railway personnel to be formed with superintendents, dispatchers, trainmasters, traveling engineers, mechanics, and telephone experts. Ten of these fourteen-man units would operate the railway between Vladivostok and Omsk. Two would control the line between Moscow and Petrograd. Therefore, on November 18, 1917, Col. George H. Emerson and his railroad men sailed from San Francisco to Vladivostok on the US Army Transport (USAT) *Thomas*. Due to the revolution, the *Thomas* did not land at Vladivostok when it arrived December 14, 1917. The *Thomas* could not wait out the civil disturbance by anchoring in the Vladivostok harbor for fear of being iced in. Instead, it sailed to Nagasaki, Japan. Stevens then went to Harbin, Manchuria, to confer with the Chinese Eastern officials to ascertain if he could put his men to work there. He was granted permission, so the Russian Railway Service Corps began its movement to Harbin on February 27, 1918,[54] and used that city as its headquarters.[55] The city's composition was a mixture of Chinese and Russian influences, and it appeared to be three separate towns. One was large and populated by Chinese. The second was Russian and provided homes for the Russian men working on the railroad. The third town was devoted to the railway officials of the Chinese Eastern Railway. The railroad headquarters dominated the center of the city.[56]

The criticality of the Trans-Siberian Railroad made it a key component in any decision to intervene. Its control would be paramount in supporting any operations in Siberia. The existence of the Russian Railway Service Corps with its mission to supervise the operations of the rail line supported a decision to intervene. The unrest in the region threatened the lives of the members of the Russian Railway Service Corps and their ability to assist the operation of the railroad.

The Decision

On November 29, 1917, the Inter-Allied Conference began with its subordinate Supreme War Council meeting on December 1 in order to coordinate the war effort. The Allies were not sure they would win and hoped to consolidate their power so as to be able to defeat the Central Powers. There was also concern that Bolshevik disclosures of secret territorial annexation agreements would harden the Central Powers' resolve to continue to fight.[57] Pressure by the Allies continued to build for Wilson to take action, while key leaders within the US government disagreed on whether to commit American troops. Even as the debate continued, events in Vladivostok began to pull American and Allied servicemen ashore. Bowing to Allied pressure, Wilson ultimately decided to commit American troops to Siberia.

Internal Debate and Allied Pressure

The factors discussed previously weighed heavily on the minds of the Allied leaders at the conference and in their capitals. Yet the Russian problem was only one segment of the World War I effort. The major problem was stopping the Germans on the Western Front. America's Allies wanted one million men in one hundred divisions for the Western Front. They also wanted to use American soldiers to replace their units' losses. War raged in France, Italy, and the Middle East. A few thousand men being sent to Russia was insignificant in comparison. However, the Allies wanted to send troops to Russia, and Wilson wanted to comply and be a good friend. His refusal to cooperate on previous issues resulted in Wilson's desire to prove he was a good ally by acceding to the demands to intervene.[58]

Gen. Tasker H. Bliss, US military representative to the Supreme War Council, forwarded a letter to US Army Chief of Staff Peyton C. March on February 20, 1918, that discussed British desires for intervention in Siberia, which favored Japanese occupation of the railroad between Vladivostok and Harbin. Bliss warned that it might be difficult to get Japan out of Siberia once allowed in. He was concerned that Russia might try to play Japan and Germany against each other. Bliss pointed out that Great Britain and France were convinced that intervention was the only way to consolidate Russian feelings favorable to the Allies. He also stated that there was no military advantage to be accrued by seizing the Trans-Siberia Railroad unless westward movement was planned. As a final note, Bliss recommended the United States stay out of Siberia.[59]

Secretary of State Robert Lansing and many State Department officers were vehemently anti-Bolshevik, but they did not encourage US military intervention. Lansing feared the Bolsheviks and refused to allow American diplomats in Russia to enter into formal or informal relations with the Soviet government. Continued Allied diplomatic pressure with subsequent support from the State Department pushed Wilson toward a positive favoring intervention. The Brest-Litovsk Treaty in March 1918 showed that the Bolsheviks would not join the Allies in fighting the Central Powers. However, in March and April 1918 British and American representatives who inspected the German prisoners of war being guarded by Bolsheviks found that the Bolsheviks had no intention of arming the prisoners and including them in the Bolshevik military forces. The Bolsheviks thought that the Germans, if armed, would attack them. Direct contact with the prisoners confirmed that only a very small number of prisoners had weapons and then only to assist the Bolshevik guard force at the camps. One investigation team was led by a William Webster of the American Red Cross and British captain W. L. Hicks, who traveled from Moscow to Irkutsk. Maj. Walter Drysdale, who was the US military attaché in Peking, conducted the investigation in eastern Siberia.[60] This no doubt reinforced the conclusions of members of the US government that armed prisoners of war were not a threat to the Allies.

Events Ashore Take Their Own Course

On April 4 several armed men wearing Russian uniforms entered a Japanese shop in Vladivostok on April 4. When the Japanese shopkeeper refused to give them the money they demanded, the Russians killed him and two other Japanese citizens in the store. Japanese warships (in the harbor since January) landed five hundred men to protect Japanese lives and property. Fifty British soldiers landed afterward to guard British subjects and property. The Bolsheviks were taken by surprise and did not resist. The US government did not know that Japan was going to commit troops prior to the actual landing.[61] Extensive operations were not mounted pending continued diplomatic wrangling over a decision to intervene.

Marines from the USS *Brooklyn* landed in Vladivostok on the afternoon of June 29, 1918, to protect the American consulate and participate in Allied patrolling of the city. The regular detachment of two officers and seventy-five enlisted men had been augmented in the Philippines by an additional fifty enlisted men. The *Brooklyn* had arrived in Vladivostok on March 1, 1918, and had to break two to four feet of ice to enter the port. By the time of the marine detachment landing in June, as many as 12,000 Czech Legion soldiers were in the city but only 2,500 were well armed. Czech, Japanese, British, and Chinese soldiers and sailors took control of the city after destroying the Bolshevik headquarters in a vicious close assault. This action followed the continuing attempts by the Bolsheviks to oppose the movement of the Czech Legion on the railroad. British and Japanese naval forces captured several Russian destroyers and submarines under the control of the Bolsheviks when the ships tried to escape the harbor. American forces remained neutral in the capture of the city government and toward the Bolsheviks and freed Austro-Hungarian prisoners of war occupying Vladivostok.[62]

American Marines, Czech Legion soldiers, Chinese sailors, British sailors, and Japanese sailors formed joint patrols to maintain order in Vladivostok in the days ahead. Most of the Czech Legion soon left to attempt to reopen the Trans-Siberian Railroad line. Czech casualties prompted the establishment of additional hospital facilities that Austro-Hungarian prisoners constructed while being guarded by ten US Marines from the USS *Brooklyn*.[63]

The American holiday celebration on July 4, unfortunately, caused some confusion during this time. The *Brooklyn* was decorated with a number of American flags for the holidays. In a completely separate action, the Bolsheviks conducted an authorized celebratory parade for their recent dead. The presence of the American flags on the *Brooklyn* inadvertently resulted in some of the Bolsheviks believing that the United States supported their cause. The American neutrality to date reinforced this belief.[64]

Previously, on June 24, 1918, a few days before the Marines landed, March had again counseled Wilson not to commit troops to Siberia. March argued that occupying the Trans-Siberian Railroad by the ten thousand to fifteen thousand Allied soldiers, which had been suggested by the president in a June 17 letter, was pointless. Such a small number would not divert German strength from the Western Front. Occupying Russia proper might accomplish that task because the minerals, oil, and grain in the Ukraine were coveted by Germany. He emphasized the war would be won or lost on the Western Front so resources should be husbanded for that effort. March pointed out that there was insufficient shipping tonnage available to supply a force in Siberia. Living off the land would take valuable resources from the Siberian population. Allowing Japan to intervene in Siberia would consolidate Russian opinion against the Allies.[65]

Final Decision

Wilson was confronted with a difficult situation. His primary concern was the Western Front, but the Allies and certain members of the government felt an intervention in Russia was necessary. Newton Baker believed that German domination of Russia was inevitable and that Germany might give up territorial gains in the west or the southeastern areas of Europe in order to gain Russia. Russia completely out of the war could allow Germany to shift thirty to forty divisions to the Western Front. Japan had initially indicated it did not plan to land troops then changed its mind and did so. Lansing encouraged intervention. March and Bliss discouraged the idea. The British and French encouraged Wilson to intervene to preclude a German seizure of Siberia, save the Czechs, and to reestablish the Eastern Front. Japan feared German submarine bases on the eastern Siberia coastline. However, all these parties were concerned that a Japanese intervention would force a racial backlash in Russia. The incident or idea that tipped the scales toward a decision to intervene is unclear. Historians have debated the issue for years and will continue to do so. The decision may very well have been a belief that the Russian people would join with the Czech Legion and reestablish an Eastern Front against the Central Powers. Japanese authorities supported using the Czech Legion to reestablish an Eastern Front. However, by September 27, 1918, the War Department would cable Graves not to assist the Czechs in moving to the west to accomplish that act. However, the failure to provide transportation to move the Czechs to Europe is an indication of this initial plan to hold the Czechs in Russia in order to reestablish an Eastern Front. As discussed previously, there were many factors influencing this decision. These factors or a subset of them resulted in Wilson's decision to intervene. The fact that the decision was made is clear. The AEF landed.[66]

Initially, Wilson agreed with March, but Allied pressure finally convinced him that intervention was necessary. Therefore, March selected the Twenty-Seventh and Thirty-First Infantry Regiments in the Philippine Islands as the core of the expeditionary force. This precluded diverting units previously slated for the Western Front to intervene in Siberia. On July 6, Wilson told Lansing, Baker, Secretary of the Navy Daniels, and March that the United States would intervene in Siberia. Seven thousand troops from the United States and Japan each were to be used. March felt that trying to limit the number of Japanese troops was futile.[67] The "Aide Memoire" was the result. Five US Army Transport ships were dedicated to transport the Czechoslovakians from Vladivostok when needed. Sufficient Russian rifles were available in the United States to equip thirteen thousand Czechs with one million rounds of ammunition on hand. Two months would be required to move the equipment to Vladivostok.[68]

The Department of State issued a press release on August 5 to explain the decision to intervene. Reopening the Eastern Front was explicitly not a reason for intervening because the effort to reestablish the Eastern Front would not help the Russian people. The press release indicated a need for the intervention in order to help the Czechoslovakian forces as well as steadying any self-governing actions undertaken by the Russians. The announcement stated that the United States, France, and Great Britain would land troops near Murmansk and Archangel in northern Russia with the United States and Japan landing troops in Siberia. The official policy promised noninterference in Russia's internal politics. In addition to armed forces, the US leadership hoped to send a commission of merchants, agricultural experts, labor advisors, Red Cross workers, and representatives from the Young Men's Christian Association (YMCA).[69]

The YMCA had actually been in Russia prior to this time. Initial operations began in 1900 and did not end in total until 1923. The largest number of representatives reached 440 between 1917 and 1920, which corresponded to the increase in Allied presence in Russia. The YMCA at first was focused on Christian social service to the people of Russia. Once World War I started, YMCA operations changed to a focus on humanitarian support to prisoners of war. In Russia, this meant support for German and Austro-Hungarian soldiers captured by the Imperial Army. The YMCA would establish operations at Kazan, Orenburg, Tashkent, Perm, Omsk, Tobolsk, Tomsk, Krasnoyarsk, Irkutsk, Khabarovsk, and other locations. The revolution and change in government would greatly complicate providing humanitarian support and ministry. With the revolution, the focus of the YMCA changed to include the Russian army.[70]

The Red Cross would eventually establish eight hospitals between Vladivostok and the Ural Mountains. Besides the doctors and other staff, 152 nurses and 42 nurses' aides would provide care and comfort to the sick and injured. In order to improve the medical care afforded the Russian people and soldiers, the Red Cross also established schools to train Russian women in nursing. Another laudable accomplishment would be an orphanage for children orphaned by the ensuing civil war.[71]

The Allied governments had different reasons to intervene. Great Britain and France were most concerned about surviving on the Western Front and were openly anti-Bolshevik. Japan sought raw materials and land for population expansion. The United States wanted to help the Russian people find democracy, save the Czech Legion (even if it really did not need saving), and protect military and nonmilitary supplies. These conflicting motivations precluded a coordinated operation since each Allied commander had to follow the dictates of his country regardless of the impact on the other Allied forces. No single commander for all Allied units in Siberia was appointed to conduct the intervention. This lack of a clear mission supported by all elements of the US government and its Allies would plague the soldiers of the AEF-Siberia throughout the intervention.

A wide range of activities was needed to maintain order and promote peace in the region. However, the guidance from the government was not clear and made the selection of specific courses of action very difficult under the circumstances. Without the instant communications of today that allow individual soldiers to call home from the battlefield, the soldiers in the AEF from Graves to the individual infantryman often had to make decisions based on their personal values and then live with the outcome. The fighting at times may have seemed similar to an insurgency that might more accurately be referred to as a civil war by the time of the Allied intervention. Regardless of the characterization, the situation was confusing with many competing factors influencing the deployment and the retention of the American soldiers in Siberia long after the World War I armistice was signed.

In order to understand the military aspects of the intervention, an explanation of the military forces is necessary. Since this discussion is focused on the American Expeditionary Force, more detail regarding its structure and equipment will be provided. Nonetheless, it should be clear that the disparate nature of the armies whose leaders were trying to coordinate their operations with one another complicated any attempts to synchronize and logistically support the actions carried out.

4
The Military Forces

As 1918 drew to a close, numerous anti-Bolshevik groups vied for power and for Allied support in Siberia. Bolsheviks dominated western and central Russia, but Siberia offered hope for other groups to establish a base of support in order to assert themselves in this civil war for control of the country. There was even a chance that Siberia might become an independent nation.[1] A discussion of White Russian groups, the Allied forces, the Bolshevik military forces, and partisan forces in Siberia follows. Finally a comparison of standard division structures will provide a perspective on how the meaning of division differed from country to country.

White Russians

A Siberian nation was not a new idea. Agitation for nationhood had occurred periodically for years. The vast distances and pioneer spirit of the settlers had fostered an independent attitude. Russian citizens who lived in Siberia experienced greater civil liberties by being so far from the national seat of power. Although there were few landlords in Siberia, which reduced landlord-peasant tensions that existed elsewhere, there was a certain amount of social and political conflict between the privileged and underprivileged.[2]

The competition among power centers in Russia affected the ability to raise military forces. As an example, in August 1917 Siberian revolutionaries began preparing for a revolt before the November 1917 revolution. A conference of revolutionary organizations was held, and in October 1917 an All-Siberian Congress convened and organized an Extraordinary Siberian Regional Congress to meet in December to set up an autonomous Siberian government. This congress met and established a provisional regional council empowered to organize a Siberian Regional Duma. Even though this body was revolutionary, it did not fully support the Bolsheviks.[3] A desire for revolutionary change or even Socialism did not always equate to Bolshevik support.

The Siberian Regional Duma was to meet at Tomsk on February 1, 1918, but the Bolsheviks seized the city and arrested several members of the Duma and the regional council. A Social-Revolutionary named Petr I. Derber convened a secret meeting of 20 of the 150 Duma delegates. This group elected a Provisional Siberian Government. Fear of reprisals prompted the government ministers to quietly make their way to Harbin, Manchuria, to establish their government.[4]

Derber's Provisional Siberian Government conflicted with another group already in Harbin. Gen. Dmitri L. Horvath, the director of the Chinese Eastern Railway, was regarded by the Far Eastern Committee as its candidate for head of a future All-Russian Government. Negotiations with the Allies were in progress; however, formation of a government had been delayed so an army could be raised. Horvath's group invited Adm. Alexander Kolchak, who was living in Japan, to come to Siberia and raise an army.[5] He did so and was to become a major player in the drama unfolding.

Other power bases in the region included various groups of Cossacks. Ataman Grigori Semenov organized a Cossack band that initially operated out of Manchuria. He was a Russian officer from 1908 until the revolution. Semenov raised an irregular army that was estimated to have reached a strength of sixty thousand soldiers. He officially recognized Kolchak as his leader but did not always obey his orders. Throughout the intervention, his loyalty was to Japan and himself. Japan supported Semenov with supplies and cooperated with Semenov in troop deployments. Semenov was well known for his brutal tactics characterized by unnecessary killing and property destruction.[6]

Ivan Kalmikov, ataman of the Ussuri Cossacks, was another Cossack leader active in Siberia. He, too, received support from the Japanese. Kalmikov's depredations were even worse than those of Semenov. He murdered and plundered at will, recognizing no authority except Semenov and the Japanese authorities. Kalmikov not only ordered murder and robbery but he personally committed these crimes. He brutally abused civilians and his soldiers. This forced many would-be supporters into Bolshevik hands. When Graves first met Semenov and Kalmikov, he did not leave with a positive impression. After the war, when describing Kalmikov, Graves considered him as "the worst scoundrel I ever saw or ever heard of." Graves speculated that there was no crime Kalmikov had not committed. He explained that while Semenov also was guilty of murder, Kalmikov enjoyed killing with his own hands, whereas Semenov would typically order someone else to commit the act. In fact Graves would write that most of the murders of civilians and prisoners were committed by the White Russians, not the Bolsheviks. He believed that the Japanese government encouraged men like Kalmikov and Semenov to commit such atrocities in order to make the United States leave Siberia in disgust. This then would leave Japan in a position to move in to "clean up the situation."[7]

After the Czech Legion seized Samara on June 8, 1918, seventy Social Revolutionaries formed another government there. This group had been part of the Russian Constituent Assembly, which had been abolished by the Bolsheviks on January 29, 1918. Viktor Chernov was president. The Samara government, also known as the Komuch, raised a People's Army and cooperated with the Czechs in several military operations. The capture of Kazan is one example of such cooperation. General Galkin headed the People's Army, which increased in size to some thirty-one thousand soldiers.[8]

A right-wing Social Revolutionary group formed another government in Omsk with P. V. Vologodsky as its president. This army grew from a few hundred men to twenty thousand. After the People's Army was defeated in the fall of 1918, the Omsk military forces were the principal anti-Bolshevik units operating in the area. The Omsk government hoped for a short period of Siberian autonomy followed by a united Russia free of the Bolsheviks.[9]

A group of former members of the Tomsk government established another governing body at Novonikolayevsk on the Ob River in July 1918. This group's policies were more moderate than Derber's and included the elimination of Bolshevism, universal suffrage, and state control of economic activities. It was supported by its Siberian Volunteer Army.[10]

Several smaller governments also formed in cities throughout Siberia including a government at Nizhneudinsk, the Ural Government at Ekaterinburg, the Kirghiz Government in Turkestan, the Bashkir Government, a Turko-Tartaric Government, and several smaller regional bodies.[11] Numerous governments claiming sovereignty illustrate the confusing political situation that existed in Siberia. The Bolsheviks could not defeat such widespread opposition immediately; however, the opposition was not united. This benefited the Bolsheviks because the inability of the opposing groups to mass against the Bolsheviks provided them time to gather strength and defeat the White elements piecemeal rather than collectively. Allied military and diplomatic contingents experienced great difficulty identifying any single person or group that might consolidate the anti-Bolshevik elements so that a collective effort might be coordinated.

The Allies were not happy with the lack of solidarity in the White camp because ascertaining who to support—who could win—was so difficult. As a means to consolidate anti-Bolshevik power, the Allies encouraged the Samara and Omsk governments to join together. Conferences at Chelyabinsk in July and August 1918 failed to bring the sides together. Red advances forced the next conference to be moved to Ufa on September 8, 1918. A compromise was reached so that on September 23, a five-man Directory would rule until a quorum of the Constituent Assembly could be gathered. All parties agreed that this meeting had to occur before January 1, 1919. Private negotiations resulted in Derber's Provisional

Siberian Government surrendering its claim to authority. Horvath relinquished power as well and was named vice regent of the Siberian Government. Kolchak became the minister of war.[12]

Omsk became the seat of the new Siberian Government in October, but conflict between the many factions did not cease. This internal conflict precluded effective government and led to Kolchak's assumption of dictatorial powers on November 18, 1918.[13] Kolchak felt he was obligated to carry on the war against Germany and support the Allies as a member of the Russian government. He also told the Allies he felt the civil war was a continuation of the war in Europe.[14] Of course, by now the Allies had an armistice on the Western Front.

In December 1918, Kolchak had three semi-independent armies under his command: the Southern Army under Gen. I. A. Dutov, a mostly Cossack force, the Western Army under Gen. M. V. Khanzhin, and the Northern Army under the Czech general Rudolph Gaida.[15] In order to obtain sufficient troops, Kolchak drafted young men, some as young as fifteen years old, to fight.[16] Kolchak then gradually lost popular support due to his cooperation with the murderous Cossack bands.[17] So many of his troops deserted with British-supplied equipment that the Bolsheviks sent a telegram to General Knox, the British chief representative in Siberia, thanking Knox for the supplies. Kolchak's corruption and ineptness were well known. His staff even reached four thousand officers, which was four times the size of the entire German army general staff and almost one hundred times the number the staff officers serving the headquarters of the AEF in France.[18]

After the November 11 armistice, Wilson and British prime minister Lloyd George hoped to have all parties in the Russian civil war attend the Peace Conference in Paris. France opposed inviting the Bolsheviks because of concern over propaganda and domestic agitation. Eventually, the Allies agreed to meet with the Whites and Reds on the Prinkipo Islands in the Sea of Marmora near Constantinople. The Bolsheviks accepted the proposal and offered the following concessions in exchange for peace:

1. Bolshevik recognition of Russia's debts. Raw materials would be used for payment.
2. Mining, forest, and other concessions to the Allies.
3. Discussion of territorial settlements.
4. Agreement not to interfere in the internal affairs of the Allies.[19]

The White Russians refused the Prinkipo proposal. They were not prepared to meet with the Bolsheviks. This peace effort drove the Whites toward the Japanese for support, complicating efforts to end the civil war and the intervention.[20]

In February 1919, with the Prinkipo proposal killed, White Russian diplomats pressured the Allies to recognize Kolchak's government. Great Britain favored recognition but the United States did not. Even though not prepared to recognize the Omsk government, the United States continued to support the Allied efforts to operate the Trans-Siberian Railroad.[21] Allies demanded that Kolchak promise election of a constituent assembly by universal suffrage with a peasant land ownership program. Kolchak's refusal to do this resulted in the United States not recognizing the Kolchak government. By the time Kolchak accepted these requirements in June 1919, it was too late. His military forces were on the defensive with the Bolsheviks steadily gaining ground.[22]

Key Allies

Great Britain had limited resources to support intervention in Siberia. Supporting forces on the Western Front as well as in the Middle East, Africa, and northern Russia was a terrific manpower drain. Britain could not deploy forces into Siberia alone.[23]

In November 1917, Britain's Twenty-Fifth Battalion, Middlesex Regiment in Hong Kong, received orders to deploy to Vladivostok, but the orders were canceled before the battalion moved out. In June 1918, the battalion was again alerted. It departed in July and landed at Vladivostok August 3.[24] The British Twenty-Fifth Battalion's soldiers were classified as "B1"—men having already seen service. The battalion was so structured because additional combat action was not expected. Brian Horrocks, who would command the British XXX Corps during Operation Market Garden in World War II, was a young officer in this battalion after volunteering for service in Siberia thanks to his having been included in a German prisoner release. Horrocks had learned Russian from a Russian prisoner while held by the Germans after he was wounded at Ypres. The First of the Ninth Cyclist Battalion of the Hampshire Regiment would also join the British forces in Siberia on November 28, 1918, minus their bicycles; they were deployed from the 116° temperatures in India. After arrival in Vladivostok, this unit would move to replace the Middlesex Regiment at Omsk and by May 1919 be supporting a training school for anti-Bolshevik forces in Ekaterinburg. Fortunately they did receive Canadian arctic clothing for the winter. This school trained a combined English/Russian brigade that never saw combat action.[25]

On the night of August 5, one-half of the battalion moved to the Ussuri River front to assist the Japanese and White Russian forces. This detachment was composed of five hundred infantrymen and a machine-gun section with forty-three men and four Maxim machine guns. The men marched four miles to the train station, which turned out to be a difficult task. By the end of the four miles, the battalion commander himself was carrying four rifles. Garrison life had not prepared the battalion for the physical strain of combat. The lack of tents, mosquito nets, and transport added to the Twenty-Fifth Battalion's woes.[26]

The Royal Navy compensated for the lack of artillery support. Comm. C. R. Payne of the HMS *Suffolk* in anchor at Vladivostok outfitted two armored trains by removing weapons from the *Suffolk*. The trains were each fitted with two 12-pounder naval guns and two machine guns.[27] The military and civilian dependence on the Trans-Siberian Railroad made armored trains essential. All forces relied on them for protected transportation of people and supplies as well as for providing machine gun and cannon fire in support of infantry maneuver. Without trains and in particular the armored trains, soldiers could not have traversed the vast distances and harsh terrain nor had any sort of supporting heavy weapons to supplement their small arms and man-portable machine guns.

As mentioned previously, Japanese troops landed in Siberia in April 1918. Eventually, Japan poured thousands of troops into Siberia. Wilson's desire to utilize a small intervention force was disregarded. Japanese soldiers occupied villages and actively fought the Bolsheviks. Allied concerns regarding Japanese intentions were well founded. The Western Allies hoped to retain an ally (Russia) to continue to pressure Germany. A strong, democratic Russian government was, therefore, important. However, Japan wanted disunity in Russia so that it could more easily exploit the resources and markets in Siberia.[28] Estimates of the number of Japanese troops vary from sixty thousand[29] to as high as seventy-five thousand.[30]

By the time the Allies intervened with large numbers of troops in Siberia, the Czechs controlled the railroad and were battling Bolshevik forces. Wherever the Czechs were located, they established democratic governments and control of local economic activities. The Czechs retained control as long as military necessity or the supply of the army required it.[31]

Troops from several other Allied nations were also present in Siberia. Estimates vary depending on the source. Table 1 lists estimates by country and source of the estimate.

China also deployed troops and took advantage of the confusion to disarm the Russian troops in Manchuria.[32] The revolution provided China the opportunity to assert dominion over her territory. The Canadian detachment arrived in Vladivostok October 26, 1918. Italy's "Black Battalion of Death" arrived October 25, 1918.[33]

A problem that would face the Allies throughout the intervention was the absence of a single commander, known as unity of command, and sometimes even the lack of an agreed upon course of action or unity of effort. No central command that was accepted by all parties was ever established. France sent Gen. Maurice Janin to Siberia to act as the commander of all Allied and Russian units.[34] Great Britain sent General Knox to Siberia to organize Russia's army. When Janin and

Table 1. Military Force Size by Country

Nationality	Coates and Coates*	Stewart**
Italian	2,000	1,400
French	760	1,076
Polish	12,000	N/A
Serbian	4,000	N/A
Rumanian	4,000	N/A
Canadian	4,000	N/A

* Coates and Coates, *Armed Intervention in Russia*, p. 207.

** Stewart, *White Armies of Russia*, p. 153.

Knox met, they decided to divide Siberia into eastern and western sections. Janin was to control western Siberia. Knox was to control eastern Siberia. France and Great Britain did not consult the Allies before making this agreement.[35] Prior to all of these forces arriving in the region, Gen. Kikuzo Otani, the commander of all Japanese units, distributed a message to Allied elements on August 18, 1918, in which he assumed command of all Allied forces. He claimed that the Allies had designated him the commander.[36] Graves had received no such instructions, so he did not abide by the order. Graves speculated that someone in diplomatic service might have misunderstood the difference in being the senior all Allied commander and the term *Allied commander*. Other than this issue being mentioned in February 1920 by Otani's successor, the matter did not come up again.[37] This lack of consensus was a distinct advantage for the Bolsheviks. The Allies' military forces cooperated but were not bound to follow the orders of a central command.

Bolsheviks

The Bolsheviks' military forces began this war with a combination of strengths and weaknesses. The Red Army initially attempted to function without formal ranks. The breakdown of discipline and control forced ranks to be reinstated. However, the Red Army also had advantages over the Allies. Red Army soldiers were enthusiastic because they were fighting for a new social order. The Bolsheviks were also fighting on interior lines[38]—their support structure came from within the country. The Allies had to bring their supplies from their homelands. Little Allied support came from within Siberia.

In order to protect their ideology, the Bolsheviks established the Cheka, the Extraordinary Commission to Fight Counter-Revolution and Sabotage. The Cheka's mission was primarily organized terror as a means of protecting the revolution. Arrests and executions were widespread.[39] This Bolshevik form of obedience through terror enforced discipline and might be described simultaneously as a source of strength and as a weakness. Soldiers feared punishment, so they carried out their assigned duties and were careful not to do something that would provoke the Red authorities. However, brutality is often not a good motivator if an opportunity ever arises for a soldier to escape that environment.

The Red Army organized along normal military lines in the summer of 1918. Previously sanctioned "soldier's committees" were abolished. The Bolsheviks decreed military service compulsory. Officers from the czar's army were invited to join, but trusted Bolsheviks had assignments to watch them. Another control technique was to threaten punishment of a soldier's family for any form of disobedience.[40]

It is difficult to establish precisely the strength of Bolshevik forces. Red Army divisions, as well as small partisan bands, operated throughout the area. When the Bolsheviks attacked the Czechs along the Volga in September 1918, the Red Army was estimated to have numbered 331,000. This number grew to 1,000,000 by the end of the year.[41] The Japanese estimated 40,000 Reds separated the Allies from the Czechs at Irkutsk in September 1918.[42]

The Bolsheviks initially relied on factory worker recruits but learned that the size army required meant a large force was needed, which required the Reds to recruit and eventually conscript peasants. Training and disciplining a large force was challenging, and supplying them was beyond the economic and administrative capability of the Bolsheviks, which then led to supply shortages. Poor provisioning then encouraged desertion with the cycle beginning once again. Massive recruiting was needed to make up for the large-scale desertions. Graves characterized the Bolshevik military forces as a combination of people committed to the ideology, criminals that escaped from prison, and peasants fighting for a representative government.[43]

When the revolution fractured the nation and the Imperial Army collapsed, towns and even trade unions formed units primarily categorized as infantry that ranged in size from 25 to 1,200. The irregular units served the Bolshevik side but eventually gave way to more organized units as resources became available. For example, as early as February 1918 when only 20,000 of an expected 300,000 volunteers materialized from Moscow, the Bolshevik leadership began to see the problem they would face in raising a large army. These mobilization challenges continued and led to conscription. Peasant resistance to conscription interrupted this effort but did not stop it. The Red Army grew from an estimated strength of 800,000 in January 1919 to 3 million in January 1920. By August 1920, there were 4,876,110 soldiers in the Red Army. However, due to training requirements, injuries, and noncombat roles for many soldiers, this probably represented an actual 494,572 combat troops. During 1918 to 1919, the Red Army conscripted approximately the same number of people as it lost through desertion.[44] Without mass mobilization, achieving the numbers required to defeat the White forces would have been problematic.

The Bolsheviks were forced to use a variety of weapons by their having to assemble an army virtually from scratch during conflict. Old hunting rifles to include elephant and tiger guns were widespread in the small partisan units. Soldiers made hand grenades from tin cans filled with such things as dynamite, stones, and bolts.[45]

The Red Army needed the technical expertise that officers from the Imperial Army could bring. Clearly there was concern over loyalty. Many former Imperial Army officers joined the Reds for no other reason than to avoid the promise of torture and injury of themselves and their families if they did not join. When an officer refused to join the Bolsheviks or joined the Reds and deserted to the Whites, retribution was merciless. The Bolsheviks and the Whites, when faced with the reverse situation, made it clear that death was the penalty for the officer and his family. An estimated fifty thousand Imperial Army officers served in the Red Army.[46]

The hard-core Bolsheviks, of course, knew their fate if captured by the White Russians was often the same as that for a deserter. The lack of quarter given then increased their fanaticism and made fighting on when there was little hope of victory the best course. The leaders of the Red Army often seeded their units with a number of dedicated Communists in order to instill this same fighting spirit and dedication in other soldiers who might not be quite so determined to support the Bolshevik cause. An example of the fury that could spring forth from the Bolshevik side was apparent in August and September 1918. On August 30, an officer killed a member of the Petrograd Cheka. That same day two women accosted Nicolai Lenin outside a factory, where he had attended a workers' meeting to hear about their complaints about harassment while riding on a train. One of the women pulled a revolver and shot Lenin three times. Cheka members captured her the following day and immediately executed her. She was known as an anarchist who had been imprisoned under the czar's rule and who had later declared herself a Social Revolutionary. These two unconnected events spurred the Bolshevik hierarchy into action. On September 3, over five hundred people were executed in Petrograd. On September 4, the commissar of Internal Affairs called for mass terror by taking and executing hostages.[47] A campaign of terror was now official.

The purpose was to punish the people who opposed Bolshevik rule. Wealthy people, landowners, former government officials, and former military officers were particularly at risk. The Cheka now had the right to execute "traitors" without the benefit of a trial to adjudge guilt or innocence. The intensity of the terror waxed and waned with the fortunes of the Bolsheviks. However, this campaign of intimidation, torture, and death would continue until the civil war finally ended.[48]

Allied relations with Lenin's government continued to be poor. Differences between Communism and the Western capitalistic systems ensured no common ground could be found. The February 3, 1918, repudiation of all foreign loans in a decree by the All-Russian Central Executive Committee was a factor in this continued the downward spiral of relations.[49]

Other Partisans

Partisan groups opposed to the Bolsheviks, the White Russian groups, and the Allies also operated in Siberia. At times, it is difficult to confirm whether a group mentioned in an official report is actually a partisan band or part of the Bolshevik forces. The successes and failures of one group or another also could result in a partisan group fighting for the Kolchak government one day and for the Bolsheviks the next. Peasants in Siberia, who were not ideologically connected to the Bolsheviks, also opposed the abuses of the czarist government. Corruption and physical abuses by Kolchak's forces resulted in these partisans turning against the White Russian government at the same time that they opposed the Bolsheviks. These "Green" forces opposed Kolchak but wanted a government that would represent the peasants and not the Bolsheviks or people from urban areas. The peasants despised the czarist regime's reliance on strict military discipline. Peasants transferred this hatred to the White Russians who employed many of the same methods of government control. The epaulettes on their uniforms came to be a symbol of this anger and intent to resist.[50]

White Russian attempts to establish state control over the villages of Siberia forced the peasants into direct conflict. Partisan groups at one point dominated an area of Siberia occupied by 1.8 million people. This accounted for about one-fourth of the total population. The Bolsheviks would not defeat the Green partisans until after the American forces departed Siberia. The White Russian leaders realized that the rural peasants could be allies against the urban-oriented Bolsheviks, but the Whites could never develop a policy to entice wholehearted support to their side. Because of this ideological difference between the Bolsheviks and the rural peasants, the Bolsheviks also had difficulty attracting support in the countryside and were suspicious of peasant motives. When peasants resisted recruiting or amalgamation into Red Army units, the Bolsheviks used a combination of reeducation and coercion to convince them. The Bolsheviks used military action to destroy the last holdouts after the Allies departed.[51]

Some of the partisans were soldiers returning home from the Eastern Front. The fighting there convinced them to oppose the old czarist elements, and these former soldiers often returned home already equipped to fight. The fighting all around them forced many peasants to band together for protection. No central government existed to protect them from the warring parties and bandits. Peasants then in some instances banded together for protection from the Whites, Reds, and lawlessness. Partisan groups often centered on a small village especially when an infraction by one villager would result in punishment for an entire village. The partisan movement attracted ethnic Russians, Koreans, Chinese, and even a few escaped Austro-Hungarian soldiers who had been prisoners.[52]

In this text, the word *partisan* at times could refer either to Green or Red forces. The record of the conflict is not always clear. This is a challenge when examining the actions by the soldiers in the AEF. Cultural differences existed, but any Russian civilian could have been Red, White, or Green. As with all soldiers in any period of history, when someone starts shooting at you, time may not allow for an investigation into the complete identity of the attacker, especially when uniforms are scarce, and elements of the civilian population are in the fight. The text descriptions, when based upon sources with a clear identification of the hostile force, include that specification. However, at times the word *partisan* will only indicate some person or group that was a combatant that was not part of a regular military force. American soldiers would find themselves shooting at people they believed to be Bolsheviks, people who were some sort of hostile and armed civilian, and at soldiers who were supposed to be allies such as the Cossacks.

Military Force Structure Review

A brief review of American and other military units fighting in Europe provides a baseline for assessing the impact of the size units sent to or found in Siberia. Each nation developed its own military forces. At times, the Allies shared equipment and cooperated with regard to tactics. Nonetheless, an American division was not the same as a British division or a German one. For example, at the beginning of the war, a 1914 German division consisted of approximately seventeen thousand soldiers. The principal maneuver element was provided by two infantry brigades each with two regiments of three battalions. The division also had seventy-two cannon and twenty-four machine guns. An Austro-Hungarian division in 1914 had approximately fifteen thousand men, seventy-two cannons, and twenty-eight machine guns. Two infantry brigades each with two regiments consisting of three or four battalions provided the primary combat element.[53]

In contrast, a 1914 French division fielded approximately fifteen thousand men, thirty-six cannons, and twenty-four machine guns. The infantry force consisted of two brigades. Each brigade had two regiments with each regiment containing three battalions. The corresponding British division had eighteen thousand soldiers, seventy-six cannons, and twenty-four machine guns. A 1914 Russian division brought twenty thousand men, forty-eight cannons, and thirty-two machine guns. Two brigades each with two regiments of four battalions provided the infantry strength.[54]

The US Army had the luxury of observing the effects of modern warfare and adapting to them prior to deploying for combat. The 1917 American division table of organization called for over twenty-eight thousand soldiers. The 1918 table of organization changed slightly but still required over twenty-eight thousand officers and enlisted men. This division fielded two infantry brigades, an artillery brigade, a machine-gun battalion, and other supporting units. There were twelve 1-pound guns in the two brigades with fifty 3-inch or 75mm guns in the artillery brigade.[55]

A 1918 American infantry brigade included two regiments. Brigades contained 8,469 men, 185 horses, and 854 mules. Weapons included twelve 3-inch mortars, 384 automatic rifles, 960 machine guns, and six 1-pound guns. The organic regiments were organized to have 3,832 men, 192 automatic rifles, 480 machine guns, and three 1-pound guns.[56]

Military Forces Conclusion

As the decision to intervene was made, the situation in Siberia was chaotic. No central authority existed. Pro- and anti-Bolshevik forces roamed the area. No central Allied command structure to conduct and coordinate the intervention existed. The "Aide Memoire" outlined Graves's missions. He was to help the Czechs attempting to leave Siberia for Europe, guard military stores, and to steady Russian attempts at self-government and self-defense. The first two missions were relatively specific compared to the last mission. This third mission would prove to be virtually impossible to accomplish. There were too many factions vying for power. None of these specified tasks included reestablishing the Eastern Front, even though that certainly was a major concern of some of the Allies. The US government never selected one particular faction, group, or person to support wholeheartedly. Graves concluded that his only alternative was to try to remain neutral. The harsh environment of Siberia also added special hardships to military operations and any activity in the region. An understanding of the geography of Siberia is necessary to understand the reasons for and the impact of decisions during the intervention.

5
Siberia's Challenges

Siberia was a land of vast extremes. Understanding the environment in which the American soldiers, their allies, and their opponents operated helps explain why certain operations unfolded as they did and the reasons for many courses of action. Climate, geography, and the rail network affected every aspect of life in Siberia. In Omsk, the temperature ranged from -48°F in the winter to 104°F in summer[1] with an average summer temperature of 65°F. Other example average summer temperatures included Khabarovsk 67°F, Vladivostok 66°F, and Irkutsk 62°F.[2] Summer also brought constant warfare with mosquitoes.[3]

Table 2 provides selected mean, minimum, and maximum temperatures for Siberian and Manchurian cities.[4] The table clearly shows the extremes in temperature that all of the soldiers and civilians in the area had to endure.

Another aspect of the environment worth recognizing is the level of precipitation that fell in the area. Table 3 lists mean precipitation. Ten inches of snow equates to one inch of rain.[5]

Winter generally began in late October. Wind was a severe problem in October and November because of the cold and snowstorms. However, the temperature was lowest in December through February, which was also usually characterized by no wind. This could lull the unsuspecting individual into a false feeling of security and quickly result in frostbitten extremities.[6] Spring started in late April; however, frost and snow occurred as late as May. June usually had warm days and cold nights. July and August comprised summer with fall beginning in September.[7]

Spring thaws turned frozen dirt streets into mud. Garbage thrown out in winter and frozen would thaw and stink in the summer. Planks were used as impromptu sidewalks. Mud would quickly dry leaving deep furrows in roads and streets.[8] Winter included storms that could kill outside sentries because, if they moved, they would get lost and freeze to death. Fine snow froze in cakes on eyes and cheeks.[9] The cold would sometimes even make the guardhouse look good as a way to avoid

Table 2. Mean Temperatures in Siberia

	Temperature (Mean °F)					
City	January	April	July	October	Minimum	Maximum
Vladivostok	5	39	66	49	−34	99
Harbin	−2	42	72	40	−39	N/A
Chita	−18	32	66	29	−46	97
Irkutsk	−5	35	65	33	−43	104
Tomsk	−3	30	66	33	−46	95

Table 3. Precipitation in Siberia

	Mean Precipitation (inches)				
City	January	April	July	October	Annual
Vladivostok	0.0	1.2	2.0	1.6	14.8
Irkutsk	1.0	0.7	3.0	1.0	16.4
Tomsk	0.5	0.4	2.6	1.3	15.3

outside duty.[10] The ground would freeze so deep that the AEF soldiers used holes dug in the ground as refrigerators in the summer.[11]

Sea transportation in and out of Vladivostok was restricted by the extreme winter cold that froze the harbor annually from mid-December until early April. Ice breakers could usually keep the harbor open. The winter cold meant that for weeks at a time water would only be available for cooking and drinking. Water was not a significant problem in the summer, though few public waterworks existed. All water, whether from wells or melted snow, had to be chlorinated before use.[12]

Temperature ranges in the Suchan mine valley northeast of Vladivostok, where an Allied guard force operated to protect the coal mines, were from -34°F in the winter to 99°F in the summer. The mean January temperature was 5°F. The mean August temperature was 69°F. Mean annual precipitation was about fifteen inches, with zero in January and approximately four in August.[13]

Natural resources abounded in Siberia. Many types of furs were trapped, including sable, sea otter, otter, beaver, mink, muskrat, squirrel, fox, skunk, woodchuck, marmot, badger, glutton, and rabbit. Vast forests provided wood for building and heating. Coal was also available, but the widespread use of wood for heating decreased the use of coal. Minerals included platinum, asbestos, manganese, gold, chrome, iron, silver, zinc, copper, and salt.[14]

Southern Siberia boasted huge agricultural lands. Crops included wheat, corn, oats, barley, and buckwheat. Beets were treated like weeds since there was no sugar refining capability.[15] Endless grain fields, grazing lands, and forests meant a person could travel for hours without seeing another human being.[16]

Vladivostok's harbor was important because it was deep enough for use by any ships sailing the Pacific. The harbor's narrow mouth was protected from the open sea by protrusions of land and islands.[17]

Much of Siberia could be described as rolling prairie land similar to the western United States.[18] However, Siberia contained many types of terrain. Low mountains and hills characterized the terrain from Vladivostok to Harbin (483 miles). Traveling west after Harbin, the terrain changed drastically as the Chinese Eastern Railroad crossed the Gobi Desert for 270 miles to the Khingan Mountains. The rail line crossed the mountains at 3,155 feet. Once across the mountains, the terrain consisted of rolling grasslands to the Siberia-Manchuria border (1,064 miles from Vladivostok). The land remained semiarid until Chita, an additional 300 miles.[19]

The area from the Siberia-Manchuria border at Manchuria Station to Lake Baikal was the Trans-Baikal Plateau. From Chita to Irkutsk, the region was hilly with steeper mountains and forests. The Trans-Siberian Railroad reached Lake Baikal at Verkhne-Udinsk. The lake was four hundred miles long and eighteen to fifty-six miles wide. Forests grew around the lake. Irkutsk was roughly 2,800 miles from Vladivostok.[20]

Wind was an important consideration when crossing Lake Baikal. Strong southwest winds in August could cause seven-foot waves that were a threat to small boats. Northeasterly winds were common in May and June. In much of June and July, little wind blew. During such periods of quiet, seaweed would cover the lake surface.[21]

Winter freezing of the lake usually began in November, but ice rarely covered the lake before late December or early January. The ice would be three and one-half feet thick in the center of the lake and thicker near the shore. For about three months each winter, the ice was strong enough to support a train. Spring, of course, ended use of the lake as a railway.[22]

Train ferries were the most important boats traveling on the lake. There were two such ferries. Both connected the city of Baikal with the eastern shore. One ran to Misovaya. The other ran to Pereyemnaya.[23]

Several ferry boats traveled the lake. The *Baikal*, an icebreaker, was 290 feet long and 57 feet wide. It could hold twenty-five rail freight cars on its three tracks. Staterooms accommodated 150 passengers. The other icebreaker was the *Angara*. It was 195 feet long and 34 feet wide. It was usually used for ferrying passengers. At least thirteen other boats and twenty-five barges of various sizes serviced the lake traffic.[24]

Continuing westward, the land remained hilly and mountainous with much timber to Krasnoyarsk (672 miles from Irkutsk). Beyond there, Siberia became a great plain with larger settlements than in the eastern section. Large wheat fields were near Novo Nikolayevst. The most densely settled part of Siberia was between Novo Nikolayevst and Omsk (3,706 miles from Vladivostok). The plain continued to Chelyabinsk and Ekaterinburg on the eastern edge of the Ural Mountains. Ekaterinburg was 4,264 miles from Vladivostok—about the same distance from New York to San Francisco.[25]

Using the route around Manchuria (the Amur line), the distance to Ekaterinburg was 4,824 miles. Rolling hills and wooded areas characterized the area north from Vladivostok near the Ussuri River. The same terrain continued westward along the Amur River. In the summer, the valleys crossed along the Amur were marshy and generally impassable.[26]

The Amur was the only river in southern Siberia that flowed into the Pacific Ocean. Part of it was navigable by river steamers. The Ussuri River joined the Amur at Khabarovsk. The Sungar River flowed north from Harbin to the Amur and was navigable by riverboats. Other navigable rivers included the Irtish, Angara, Yenesei, and Obi Rivers, all of which flowed north to the Arctic Ocean.[27]

Wagon roads, except on the plain, were few and in poor condition. American vehicles and carts had difficulty using the roads due to the width of ruts in them. Russian carts were usually of a more narrow tread than American vehicles and cut ruts that were difficult for American vehicles to use.[28] Mud was one of the biggest problems when trying to use roads in Siberia. The worst time to travel by road was the middle of April to the middle of May. Melting snow turned roads into seas of mud. When roads became impassable due to deep ruts or mud, wagons would only make a new track running parallel to the old.[29] Drifting snow was a winter problem, especially east of Irkutsk. Drifts up to twenty feet deep were common. Regions where the wind blew away most of the snow leaving only a thin coating were interspersed with deep drifts, making road movement often impossible.[30]

Rivers were common throughout Siberia. In the summer, they provided excellent transportation arteries. In the winter, when frozen, they again provided excellent routes. However, between mid-November to mid-December or early January, the rivers were in the process of freezing and made poor roads. The mid-April to mid-May thaw also made the rivers impassable.[31]

The Suchan valley northeast of Vladivostok sits between two spurs of the Sikhota Alin (or Coast Range). The valley is approximately sixty miles long and sixteen miles wide. Crops included wheat, rye, and vegetables. Livestock included dairy and beef cattle, hogs, and chickens. The few people who populated the fertile area were peasants, who occupied small villages and farmed small, outlying strips of land. The small villages had one or two parallel roads and possibly one crossing lane. Fencing closed off the roads so cattle could be herded into the protected area at night.[32]

Log houses with enclosed courtyards were the norm. Larger villages sometimes had a community steam bathhouse. Peasants in smaller villages were forced to bathe in streams—usually only in the summer. This lack of sanitation facilities resulted in vermin-ridden housing. Bed bugs and lice were common, and disease was a significant problem.[33]

On a "special" train, a trip from Vladivostok to Omsk could take nineteen days. Using a "regular" train could result in a thirty-day journey. Few locomotives were operational. The various armies in Siberia commandeered the better railway coaches. Transportation costs significantly increased the cost of goods. For example, a pack of twenty cigarettes cost three cents in Manchuria Station but eighty cents in Chelyabinsk. Sheepskin sold for seven dollars in Harbin and thirty-five dollars at Irkutsk. Salt, tea, and rice were luxuries.[34] However, some goods produced in Siberia were inexpensive. Roast goose sold for eighteen or twenty cents per pound. Butter was available at prices ranging from nineteen to twenty-five cents per pound.[35]

Economic conditions varied throughout the area. Grain and meat were plentiful between Vladivostok and Manchuria Station. Near Lake Baikal, however, starvation was widespread. Traveling westward from Irkutsk, butter, meat, bread, and fish were readily available. Throughout Siberia, household furnishings and clothing were scarce. The naval blockade of Russia that continued after the peace treaty with Germany had a continuing negative effect on living conditions in all of Russia. The Allies established and maintained a blockade at Vladivostok, Murmansk, and Archangel.[36]

Siberian cities had at least one market place—a large square filled with small stands allowing customers to purchase small items. Most finished products, which were displayed on wooden tables or the ground, were secondhand. These markets, or bazaars, served as social as well as business centers. Peasants used the bazaar as forums to discuss such topics as the war, politics, and food prices.[37]

The revolution and civil war resulted in millions of refugees. Currency included a variety of paper bills and postage stamps. Coins were not in circulation. Paper notes included those issued by the czar, Alexander Kerensky's government, the Omsk government, and the Bolsheviks.[38]

As mentioned earlier, travel by train was a challenge but also a necessity. Boxcars were standing room only and had a stove in the center of the car for heat. People would stand in line for eighteen to twenty hours waiting to purchase a ticket. Russian trainmen used whips to control passengers. On the other hand, "special" trains were composed of true passenger cars and dedicated to a particular agency, such as the American Red Cross, or army. No reliable timetables existed. Trains ran when the tracks were clear. Intracity transportation consisted of droshkies (four-wheeled, open, one-seat carriages pulled by Siberian ponies) and sleighs.[39]

Supporting an expeditionary force in Siberia required using the railroad lines for transportation. Additionally a caravan route linked Kalgan, China, to Verkhne-Udinsk. The caravan route was long and difficult to negotiate. It was only useful in a severe emergency. The significant point to note is that all the routes converged in the Lake Baikal area. The main line of the Trans-Siberian Railroad provided the link to western Russia.[40]

The main rail line passed through the valley of the Angara River, which flowed out of Lake Baikal between Verkhne-Udinsk and Irkutsk. There was no route to support a military expedition in Siberia north or south of this valley. A wagon road and a rail line ran around the southern end of the lake. The rail line passed through many tunnels and over many bridges. A few determined men could have easily interdicted the railroad in this area. A 1918 War Department monograph considered this area between Verkhne-Udinsk and Irkutsk the "most critical point between the Pacific Ocean and the German frontier."[41]

Siberia was a difficult place to live. The climate had a wide range of temperatures. Natural resources were plentiful; however, the civil war had destroyed the economic livelihood of the people. Simple necessities such as food and clothing were difficult to find, poverty and filth were rampant, and disease was widespread. Transportation was slow and dangerous due to roving armies. No one group controlled the region. Violence was ever present. Peasants were abused by anyone more powerful than they. Into this confused morass marched the US Army. The AEF deployed to Siberia with the best of intentions—to help the Russian people find democracy and protect America's Czech allies. These good intentions were not universally well received as subsequent pages will show. One group not officially part of the US Army played a central role in the intervention. The Russian Railway Service Corps deployed to Siberia to provide advice and sometimes to supervise the operation of the Trans-Siberian Railroad. After the war these veterans were ignored for years,[42] but without them it is questionable if anyone could have consistently used the rail lines.

6
Russian Railway Service Corps

The Russian Railway Service Corps was a remarkable organization. While not directly part of a military organization, the members dressed in military-style uniforms. Many of the members of the organization believed that they were part of the US military forces. They arrived before the AEF and often supervised the operation of the Russian railroad system, which put them in great danger at times. Their story is an integral part of that of the American soldiers in Siberia and must be understood to gain an appreciation for the American efforts to stabilize the region.

Motivation

The railroad was a critical transportation asset in World War I Russia and especially in Siberia. Distances were great, few roads existed, and horse-drawn transportation was common. Russian farmers could grow food to sustain the population but without the railroad that food could not reach the people who needed it. Therefore, one of the first problems that the Provisional Government had to overcome upon coming to power was a method of food distribution over a railroad system that was in poor condition. The American ambassador notified the US government of this problem. The French and British governments confirmed it. Clearly something had to be done or the lack of food would doom any hope of democracy taking root when the people continued the revolution while seeking food in order to survive.[1]

In 1916, Daniel Willard, who after the war would be the president of the Baltimore & Ohio Railroad, was appointed by Wilson to the Advisory Commission to the Council of National Defense. His position was elevated to that of chairman of the same advisory commission on March 1, 1917. During that month, Stanley Washburn visited Willard and explained that conditions in Russia were deplorable with the Trans-Siberian Railroad near collapse as a transportation network. Washburn, a reporter for the *Chicago News*, had been a war correspondent in the

Russo-Japanese War and had just returned from being with the Russians on the Eastern Front. He argued that the railroad was necessary for Russia because with Archangel iced over and the Black Sea closed due to the war, Vladivostok was the only seaport available through which to pass any sort of supplies to Russia. The Trans-Siberian Railroad then was the lifeline for Russia as the transportation means between a seaport and the rest of the country. Keeping Russia in the war was required in order to occupy the Germans on both fronts.[2]

On March 31, 1917, Washburn testified to a joint meeting of the Advisory Commission and the Council of National Defense regarding the sad state of affairs in Russia. During this same general time, Sir George Drury of Canada also visited and provided a similar opinion. These reports led the members of the Council of National Defense to conclude that they should recommend to the president that he send a small group of railroad experts to Russia in order to confirm the need for assistance.[3]

The Council of National Defense, chaired by the secretary of war, also organized and sent several regiments of railroad men to France in order to support the Allies and the AEF there under the command of Gen. John J. Pershing. S. M. Felton, director general of Military Railways, organized these units that were considered part of the US Army. Even though Felton was a key agent in organizing the Russian Railway Service Corps, he would later contend that the unusual nature of their duties meant that they were not members of the army.[4]

When Ambassador David Francis also telegraphed for railroad men to be sent to Russia to supervise the operation of the Trans-Siberian Railroad, Willard discussed this with the Russian ambassador to the United States and Felton. They even discussed Felton diverting some of the men then being selected for duty in France to Siberia instead. He planned to do that. However, the men who went to France deployed as regiments, typical military units of all ranks. The men deploying to Russia all went as officers with what turned out to be a dubious commission (at least with regard to its military nature), and the Russian government had agreed to pay their salaries.[5]

Wilson decided to send a commission of railroad experts to Russia in order to clarify the situation. John F. Stevens, W. L. Darling, John Greiner, George Gibbs, and Henry Miller of the Advisory Railroad Commission to Russia were appointed by Secretary of State Robert Lansing, traveled to Vladivostok, and developed the report that resulted in the deployment of the Russian Railway Service Corps. Stevens served as the chair. Darling provided maintenance expertise. Greiner focused on bridges and other structures. Gibbs and Miller reviewed equipment and transportation coordination, respectively. The commission was formed in Chicago and left there in early May 1917 to arrive in Vladivostok on May 31. They briefed the Russian Railway Ministry of their findings and recommendations on July 23,

1917. After seeing Prime Minister Alexander Kerensky on August 10, the commission returned to Vladivostok and then the United States. Stevens remained in Siberia so that he could continue to gather information about the railroad. The revolution in February 1917 had delayed the arrival of the railway experts, but eventually the Russian Railway Service Corps went into action with the understanding among the Allies as well as the Russian government that they were in the country to provide expert advice in railroad operations.[6]

The relationship of the men of the Russian Railway Service Corps to the AEF and the US government would remain a question for years. Stevens and his men were not officially in any element of the US military forces. However, they went to Russia as agents of US government policy in an advisory capacity to the Russian government. Their rights to receive military benefits would remain contentious.[7]

Willard notified the secretary of state in September 1917 that mechanics and engineers would be sent to assist Stevens in Siberia. One letter indicated that the secretary of war considered the men to be part of the "engineering forces of the Army."[8] Willard again wrote the secretary of state in October 1917 that George Emerson, who was the general manager of the Great Northern Railroad, would soon deploy with three hundred railroad men to join Stevens. Emerson was to be a lieutenant colonel of engineers. These initial communications implied that the men of the Russian Railway Service Corps were an integral part of the American military establishment. However, this view was not to last. In February 1918, the State Department notified Emerson that the War Department had decided that the railroad men were not part of the military service. This saga of how to define the Russian Railway Service Corps would continue to evolve. Once the AEF was in country Graves received authorization to sell clothing to the railroad men and also to provide medical support and other supplies as if they were in the US Army.[9]

Emerson later would be considered a colonel in the Russian Railway Service Corps. When he originally received the task to raise the railway corps, he traveled to Washington and began to review approximately two thousand applications for rail service. After spending one evening in the Willard Hotel with this mountain of papers, he concluded that a different approach was needed. Emerson then wired the president of the Great Northern Railroad and asked that he call a meeting of the presidents of twelve to fourteen railroads operating in the northwest United States, whom he planned to meet with when he departed Washington, DC. He asked each president to provide a standard set of railroad men, which they did. In this manner Emerson was able to meet the timeline required.[10]

The Russian Railway Service Corps was to be supported by the Russian government. However, the revolution in Russia caused a break in this support. Even after the Bolshevik revolution the Russian railway mission in the United States provided financial support, but even that money could be traced back to an allied technical board in Harbin, China. That board received its financial support from the United States, Japan, and China. Therefore, the Americans in the Russian Railway Service Corps found themselves in a hostile foreign land with a tenuous line of support.[11]

The Red Cross had faced a similar issue of uniforms and some form of rank to ease the integration of its activities with the military forces deployed in Europe. Employees of the Red Cross received "assimilated rank" with no corresponding military duties. Their commissions served as "certificates of identity" in order to ensure appropriate "courtesy and respect" in the discharge of their duties.[12]

The initial recruitment for the Russian Railway Service Corps was for 288 men. Their uniform was similar to the US Army uniform though the collar resembled that of the British uniform. The men wore the same rank insignia as officers in the US Army. The Baldwin Locomotive Company provided 72 of the men so that they could assemble locomotives provided by that company in Vladivostok. Recruiting was conducted in Saint Paul, Minnesota. On November 19, 1917, the corps left San Francisco on the US Army Transport (USAT) *Thomas* en route to Honolulu and Vladivostok. The stopover in Honolulu provided the men an opportunity to see parts of Hawaii. When they arrived at Vladivostok on December 14, the situation was unsafe, so most of the men remained on the ship. A few men went ashore at their own risk using sampans hired for a dime. Due to concerns about the port icing over the *Thomas* then sailed on December 17 to Nagasaki, Japan, arriving on December 24.[13]

As noted, the status of the railroad men with regard to the US Army would remain in question for years. The War Department did not consider them to be soldiers; however, several officers of the corps received treatment in military hospitals in the United States and discharge as if they were in the army. The men serving on the railroads thought they were part of the army. Had they not, some would not have volunteered to serve. Congressional hearings would occur years after the war to resolve their official status.[14] However, that problem was for the future. Right then the men of the Russian Railway Service Corps had a railroad to organize.

Railroad Men in Japan

Emerson, Stevens, and the men of the Russian Railway Service Corps sailed to Japan. Upon arrival, Stevens traveled to Yokohama in order to report the conditions of Vladivostok to the American State and War Departments. Emerson stayed with the men aboard ship. On January 10, 1918, the men were allowed to disembark and occupy quarters in Nagasaki. Shortly thereafter, Stevens ordered Emerson to join him in Yokohama.[15]

Fortunately for the men of the Russian Railway Service Corps there was a small group of Americans who were missionaries and ran the local YMCA in Nagasaki. The missionaries hosted the men and helped them pass the time. The YMCA provided Russian language lessons. The Japan Imperial Railway Board provided travel passes so that the men could tour the country. Dances were held onboard the *Thomas*. The bowling alley of the Nagasaki club was cleaned and re-opened. The operations crews stayed in several hotels—the Nagasaki Hotel, the Bellevue Hotel, the Cliff House, and the Japan Hotel. The men from the Baldwin Locomotive Company were housed in the Ikkakuro Hotel in Obama, about forty miles distant and a seaport.[16]

As often is typical when groups of soldiers are a long way from home, athletic events became a main activity during leisure time. Tennis, baseball, and soccer helped pass the time. The Russian Railway Service Corps teams played groups from the Nagasaki Higher School of Commerce, the Medical College, and Mitsubishi. One group went to Yokohama for a baseball tournament. However, volleyball became the sport of choice once the seats in the YMCA auditorium were removed making room for three courts.[17]

Boredom was a major problem. Recreational activities were the only outlet for this group of men who were accustomed to work hard and expected to go to Russia. Donated books helped. Some men took lessons in using chopsticks. Two men from the group in Obama even walked to Nagasaki once just to pass the time. Wives and daughters of the local missionaries helped reduce the boredom by hosting and attending dances, concerts, and afternoon teas. The men of the Russian Railway Service Corps helped raise money for a piano for the local YMCA. They also organized a jazz band and minstrel performances. The *Nagasaki Press*, the local English language newspaper, ran an article praising the February 15, 1918, minstrel performance held at the YMCA as a benefit for the Red Cross.[18]

Nagasaki was picturesque from the sea when the American railroad men arrived aboard ship. The city sat on the edge of the harbor with a narrow entrance into the bay. Hills surrounded the city. The local population planted small gardens if the hills were too steep for houses. Stone walls encircled many of the terraces. Open-air sewers resulted in an unpleasant smell throughout the city. Streets were a combination of dirt, paved with concrete, or made from stones. There were no automobiles or sidewalks. Transportation was either from an animal-drawn wagon or cart, human-powered rickshaw, or bicycle. Houses were built from wood with paper screens. Few houses had glass windows.[19]

While the railroad men were setting up quarters in Nagasaki, Emerson and Stevens crossed to Korea in order to work their way into Manchuria and China and determine when they could transfer the men to Siberia. Taking the South

Manchuria Railroad, they reached Chanchung and then Harbin. A representative of the Kerensky government met them with assurances that his government had made an agreement with the Bolsheviks regarding the railroad. The men agreed to carry out the original plan to support the Chinese Eastern Railroad. In March, slightly over one hundred men left Japan for Manchuria. Then the Kerensky representative announced that the deal with the Bolsheviks had fallen through. The men of the Baldwin Locomotive Company returned to the United States when it became apparent that they would not be needed in Vladivostok. They left Nagasaki in April 1918 in small groups on three ships, the *Empress of Japan*, the *Empress of Asia*, and the *China*. Two more months of negotiations ensued regarding the Russian Railway Service Corps men still scheduled to go to Russia. In July, another group of approximately eighty left Japan for Vladivostok. They docked before the American infantry regiments arrived and landed in conjunction with the Japanese forces. By December 30, 1918, there would be 194 Russian Railway Service Corps men in Siberia.[20]

Initial Actions in Siberia

Emerson received a request from the State Department to link up with Ambassador Francis and ascertain if the Allies could do anything to stabilize the situation in European Russia. Emerson went to Vladivostok and met Adm. Austin M. Knight, who was the senior American in the city. Knight told Emerson that he had no means to assist Emerson in his mission to travel through Siberia to European Russia. The American consul also told Emerson that the US government had no agreement with the Bolsheviks for his safe passage.[21] Undeterred, Emerson concluded that he had best meet with the local Bolshevik leader.

Upon meeting the Russian peasant who was the senior Bolshevik representative in the area, Emerson received assurances that Leon Trotsky had decreed that the Bolsheviks would provide safe passage and support him in his mission as necessary. Emerson then chose seven of his Russian Railway Service Corps men to accompany him on the trip. Before they could depart, Emerson coordinated with Knight to inventory all of the military supplies in Vladivostok as all of the Allies wanted to know the status of military equipment available.[22]

Cossacks under Ataman Grigori Semenov's command had cut the Chinese Eastern Railroad line by the time the inventory was completed. Therefore, Emerson decided to travel up the Amur line that paralleled the Amur River north of Manchuria. At Khabarovsk, Emerson met a Bolshevik leader who claimed to be in charge of all soviets in Siberia. This man also told Emerson six months before he had been practicing law in Chicago. As Knight had asked Emerson to collect information on all munitions along his route, Emerson asked this Bolshevik leader for permission to do so. The Americans and Bolsheviks were not in conflict yet, so the request was granted. Emerson also made a survey of the condition, grades, and stations along the rail line that he later passed to the AEF.[23]

Numerous breaks in the rail line slowed his journey westward. Emerson and his party spent about two weeks traversing the Amur line. Once he reached the junction with the Trans-Siberian Railroad coming out of China at the Karinskaza junction, the rail line was in much better condition. At Verkhne-Udinsk, the party of Americans encountered a group of German former prisoners of war who were boarding a train to travel home. A German officer met with them and said that Germany and Russia were now at peace, so they were going home. This officer said he had been a professor at Chicago University for fourteen years prior to the war. After a short delay, the Germans allowed Emerson to continue westward to Lake Baikal.[24]

Emerson discovered that there were forty-one tunnels around Lake Baikal. The Bolsheviks were mining them as protection against a Cossack attack to the east. Emerson continued westward to Irkutsk and met the American and French consuls. There he learned that the movement of the Czech Legion toward Vladivostok was encountering opposition from the Bolsheviks. Ernest L. Harris, the American consul general at Irkutsk, and the French consul general asked Emerson to continue to the west and mediate the dispute between the Czechs and the Bolsheviks. Emerson wired both sides that he was on the way to the front line four hundred miles to the west. The Czechs and Bolsheviks agreed to allow Emerson to mediate.[25]

The Czech Legion, by one estimate fifty thousand strong at this juncture, was in a difficult situation. As they understood the situation, Russia and the Central Powers were no longer at war and all soldiers of the Austro-Hungarian Empire were to be disarmed and repatriated. Since the officers and men of the Czech Legion had actually deserted from the Austro-Hungarian forces and joined the Russians, surrender such as this was a death sentence. Emerson encountered this problem when he met with an officer from the Czechs to begin his negotiations.[26]

Negotiations resulted in a truce between the Bolsheviks and Czechs being declared for six days in the area east of the meeting, Marinsk. West of Marinsk, the Czechs were free to operate as they decided. Consequently, the Czechs, who had been in part disarmed, attacked to the west to seize an arsenal. This allowed them to rearm with small arms and even field artillery. The Czechs captured Omsk and continued to the Ural Mountains. Emerson found himself a virtual prisoner of the Czechs because they had connected the railcar he was using to one of their trains to help him move around during the negotiations. Once at the Urals, Emerson finally convinced the Czechs that his mission really was to run the railroad and that he was trying to make contact with Ambassador David Francis. The Czechs then allowed Emerson to contact the Bolsheviks to be allowed to proceed to the west. The Bolsheviks refused. Consequently the Czechs ordered Emerson back to Omsk. The day Emerson reached Omsk this time a French officer arrived and told him that the Allies had decided to intervene in Siberia. The Czechs were to remain in place. Previously with little information on the war and reports from the Central Powers former prisoners that they had won the war, Emerson had decided to stay with the Czechs who had vowed to fight their way to Vladivostok, approximately four thousand miles distant.[27]

When Harris confirmed the report of the French officer, Emerson offered to support the Czechs. They agreed. The Czechs had the Americans join their engineering department to prepare armored railcars to lead the attack to the east and also to be prepared to rebuild bridges. Emerson estimated that about three hundred bridges required reconstruction. The Czechs and Americans constructed the armored cars by plating steel gondola cars with steel rail and pouring concrete inside the cars. Holes cut in the sides allowed machine guns to fire. A 3-inch gun was placed in the front of the car to clear the path straight ahead.[28]

Emerson and the Czechs then began the attack to the east to clear the path to Vladivostok. Upon reaching Irkutsk and Lake Baikal, they encountered the tunnels mentioned previously. The Bolsheviks had blown one of the forty-one tunnels, so Emerson and the Czechs began to clear it with the aid of approximately 450 German prisoners used for labor. However, that required twenty-eight days of difficult work while under fire from the Bolsheviks. Besides their ground forces, the Bolsheviks had two icebreaker ships on Lake Baikal that shelled the Czech force while they were clearing the destroyed tunnel.[29]

The lead element of the Czechs numbered around two thousand men. After several days of clearing operations, a major element flanked the Bolsheviks, cut the rail line, and seized nine trains, forcing the Bolsheviks to retreat. While this was underway, the commander of the Czech force rear detachment raised a sunken raft, mounted a 5-inch gun on it, and started across the twenty-two miles of Lake Baikal in a fog that had settled over the lake. Once he sank the two Bolshevik icebreakers, clearing the tunnel became much less dangerous. At least the Bolsheviks could not shell them anymore.[30]

After clearing the tunnel area around Lake Baikal, the Czechs continued to push eastward defeating any Bolshevik force and reportedly one large group of released German prisoners. As Emerson described it, this "running fight" continued until they linked up with Japanese forces in Manchuria in November 1918. Emerson also believed by then that the situation in Siberia was relatively peaceful right after this occurred since the Czechs had defeated every sizeable force that had tried to interfere with their movement. Emerson and Maj. H. H. Slaughter, a Regular Army officer who had been traveling with him; prepared a report for John Stevens, Knight, and Graves once they reached Vladivostok.[31]

At this time, the Allies had signed the armistice ending combat operations in Europe, but the chaotic situation in Siberia and the recently arrived Allied forces meant there was still a need for the Russian Railway Service Corps. Emerson and his men stayed though the men from the Baldwin Locomotive Company departed because they had finished their work assembling locomotives. Emerson organized his remaining group of approximately 160 men to run the 4,000-mile rail line. Operating in groups of two to three men with little protection from American or other Allied military forces, these tough railroad men strove to keep the trains rolling. Their independence and adherence to American ideals were critical. They would often be required to act with little but American values[32] and their technical expertise as a guide.

Importance of the Railroad

The railroad was the transportation lifeline for everyone regardless of nationality or ideology. Protecting the railroad was a critical military task in order to ensure that the military forces of the Allied nations could move large distances and be supplied. Protecting the railroad also sustained civilian life because the only assured means of travel in all weather was a train. Therefore, the Russian Railway Service Corps men were a crucial element in the American and Allied military forces' own survival and their ability to accomplish any mission.

The American Expeditionary Force–Siberia (AEF-Siberia or simply AEF when clearly referring to the American forces in Siberia) was the US military element of the Allied intervention in Siberia. A description of the AEF-Siberia's composition follows as a means of explaining the capabilities available in this deployment such a long way from home.

7
American Expeditionary Force

Even before Graves received notification of his selection as the AEF-Siberia commander, the War Department staff was planning the structure of the forces that were to be at his disposal. Detailed planning went into the preparations of the expeditionary force. The men deploying into Siberia would need cold weather equipment and sufficient arms to combat the potential enemy forces. They also needed support from other military services and a variety of nonmilitary groups. No one knew the amount of time the soldiers of the AEF-Siberia would remain, so they had to be ready to function independently from any higher headquarters. Even while the US forces were still moving into Siberia, the first Americans would go into action. The deployment sequence, organization, equipment, supporting nonmilitary organizations, and tactics employed by the AEF were key elements in determining the success of the mission. The fate of the imperial family and initial effects of the foreign intervention would continue to color the operations of America's soldiers in Siberia. The lack of a clear mission supported by all agencies of the US government and the Allies with forces in Siberia would continue to cause problems for Graves and his soldiers.

Deployment

A July 6, 1918, memorandum to the army chief of staff recommended the use of the Twenty-Seventh and Thirty-First Infantry Regiments in the Philippine Islands as the core of the AEF. As both were understrength for a combat mission, the recommendation included supplementing the regiments with additional soldiers after they arrived at Vladivostok. The State Department had already recommended the immediate deployment of the two regiments. Several reasons argued for the dispatch of the understrength regiments. The memorandum pointed out the utility of an American force serving as a rallying point for anti-German forces whether Russian or Czechoslovakian. An Allied force moving into Siberia with an American component would be viewed as a rescue force, though the author of the memorandum did not point out the unit or persons to be rescued or the people who would view the force in this manner. Finally, since combat was not expected, waiting for replacements to arrive was not necessary. The "moral effect" of the deployment of the two regiments outweighed any argument for waiting for replacements who would be new recruits.[1] Supplementing units with additional soldiers is not a novel concept; however, such techniques affect unit cohesion until the new members fully integrate into the unit and become accepted members.

Plans included a nine-day voyage from the Philippines to Vladivostok aboard US Army Transport ships. Additional augmentation included a field hospital, ambulance support, engineers, and communications support. The plan called for dispatching the two regiments in early August to arrive at Vladivostok around August 20. Two groups of three hundred men each would be sent from the American Pacific Coast as reinforcements. One group would sail in early August and arrive at Vladivostok near the end of August. The second would sail from the United States once transports were available. The War Department expected to complete troop deployments to bring the AEF to full strength by mid-October.[2]

Winter clothing and the additional weapons and equipment to outfit the AEF were expected to be available whenever needed for shipment from the United States. One shipload of supplies was projected to provide seven months' sustenance. Fresh beef was available at Tsing Tau, China, which was already supplying US troops in the Philippines. Should ice blockage of the Vladivostok harbor become a problem, three other ports were available with rail lines to Vladivostok through Mukden, China. The ports were Fusan in Korea, Chinwangta in China, and Darien in Manchuria. Rail lines connected all three through Mukden to Harbin and then Vladivostok. Even though the railway was not in superb condition, the railroad reconstruction being undertaken was expected to keep the line open.[3]

Another significant event occurred on July 6. The Allied forces in Vladivostok issued a proclamation telling the citizens of Vladivostok that the Allies were instituting "all necessary measures" to safeguard the city and Allied forces from "external as well as internal danger." The city government would still be allowed to administer local civil affairs. But the Allies promised to take military and police action as necessary to protect the city from "Austro-German prisoners, spies, and emissaries." Adm. Austin Knight, commander in chief of the Asiatic Fleet of the United States, as well as Japanese, British, French, Chinese, and Czechoslovak representatives signed the proclamation.[4]

These plans were followed by messages to the Philippines and Camp Fremont in California to make the AEF a reality. The War Department cabled the commanding general of the Philippine Division on August 3, 1918, to send the Twenty-Seventh and Thirty-First Infantry Regiments to Vladivostok on the first available

US Army Transports (USAT). A field hospital, ambulance company, and telegraph company were to accompany the regiments. USATs *Warren*, *Merritt*, and *Crook* were designated for use. The telegram named Graves as the AEF commander and stated five thousand men would be sent from San Francisco to Vladivostok to complete the regiments' authorized strengths.[5]

The War Department cabled Graves on August 3 and informed him of the instructions to the Philippine Division. The War Department also instructed Graves to select five thousand men from the Eighth Division at Camp Fremont for service with the AEF. Additional instructions included taking his "Chief of Staff, Assistant Chief of Staff, necessary intelligence officers, and such members of his division staff" as he deemed necessary. Graves was to coordinate directly with the commanding general of the Philippine Division regarding assignment of staff officers to support the AEF from the Philippines.[6]

Subsequent to the above-noted telegrams, the War Department told the Eighth Division to provide thirty-nine first lieutenants and twenty-four second lieutenants for the AEF. Additional officer vacancies in the Twenty-Seventh and the Thirty-First Regiments were to be filled by appointing enlisted men from the regiments as second lieutenants.[7]

Pursuant to orders, the Twenty-Seventh Infantry under the command of Col. Henry D. Styer sailed from the Philippines August 7, 1918, aboard the USATs *Crook*, *Warren*, and *Merritt*.[8] The Thirty-First Infantry under Col. Frederic H. Sargent sailed from the Philippines on August 12 aboard the USAT *Sherman* for Vladivostok.[9]

On August 14, Graves with the first of his California-based troops left Camp Fremont on two trains for the transport dock at Fort Mason, San Francisco.[10] This group left the same day on the USAT *Thomas*. Lt. Col. O. P. Robinson accompanied Graves as chief of staff with Maj. Robert L. Eichelberger as assistant chief of staff. The US battleship *Oregon* and the US gunboat *Vicksburg* accompanied this element.[11]

A recapitulation of the AEF forces en route by August 14 is provided in table 4.[12]

On August 15, the *Warren* and *Crook* arrived at Vladivostok. The *Merritt* docked the next day.[13] When the first troops arrived they did not know their mission. Rumors included such ideas as establishing a new Eastern Front, killing Bolsheviks, capturing escaped prisoners of war, and helping the Czech Legion.[14] This confusion grew when Gen. Kikuzo Otani, the Japanese forces commander, informed Colonel Styer that the Allies had entrusted command of all Allied forces to him.[15] Styer, having no order to the contrary, and knowing he was allied with the Japanese, agreed to support Otani until Graves arrived.

Meanwhile, the remainder of the AEF continued to sail for Vladivostok. The Thirty-First Infantry arrived on August 21.[16] The *Vicksburg* had ceased its escort duties and returned to San Francisco on August 16.[17] The *Oregon* followed the

Table 4. AEF Siberia Forces in Transit, August 14, 1918

Element	Officers	Men
USATs *Crook, Warren,* and *Merritt* sailing on August 7	53	1,537
USAT *Sherman* sailing August 12	45	1,379
USAT *Thomas* sailing August 14	47	1,889
Total	145	4,805

Vicksburg's example and stopped escorting the USATs in transit on August 17. Afterward, the troops on the transport ships manned Browning machine guns and 1-pounder cannons on deck for self-protection.[18] The *Thomas*, with Graves, docked at Vladivostok on September 2.[19] Unknown to Graves, during his passage to Siberia the Twenty-Seventh Infantry conducted the AEF's first combat action as part of an Allied force under Japanese command attacking Bolsheviks. Before Graves could prevent it, his command violated the spirit of the "Aide Memoire" by taking sides in the civil war.

Organization and Equipment

Additional trips by the army transport ships supporting the AEF delivered the remainder of the forces to Siberia. On September 14, the USATs *Warren* and *Crook* disembarked Ambulance Company Number Four and Field Hospital Number Four from the Philippines. The ambulance company set up operations at Ulysses Bay. The field hospital established an evacuation point at Khabarovsk. A total of 7 officers and 129 enlisted men were included in the two medical elements. The field hospital at Khabarovsk was upgraded to a one-hundred-bed hospital November 11, when the Twenty-Seventh Infantry's medical detachment combined with Field Hospital Number Four. A fifty-bed hospital began operations at Spasskoe on November 22 by transferring personnel from Khabarovsk. The Twenty-Seventh Infantry had earlier established another one-hundred-bed hospital at the German prisoner of war camp at Krasnaya Rechks November 8.[20]

By January 1919, a substantial number of medical personnel had arrived in Vladivostok as members of the two infantry regiments, Ambulance Company Number Four, Field Hospital Number Four, Evacuation Hospital Number Seventeen, and Medical Supply Depot Number Seventeen. A total of 76 officers, 27 nurses, and 629 enlisted men would man and operate the hospitals, ambulances, veterinary facilities, dental clinics, and medical supply depot. Twelve animal-drawn ambulances and four motor ambulances were available with Ambulance Company Number Four to supplement regimental ambulances. Two hospital trains, one made from six boxcars and the other from four boxcars, were used on the rail-

Table 5. AEF Siberia Hospitals, January 1919

Location	Beds
Base (Vladivostok)	431
Khabarovsk	74
Spasskoe	50
Harbin	8
Razdolnoe	21
Suchan Mines	12

ways. One boxcar on each was used as a ward with a kitchen and another boxcar was devoted to supplies. Hospitals as of January 1919 are listed in table 5.[21]

Disease would take a large toll on AEF soldiers. The most prevalent diseases were plague, typhus, typhoid fever, scarlet fever, relapsing fever, and malignant sore throat. Venereal disease was a particular problem and incapacitated many.[22]

Replacements from Camp Fremont arrived at Vladivostok September 29 on USATs *Sheridan* and *Logan* with an additional 3,682 soldiers. This group included an evacuation hospital, a medical supply depot, an ordnance detachment, and dental and veterinary elements. These replacements were used to bring the two regiments up to full strength, form an AEF headquarters detachment, and organize a replacement battalion. The headquarters detachment contained 1 officer and 64 enlisted men. The replacement battalion consisted of 6 officers and 250 enlisted men.[23] The 1918 table of organization and equipment called for an infantry regiment to have 3,832 men.[24]

The AEF headquarters formed an intelligence section from the officers and men arriving on the *Sheridan* supplemented by soldiers that had arrived earlier. The recent arrivals from the *Sheridan* included sixteen members of the Military Intelligence Division, Washington. Four officers and fifty-one enlisted men had arrived earlier and were assigned because of their knowledge of Slavic languages, Japanese, or German. A detachment of one officer and eighteen enlisted men from the Corps of Engineers was assigned for mapping. Another group of eighteen enlisted men was assigned to the Intelligence Section from the Signal Corps for communications support. With the fifteen clerks assigned, this section totaled 123 soldiers.[25]

Intelligence is crucial in any military operation. Given the limited information available before the deployment, the AEF would need good intelligence work once in Siberia to identify and separate friend from foe. The changing nature of the AEF's allies would make intelligence that much more critical to the understanding of the situation.

This large number of personnel supported a code and cipher section, a map section, a censorship section, and a counterespionage section. The Intelligence Section worked with the other allied forces regarding telegraph and postal censorship. Passport control was a cooperative venture with the other Allied forces but did not produce any important results. The Intelligence Section accomplished little counterespionage work beyond establishing a list of suspected agents. The engineer detachment was successful at collecting and reproducing maps. The translators, who were of high value in supporting AEF operations, provided the means for AEF elements to converse with the local population and captured enemy soldiers. Only one officer who spoke Japanese was available, which was a source of much concern. Many of the soldiers who were language interpreters happened to be Jewish, which was often a problem in working with Russian officers, who often exhibited a high level of prejudice against Jews. The Intelligence Section also produced translated copies of local newspapers that provided valuable information about local events and opinions. A censorship office supervised the review of incoming and outgoing communications for all Allied forces under the leadership of a British officer. The AEF leadership decided that there was insufficient intelligence work to keep such a large group busy and eventually reduced the size of the section.[26]

Communication support is another critical function in any military operation. The poor infrastructure in Siberia increased the importance of maintaining the available assets. Redundancy would be hard to find. The signal detachment accompanied the Twenty-Seventh Infantry from the Philippines to Vladivostok. The eighteen soldiers were from Company D, Fifty-Third Telegraph Battalion. The remainder of Company D, one first lieutenant and fifty-one enlisted men, arrived September 18. Later reinforcements increased the number of enlisted men to eighty-one. Telephone communication in and around Vladivostok was established September 19. The section established telegraph communication between Vladivostok and Khabarovsk on August 22 and later with Chita. The Vladivostok telegraph office handled approximately two thousand words daily.[27]

On November 4, 1918, two officers and four enlisted men arrived as a Signal Corps photographic unit.[28] During its first three months of operations, the photographers took 1,200 still negatives and 12,000 feet of motion picture film. These visual records included parades, foreign soldiers, and all aspects of AEF operations.[29]

A quartermaster detachment of eleven officers and ninety-one enlisted men supported the AEF initially.[30] Winter clothing had to be provided because some soldiers were shipped to Siberia without any.[31] Sufficient winter clothing soon arrived to outfit the AEF.[32] The issued winter clothing was similar to that used in Alaska and included the following items:[33] three-quarter length wool-lined coat, fur cap, fur mittens, wool blouse, wool trousers, knit underwear, light wool underwear, wool shirts, lumberman's knit socks, shoe packs, and parkas.

Regular marching shoes had tops that were too short and soles too thin. The standard wrap puttees were not durable or waterproof. Issue gloves were also not durable in the harsh Siberian winters. Standard shelter tents were judged of no value in the winter. Exposed piping on the rolling kitchens froze in the cold and made this piece of equipment worthless.[34] Graves later reported the fur-lined coat to be too short. He suggested any coat issued for use in Siberia extend at least four inches below the knee. He also noted the rolling kitchens and escort wagons were too heavy for use in Siberia.[35]

Monthly shipments from San Francisco ensured that a six-month supply of necessities could be maintained except for milk and tomatoes. The mules and horses supplied from the Philippines were in good condition. The AEF purchased wood in Siberia, while coal was available from Japan and San Francisco. Mineral oil for lamps and gasoline were purchased locally and from the Philippines. A limited amount of materials for construction and building were available. Hay purchased locally for enlisted men and animal bedding was generally satisfactory.[36]

Motor transportation assets included nineteen automobiles and trucks, twenty-five motorcycles, and fourteen motorcycle sidecars. Ten of the automobiles were procured locally and did not function well. These 1915 Mitchell seven-passenger touring cars apparently sat on the beach at Vladivostok two or three years before the AEF arrived. The quartermaster detachment supervised construction and repair work, stevedore work, road building near Vladivostok, water-distilling plants, bath facilities, a steam laundry, and a facility to repair shoes as well as to manufacture and repair uniforms. Russian workmen and prisoners of war provided the labor force.[37]

The ordnance detachment initially consisted of one officer and two sergeants that arrived September 2, 1918. Six additional officers (later reduced to four) and seventy-eight enlisted men arrived September 29. The infantry regiments possessed a full authorization of weapons except for trench mortars. Soldiers were armed with M1903 bolt action rifles. Additional small arms included machine guns and M1918 Browning Automatic Rifles (BAR). The infantry regiments were also equipped with 37mm guns.[38] No field artillery was assigned to the AEF even though 2.95-inch mountain guns and 3.2-inch guns with limbers and caissons were available in the Philippines.[39]

After all requisitions of equipment were filled, the ordnance depot possessed an abundance of material. The AEF stockpiled over 10 million rounds of .30-caliber ammunition and 350,000 rounds of .45-caliber ammunition. Spare weapons included 16 heavy Browning machine guns, 46 Vickers machine guns, 370 automatic rifles, over 1,000 pistols, and over 7,000 rifles. The stocks exceeded the AEF requirement.[40]

Machine guns and automatic rifles were issued to support AEF units and the AEF's machine-gun school established at Churkin. The Model 1918 automatic rifles performed satisfactorily. The Model 1917 machine guns performed well but did experience an excessive number of bottom plate breakages while being fired at the machine-gun school. The Twenty-Seventh and Thirty-First Infantry arrived with Model 1919 Benet Mercie machine guns that were replaced and returned to the Philippines. The regiments arrived at Vladivostok without automatic rifles because none were available in the Philippines. Replacement and resupply ships from the United States provided the M1918s issued by the ordnance detachment. Both regiments also arrived with obsolete 37mm pompom guns that were replaced with the new 37mm gun December 1918 to January 1919.[41] As of 30 June 1919, gas masks were held in reserve by the ordnance depot.[42]

The Model 1918 BAR had a selector switch for semiautomatic or automatic fire. Ammunition was provided by a magazine holding twenty or forty rounds. The BAR rate of fire was five hundred rounds per minute. The weapon weighed fifteen pounds, eight ounces empty. Theoretically, a soldier armed with a BAR could engage targets out to a range of 1,600 yards.[43] Best results were obtained using rates of fire of eight to one hundred rounds per minute standing and fifty and sixty shots per minute prone. The standard BAR crew included three soldiers: a gunner, first ammunition carrier (loader), and second ammunition carrier (scout).[44]

The term "machine gun cart" referred to three different carts: gun carts, ammunition carts, and spare gun carts. All were one-mule carts, but they differed by the number of ammunition racks, gun carrying cases, tripod supports, and a few minor characteristics. A special metal towing pole and emergency rope provided the ability for the carts to be towed by hand if needed. Pioneer tools carried on the gun and ammunition carts included a shovel, pick mattock, and broad hatchet. The only pioneer tool on the spare gun cart was the hatchet.[45]

The gun cart carried a machine gun in a box running the length of the cart. The water-cooled Browning Model 1917 and Vickers Model 1915 machine guns fit snugly inside the box with a special cover fitting around the water jacket. The ammunition rack held seven boxes of ammunition.[46]

The ammunition cart carried fourteen ammunition boxes and two tool chests. Each ammunition box contained 250 rounds in loaded belts. Two water boxes were also included. The spare gun cart carried two gun chests, and two tripods could be carried on the cart between the two gun chests. Each machine gun company received two spare gun carts to carry their extra four machine guns.[47]

The Model 1916 37mm gun was mounted on a tripod but could be mounted on wheels. A light wheeled cart was available as a limber and caisson for ammunition. One animal (such as a horse) would pull the gun and limber. Each weapon required an eight-man crew. Cast-iron, armor-piercing, and shrapnel shells were available with weights of 0.665, 0.720, and 0.770 kilograms, respectively. Maximum range was 2,400 meters with a 10.1-second time of flight. Each crew carried 144 shells on the cart.[48]

American weapons generally performed well in Siberia. For example, US rifle bullets could penetrate railroad rails. Bolshevik bullets could not.[49] The M1903 .30-caliber rifle had a maximum effective range of six hundred yards and a maximum rate of fire of ten aimed shots per minute.[50] The M1911 .45-caliber pistol earned quite a reputation. The "Amerikanski Colt" was even known to disperse crowds just by the mention of its name.[51] The M1911 was officially listed as accurate to seventy-five yards.[52]

Machine guns and 37mm guns were transported by animal-drawn carts that proved to be a problem. Axle eyes and stay hooks frequently broke. Soldiers improvised packs for both weapons from wood and canvas to relieve the need for the carts. The lack of field artillery was later to prove a difficulty when facing enemy forces equipped with guns on armored trains or with field artillery.[53]

Armored trains played an integral part of combat action throughout Siberia. Armaments on them varied. Machine guns and light cannons were standard. Rifle-firing ports cut in the armor plating that lined the boxcars and gondolas provided soldiers riding in the cars the ability to fire from the trains. Sibley stoves heated the boxcars in winter.[54] Armored trains provided a protected base of fire or functioned as armored assault vehicles. The specific armaments on such trains and the tactics concerning their use will be described in later pages when various battles are discussed.

It is impossible to assemble a large group of people such as the AEF and expect everyone to act properly. The AEF was authorized to appoint General Courts-Martial as early as August 1918 when the Twenty-Seventh Infantry Regiment landed. An Office of Judge Advocate began operations on September 3, 1918, with one officer, one clerk, and one sergeant-major. The first General Court-Martial began September 14, 1918, for an enlisted man's trial.[55] Other courts-martial occurred as necessary. Punishments were not light. For example, one soldier that deserted to the Bolsheviks for a Russian girl in Khabarovsk turned himself in to the AEF in the spring of 1919. He was tired of being with the Reds. His General Court-Martial sentenced him to twenty years confinement for desertion in time of war.[56] The ease with which alcohol could be obtained in the local community fostered many of the courts-martial.[57]

Nonmilitary Support for the AEF

Several morale support agencies operated with the AEF in Siberia. The American Red Cross mission first arrived in Petrograd on August 7, 1917. It ministered to all in need, even cooperating with the Bolsheviks when necessary to ensure the safe delivery of supplies.[58] Dr. Raymond Teusler, cousin of Mrs. Woodrow Wilson, headed the American Red Cross mission in Vladivostok.[59] To supplement military supplies, the Red Cross furnished the AEF soldiers with socks and other winter clothing.[60] The Red Cross provided aid to the Russian people, White Russian soldiers, and Czechoslovakians as well as the AEF. The Red Cross ran relief trains carrying food, clothing, and medicine to stations located along the railway. Three sanitary trains and one dental train also circulated through the area. One Red Cross antityphus train shuttled between Vladivostok and Perm, bathing 105,000 people and disinfecting 1 million articles of clothing. The Red Cross mission eventually grew to a staff that included more than 300 Americans and over 1,000 foreign national workers. This included 146 nurses and 43 nurse's aides. Total expenditures included donated materials exceeding $23 million.[61] Dr. Teusler was decidedly pro-Kolchak; he was even later accused of being the virtual surgeon-general of Kolchak's army. The Red Cross provided little or no support to the Bolsheviks.[62]

The Red Cross worked hard to support soldiers and civilians in Siberia. Col. George Emerson reported an example that he encountered on a train of the Russian Railway Service Corps in December 1918. The train was under the control of the Czech Legion but carried a large number of prisoners the Czechs wanted to hand off to someone. The escort of 118 men included 15 soldiers who were sick, but the Russian authorities in Vladivostok refused to take the prisoners into hospital facilities. The train had thirty-eight cars, twenty-six carrying prisoners with thirty-two to thirty-three prisoners per car. When Emerson checked the train in Harbin, he noted that it had meat and bread for about a day and that the guards had no money to use to buy food. He also reported that human excrement and blood poured out the doors of the railcars. Diseases included dysentery, typhoid fever, syphilis, pneumonia, rheumatism, burns, and bullet wounds. Emerson notified Graves and the Red Cross in Vladivostok seeking help for the prisoners and guards.[63]

The Allied leadership encouraged sports competition as a morale builder. Baseball and football fields and tennis courts were established. Crafts such as pottery, machine shop, and art were available for a soldier to learn.[64] The Canadian forces hosted an Allied sports contest at the Hippodrome in Vladivostok. The Twenty-Seventh Infantry held a Wild West show in Khabarovsk.[65] Contests were also held to display soldier skills. One representative from each of the Allied forces was selected to compete in front of a board of staff officers. The competition judged military bearing and the ability to assemble and disassemble a rifle, pack, and associated equipment.[66]

Alcohol was a problem; however, it was not the only problem that faced the AEF leadership. Illegal drugs were also available. American soldiers caught a Chinese cocaine peddler in Spasskoe trying to sell his product to Americans. The AEF leadership transferred him to the local Chinese garrison. They whipped him and banished him from the town.[67]

The American Library Association shipped over sixteen thousand books to the

AEF. Periodicals such as *Atlantic Monthly*, *Scientific American*, *The Police Gazette*, and many more were sent. YMCA representatives and unit morale officers distributed these materials. The YMCA had remained in Russia to support the Russian army. Its representatives tried to remain neutral in the civil war that erupted between the White and Red Russians. The YMCA leadership recruited new secretaries and continued to expand operations through the Allied intervention. However, the Bolsheviks never accepted the YMCA as being truly neutral, which forced the YMCA representatives in Russia to rely on the Allied armies including the Czechs for their safety and eventual escape and evacuation.[68] Young Women's Christian Association (YWCA) representatives also were in Siberia working with the AEF.[69]

The Knights of Columbus was active in Siberia as well. Vaudeville acts, musical performances, and motion picture shows were provided free of charge to soldiers. The Knights of Columbus operated two cafes that served free meals to American troops. During one of the revolts that occurred in Vladivostok, Knights of Columbus representatives provided hot coffee and sandwiches to American guards, even though such actions involved personal risk.[70] Gifts such as cigarettes, tobacco, candy, crackers, cake, toothpaste, chocolate, wool mufflers, and mittens were distributed. The 1919 Christmas shipment even included one thousand footballs.[71]

One concern regarding such nonmilitary agencies arose during the AEF's operations. The Red Cross, YMCA, Knights of Columbus, and Russian Railway Service Corps personnel all wore uniforms similar to the US Army. However, these individuals were not subject to army regulations. Foreigners had difficulty differentiating between the groups. Improper action by certain civilians had a negative impact on the army's image with the army having no way to correct the error. This problem was common enough for a few soldiers to use alleged lack of recognition as an excuse for not following an officer's orders. Graves felt that all civilian organizations should have distinct uniforms in order to preclude such confusion in the future. Allowing people who were not in the army to wear uniforms similar to the army caused problems ranging from soldiers and civilians not knowing whether someone was in the army to uniform wear violations that made the army appear undisciplined.[72]

Tactics

Military tactics selected differed to some degree for each situation encountered and the leader concerned. However, there were several tactics and techniques employed by the AEF, other Allied forces, and the partisans that are worthy of note here. Actions taken in specific operations will be discussed in subsequent chapters.

The use and type of fire support assets differed among the various combatants. The largest support weapon organic to the AEF units was the M1916 37mm gun.

However, the AEF may have been able to obtain some form of cannons for its armored trains. The source of these is unclear. But photographs of the AEF do occasionally show American soldiers on armored trains mounting artillery pieces.[73] At the battle of Dukoveskoie in August 1918, British and Japanese forces faced a hostile force of Bolsheviks. The Bolshevik and Japanese forces had field artillery, and the Bolshevik and British units had several armored trains as well.[74] The Japanese forces used gunboats for river patrols.[75]

The major tactical innovation that characterized combat in Siberia and differentiated it from the Western Front was the reliance on armored trains for fire support and movement. Armaments on armored trains differed widely. Cossack ataman Grigori Semenov's the Destroyer had ten machine guns, two 1-pounder howitzers, and two 3-inch guns mounted behind steel plate and eighteen inches of concrete.[76] At least one Czech armored train car contained eight water-cooled machine guns mounted in an open-top car. The machine guns, four to a side, were mounted behind a protective barrier. The gunners stood in a chest-deep well running the length of the car.[77] British soldiers faced a 6-inch Bolshevik gun on an armored train in the Ussuri River area.[78] One of Cossack ataman Ivan Kalmikov's trains consisted of one first-class coach, two second-class coaches, and an armored car. Two soldiers rode on the outside of the engine in front of the smokestack.[79] The two soldiers must have only done this in warm weather since the often frigid winter temperatures would have precluded survival using such a technique year-round.

In March 1919, Semenov had four armored trains, each consisting of one or two armored cars, one or two platform cars mounting guns and howitzers, and one or two other cars for personnel and supplies. Three of the trains' armored cars were made of concrete. One train's armored cars were steel plated. Kalmikov had two similar trains. Semenov and Kalmikov often used one train preceding and one following their headquarters train during movement.[80]

The White Russian forces used many armored trains. One train constructed at the Vladivostok Naval Arsenal had a gondola car, whose steel sides were reinforced with five inches of concrete. It had a 7/8-inch steel plate for the roof. A 4.7-inch naval gun was mounted in the front of the gondola. Steel doors 5/8-inch thick protected the magazine.[81] Loopholes for machine guns were also cut in the sides of some armored cars.[82]

Armored trains were first used on the Eastern Front. The plans for the first Russian armored trains were derivatives of observations of German armored trains. One design included an armored flat car in front of a locomotive and one behind. Each of these flat cars might have a 3-inch gun, one firing forward and one firing rearward. Other cars might be attached and armored to protect the weapon crews and other personnel assigned to the train. One armored car developed had two turrets, each with a 5-inch naval gun. The turrets could rotate 360° and even elevated to fire upward against aircraft. The compartment between the twin turrets included machine gun positions and an observation tower with periscope.[83]

Even with such massive, concentrated firepower, armored trains had limitations. They were not effective at engaging hostile field artillery systems on the Eastern Front. Broken track could halt their movement and allow hostile infantry to maneuver against them. A derailed car made an armored train very vulnerable until the car could be pulled back onto the track or abandoned. The steel plate used for armored protection often was not sufficiently strong to stop cannon fire and even certain types of rifle ammunition.[84]

Armored trains were particularly effective in breaking the morale of an opponent, especially when moving rapidly. Camouflage to match the surrounding terrain was useful. Some means of protecting the track to the rear of an armored train was also important. Armored trains were also useful in providing supporting fires for soldiers withdrawing along the railway line. Such trains also provided a means to carry demolition supplies to support the destruction of railroad tracks, bridges, and tunnels.[85]

The importance of the rail line made its interdiction a key objective. Bolsheviks would destroy small bridges, chop down telegraph poles, cut telegraph lines, remove spikes from the rails on curves, and invert rails then spike them down as ways to interfere with rail operations. American soldiers were often involved in repairing such damage. It was difficult to catch the Bolsheviks in their destructive acts. Trains provided the most rapid means of moving from one point to another along the railway, but the noise and smoke rendered surprise impossible.[86]

Bolshevik fighters learned to use deceptive communications to set up ambushes against their White Russian opponents. For example, the Bolsheviks would splice into a telephone line and, posing as railway officials, tell American railway station guards to stop a White Russian train. After setting up the ambush on the train route, the Bolsheviks would tell the Americans the line was open and to release the train. When the train reached the chosen site, the trap would be sprung. This coupled with anti-American propaganda by the Japanese caused some White Russians to believe the AEF was pro-Bolshevik.[87]

Japanese tactics included brutal suppression of anyone they believed was a threat or in opposition to their plans. No mercy was given. Even when faced with American soldiers pleading that they stop, the Japanese soldiers continued. One example of this conduct involved five Russian citizens (alleged Bolsheviks) who were required to dig their own graves. A Japanese officer then cut off the heads of the three men and two boys. Americans and villagers watched but could not prevent the execution. The next day the villagers dug up and reburied the bodies. Such brutality solidified opposition and resulted in Japanese prisoners suffering a similar fate at Bolshevik hands. Bolsheviks would exchange American prisoners of war but kill captured Cossack and Japanese soldiers.[88]

Bolsheviks were also known to be brutal. For example, in December 1918, at Kansk, several Bolsheviks killed a schoolmistress. Then they poured cold water over her naked husband and made him run through the snow until he froze to death.[89]

The Reds used disguises such as imitating friendly peasants as a way to lure AEF soldiers into relaxing their guard. Then the Bolsheviks would seize any carelessly placed weapons, start shooting, and run away. Americans soon became suspicious of everyone. Americans in isolated guard stations were regularly attacked.[90] Constant vigilance was necessary to protect the American positions. The difficulty of separating friendly and hostile civilians in an insurgency or similar situation was not new and remains an issue today in such environments. When the hostile force looks and speaks like the civilians whom they operate around, then an outside military force will always be at risk of deception and confusion in identifying the real threat.

Undoubtedly, the clash between the different cultures bred some of the animosity, confusion, and brutality that characterized 1918–20 Siberia. For example, American soldiers captured three Chinese bandits from Kraefski and gave them individual mess kits, forks, spoons, and knives to use to eat. But the Chinese did not understand what to do. A soldier with experience in China made three pairs of chopsticks and dumped all the food into one pot. The Chinese happily surrounded the pot and ate the food.[91]

AEF soldiers also used their imaginations to deceive the enemy. A "fighting turret" was a raised platform built on four poles as a tower for better observation and fire used at railroad guard stations. A hedge of branches nailed to boards or a lumber palisade would provide concealment and/or cover on the platform.[92] When building a fighting turret at Kraefski, the American soldiers decided machine guns and field artillery were needed but were not available. Not to be discouraged, the Americans spread a rumor that machine guns and artillery would soon be emplaced. An elaborate scheme was hatched. The soldiers installed and operated fake weather vanes and instruments. Great commotion accompanied raising ropes, chains, and boards at the tower. Eventually, fake gun tubes could be seen. The soldiers claimed to have six machine guns and two light field guns in the turret. Pre-emplaced hand grenades and powder charges were used to demonstrate the artillery firing for the local population. Five BARs simulated the machine guns. The local population was thoroughly convinced by the ruse.[93]

Americans also developed innovative ways to convince prisoners of war to cooperate. For a time, E Company, Twenty-Seventh Infantry, guarded the prisoner of war camp at Krasnaya Rechks (also known as the Red River prisoner of war camp). One winter, several of the Austro-Hungarian officers threatened to mutiny. The leaders of the group worked outside the camp for seventy-two hours without food or shelter. When allowed to reenter the camp, the prisoners of war concluded that a mutiny was inappropriate.[94]

The AEF's operations in Siberia were characterized by small units engaging an enemy that often avoided action against an armed force and never massed large numbers of soldiers for an attack. There were no large-scale battles as seen on the Western Front. Small units and junior leaders had to make instantaneous decisions with consequences that could reach international proportions. Communications were primitive by the standards of today. Telegraph and couriers provided the standard communications network. Boredom was a problem as were confusion and uncertainty.

The different reasons prompting each country to intervene in Siberia naturally affected the actions of military forces deployed. Japanese and Cossack brutality exacerbated the poor relations among the supposed allies and seriously endangered any attempt to convince the local populace to support the Allies and the White Russian forces. The Allied leadership wanted Graves to take sides in the civil war, but he steadfastly refused. Graves was determined to abide by his orders. Open warfare between the Allies remained a threat throughout the deployment.

Combat between the Allies accidentally occurred in Sviyagino in June 1919. Japanese forces unexpectedly moved into the town. AEF and Japanese elements divided the town into sectors for each to guard. On June 25, Japanese and American patrols blundered into each other when a Japanese patrol wandered into the American sector. The Japanese soldier wounded one American officer. An older Russian peasant woman was wounded by a stray bullet. The Americans killed one Japanese soldier and wounded two.[95] The lack of a single commander for all of the Allied forces with the resulting lack of coordination certainly contributed to this incident. Even separating the two independent groups in different sectors could not prevent this inadvertent fratricide between allies.

Relations with Cossack forces steadily deteriorated throughout the AEF's time in Siberia. Ataman Kalmikov eventually boasted he would drive the AEF out of Siberia. His soldiers abused civilians who were friendly to the Americans. An example was an incident in which several of Kalmikov's men seized three Russian girls walking with American soldiers at the Shmakovka railway station. The Cossacks beat the girls with ramrods and tossed them off the train at Kraefski—without stopping. This and other such actions prompted a September 12, 1919, message from AEF headquarters in Vladivostok warning of potential armed conflict with the Cossacks. The AEF units were ordered to destroy any organized actions against American forces.[96] While understandable after the depredations committed by a number of the Cossacks, this order is indicative of the ill will and lack of coordination and cooperation among the supposedly allied forces in Siberia. The AEF leadership ultimately had no choice but to accept the fact that the AEF's goals differed from its allies.

All displays of animosity or conflicting objectives were not lethal in nature. A Japanese unit showed its displeasure with the AEF in an interesting manner at Ussuri. While passing through town, they dumped a dead horse at the camp of Company D, Twenty-Seventh Infantry, with no explanation given.[97] A dead horse is an unpleasant sight and unsanitary, but it is difficult to remove.

Such negative aspects of American-Allied relations did not exist everywhere. For example, an American soldier contracted anthrax in Khabarovsk reportedly after being shaved by a Chinese or Korean barber. American medical facilities at the time were inadequate. Three Japanese doctors responded to the plea for help and saved the soldier's life.[98] In general, however, relations between the Allied forces were not satisfactory. The discord that characterized the Siberian intervention doomed any attempt to help the Siberian people establish self-government. The Allies could not agree on the real mission for the military forces deployed to Siberia. Therefore, the support provided by the Allies was fragmented and uncoordinated.

The Imperial Family

As the final decision was being made on the AEF's deployment to Siberia, the fate of Czar Nicholas and his family was being decided. After the abdication, Nicholas and his family were captives in a former imperial home and then in Tobolsk in Siberia. Their last prison was in Ekaterinburg. The Provisional Government originally moved the czar and his family to Tobolsk for their protection. In Tobolsk, the family stayed in a former governor's residence. Once the Bolshevik revolution occurred, their situation took a turn for the worse. Communications were slow and the revolution did not spread overnight, yet once the guards learned of the change they became less respectful of the royal family and less willing to allow the family to receive any acknowledgment of special privilege. The guard force restricted interaction with others including religious observances. Butter and coffee became luxury items that were not provided.[99]

In March 1918, a Red Guard detachment arrived in Tobolsk. More Bolsheviks arrived after that resulting in discussions regarding movement of the imperial family. A Bolshevik named Yakolev eventually arrived and started the czar and czarina on a train toward Omsk. The story is not clear, but there were accusations that he was trying to help them escape. After other Bolsheviks apprehended the group, the czar and his family found themselves under guard of Bolshevik former factory workers in Ekaterinburg.[100]

This new set of guards seemed to look for ways to show disrespect to the czar and his family. Tea and black bread served as breakfast. A lack of beds forced the princesses to sleep on the floor. Many of the Bolshevik leaders wanted to try the czar and czarina with an expectation that the verdict would likely result in both of their executions. However, the fortunes of the civil war would speed up and change this initial plan.[101]

White Russian and Czech forces were having great success in the area near Ekaterinburg. The White Russians had not claimed to want the czar reinstated, but the proximity of these anti-Bolsheviks elements forced the Bolsheviks to make a decision regarding the disposition of the imperial family. The Ural Territorial Soviet concluded on July 12, 1918, that Ekaterinburg could not withstand the assault by the White Russians and Czechs beyond a few days. The Cheka sent a replacement guard force that on the night of July 16 escorted the family, the czar's physician, and three servants into the basement. After shooting the czar, the guards slaughtered the entire group. The executioners tried to destroy the bodies and bury them so that no one might find them. Initial announcements did not disclose the execution of the entire family, possibly as an attempt to avoid public scrutiny of the decision to kill the children.[102] Regardless of the motivation in initially obscuring the extent of the killings, Lenin apparently wanted the imperial family eliminated as a possible rallying point for the White Russians. Rather than try to move them to a safe place where the Czechs or White Russians might free them, executing the family and hiding the remains seemed the simplest solution.[103]

By now, White and Red Russian forces were fighting each other all through the country. The scattered nature of the forces for both sides made coordination difficult. The White Russians and Czechs continued to experience difficulty in defeating the Reds. However, in August, Czechs under the command of Gen. Rudolph Gaida secured the Lake Baikal area. The Bolsheviks initially held a strong position in the mountains and tunnels around the massive lake that the Trans-Siberian Railroad line transited. Gaida split his force in order to set an ambush by enticing the Bolsheviks into following his main body into a kill zone. Once the ambush force was in place, the Czechs attacked on August 4 and then retreated as if defeated. The Reds counterattacked the retreating force with infantry, cavalry, field artillery, and three armored trains. The Czechs patiently waited for the Bolsheviks to enter a valley so the ambush force could cut the rail line behind the Reds. Rain and the difficult terrain of the mountains, tunnels, and forests made the combat miserable for both sides. By August 6, the Czechs had turned the tide and cleared their line of communications to Vladivostok by securing the railway near Lake Baikal.[104]

Gaida's success now gave rise to visions of a westward advance to the White Russian forces fighting elsewhere. The Czechs were in position to control the entire Trans-Siberian Railroad. Instead of rescuing the Czechs, using them to defeat the Bolsheviks seemed to be a real possibility. While the Czechs were securing the railroad, other Czech and White Russian forces were capturing Kazan. This also resulted in the Samara White Russian government finding itself in possession of the imperial gold reserves that had been shipped to Kazan. Unfortunately for the Samaran government, efforts to safeguard the gold from further Bolshevik attacks resulted in Adm. Alexander Kolchak's government in Omsk finding itself in possession of the gold in the end.[105] This gold would come into play later in the saga of Kolchak's government and his relationship with the Czechs.

Initial Impact of Foreign Intervention

The Allied intervention would now serve to help motivate the Bolsheviks and harden their resolve to establish their form of government. The arrival of foreign soldiers in Siberia such as the Japanese and British forces provided the Bolsheviks with a propaganda coup allowing them to argue that they were fighting to preserve Russian independence from foreign domination. The Bolshevik leadership portrayed the arrival of the Allies as an attempt to reinstate imperial rule. Killing the imperial family helped clarify the Red message that a new day had come for Russia. There would be no going back. The White Russians hoped to benefit from the Allied intervention, which reinforced the Bolshevik message that the Allies were related to the old regime and not part of the change for the better. Other partisan forces only wanted to survive. When the civil war did not go well, White Russian leaders then blamed the Allies for not helping more. Unfortunately for the White Russians, the Allies were not of like mind regarding an appropriate course to follow.[106] The first AEF-Siberia forces that arrived supported the efforts of the other Allies to destroy the Bolsheviks. However, Graves's arrival changed the situation dramatically.

8
Initial Operations

Graves was not yet in Siberia when the initial AEF units arrived. Allied forces, as well as US naval forces, had been in and around Vladivostok for months while their respective governments argued about the intervention. The lack of the senior AEF command element being on the ground resulted in operations of a type that would not be sanctioned later. The Twenty-Seventh Infantry joined an Allied attack against the Bolsheviks as a supporting force. The Thirty-First Infantry provided a mine guard force when it arrived in country, and when AEF headquarters arrived, it took control of US military actions. The situation throughout Russia remained chaotic.

Twenty-Seventh Infantry Regiment—The Ussuri and Amur Campaigns

Upon arrival in Vladivostok, the Twenty-Seventh Infantry Regiment immediately went to work. As the senior American army officer present, Col. Henry D. Styer commanded the expeditionary force until Graves arrived on September 2. Lt. Col. Charles H. Morrow commanded the regiment, while Styer commanded the AEF. The Twenty-Seventh Infantry's transports arrived on August 15 and 16, but the troops initially remained aboard ship. On August 18, Companies F and G under the command of Maj. Earle G. Buck disembarked and assumed railway station guard positions from Vladivostok to Nikolsk replacing the Czechoslovakian troops. The regimental colors disembarked August 19 with the regiment conducting a parade through Vladivostok in front of the senior Allied officers present: Gen. Kikuzo Otani, Imperial Japanese Army; Adm. Austin Knight, US Navy; Gen. Milo K. Dietrichs, Czech Legion; and Styer, AEF commander. On August 20, the remainder of the regiment moved ashore.[1]

The AEF Intelligence Section issued a report on August 17 that noted the arrival of the initial elements of the AEF on August 15. This same report provided an estimate of Czech soldiers as 14,500 east of Lake Baikal and 45,000 west of the lake. An estimated 4,000 Japanese soldiers had landed. British and French troop strength totaled 800 and 1,100, respectively. Capt. Frank Brezina of the Philippine Scouts, who authored the report, also indicated 40,000 Bolshevik fighters were in Siberia.[2]

Brezina also noted that Czech, British, French, and a few Cossack units generally held the front north of Vladivostok. Approximately 200 Russian militiamen were in Vladivostok under the command of a Colonel Tolstoff. The Russian Railway Service Corps had 85 engineers in Vladivostok and approximately 100 at Harbin. The Allied naval commanders had established a guard force of 30 men ashore at the Navy Yard. A guard force of 100 men from the USS *Brooklyn* guarded the harbor eastern entrance and 125 men from the HMS *Suffolk* guarded the western entrance. A French cruiser and a Japanese battleship were also in the Vladivostok harbor. Brezina reported that the YMCA had approximately 20 people in the city. The American Red Cross had already set up a hospital on Russian Island in the harbor. At this early stage of the intervention the local civilians were friendly toward the Allied soldiers.[3]

Early AEF activities included establishing a temporary camp near Vladivostok and unloading the transport in the harbor. No laborers were available, so the regiment's soldiers were pressed into service to unload the AEF's supplies. Other soldiers were busy cleaning and repairing railroad yard buildings for use as barracks. F and G Companies deployed 214 soldiers in small groups to guard elements of the rail line. The groups ranged in size from 6 to 56 soldiers.[4]

On the evening of August 19, an element of F Company became the first AEF unit to come under hostile fire. The guard detachment at Razdolnoe received word that Chinese bandits were looting a village near them, so 1st Lt. George F. Herrick selected forty men and responded to the call for help. Near midnight, a small group of bandits was discovered by a flank patrol. The Americans fired five rounds per man at the bandits, hoping to determine the size of the bandit force by the amount of return fire. The Chinese bandits fired an estimated six shots and left the area. No trace of the bandits was found. The first AEF casualty occurred in this brief fight. A bullet that glanced off a rail wounded Pvt. Stephen Duhart in the head.[5]

Since the Czech and Cossack forces fighting in the Ussuri area were having little success against the Bolsheviks or other partisans, General Otani decided to mount an expedition to that area. Graves later wrote that the Japanese claimed there were fifteen thousand hostile Bolshevik troops between Vladivostok and Khabarovsk with an additional forty thousand Bolsheviks between the Allies and Irkutsk, where the Czechs were stranded and almost out of ammunition. Otani wanted American support in order to reach the Czechs; however, subsequent reports, including those of the Russian Railway Service Corps, would show that the

Czechs needed no immediate assistance. In fact, the Bolshevik leadership wanted the Czechs to leave in order to ensure that these veteran soldiers were out of their way. On August 24, the Twenty-Seventh Infantry began moving from Vladivostok to Sviyagino (see map 2) to operate in conjunction with the Japanese Twelfth Division commanded by Gen. Shigemoto Oi. The movement to Sviyagino was completed August 27.[6] The regiment's effective strength was 49 officers, 1,375 enlisted men, 86 horses, 152 mules, and 27 vehicles (including 3 ambulances).[7]

Before the operations began, Styer requested three trains to transport the regiment from Vladivostok to the front and evacuate casualties to Vladivostok. He also directed that messages affecting operations be sent to him at the front and that administrative and supply matters be conducted by the Base and Line of Communications commander in Vladivostok. To facilitate message traffic, Styer ordered that a telegraph line using poles along the railroad be run from Vladivostok to Sviyagino as the forces progressed. The regiment carried ten days' rations and five hundred thousand rounds of ammunition in the trains. The railway guards rejoined the regiment and the Thirty-First Infantry Regiment replaced the railway guards.[8]

The regiment was used by the Japanese as a reserve. Sviyagino was an important village because its railway station served approximately twenty villages. Sviyagino's principal industry was a sawmill.[9] As the Japanese and Americans moved into the Ussuri area, the British Twenty-Fifth Battalion, Middlesex Regiment, and the French Tonquin [Tonkin] Battalion moved out.[10]

On August 30, the Twenty-Seventh Infantry departed Sviyagino with orders to move through Runovka and Uspenka to the Nikolsk monastery. This operation involved the regiment covering the right flank of the Allied forces moving toward Khabarovsk. The regiment also had to repair nine railroad bridges that had been destroyed by Bolsheviks retreating from the August 25 battle at Kraefski. Japanese, Cossack, French, and Czech elements had defeated the Bolshevik force and forced the enemy's withdrawal. This early combat already was proof that the AEF was to operate in Siberia under very different rules and with a different mission from its allies. Supply and hospital trains were to follow the Twenty-Seventh Infantry once repairs were completed.[11] A report from one Russian source indicated that the Bolsheviks were surprised by the Allied advance. The Bolsheviks apparently were unaware that the Japanese forces had placed a major force in the field to attack them prior to August 27. This surprise resulted in the partisans retreating in disarray and made possible the capture of much of the equipment reported including armored trains, machine guns, and cannon. However, the partisans took time to poison wells and destroy bridges and other property when possible as they retreated.[12]

By the end of the first day's march, the Twenty-Seventh Infantry reached Nikotofka, a distance of thirteen miles. The regiment arrived at Runovka, an additional fourteen miles away, on August 31. Swamps and marshes interfered with the second day's march and the roads were in a poor state. Soldier's continually put logs and brush covered with hay in the road to keep wagons from becoming bogged down in the mud.[13]

Between September 1 and 4, the Twenty-Seventh Infantry marched from Runovka through Uspenka, Ordejefka, and Tikmanova to Ussuri. The regiment arrived at Ussuri at 3:30 P.M. on the September 4, approximately sixty miles from Sviyagino. Japanese general Oi complimented the American support as essential to the success of the Allied advance. On the day before the Twenty-Seventh Infantry reached Ussuri, the Japanese forces reported that the enemy forces totaled four thousand infantry, two cavalry squadrons, and nineteen artillery pieces in addition to several armored trains and ammunition cars.[14]

The Japanese command notified the Twenty-Seventh Infantry on September 7 that the Japanese cavalry and Kalmikov's Cossacks had reached Khabarovsk. The Twenty-Seventh Infantry sent E Company to Khabarovsk to take part in the Allied formal occupation parade in the city on September 10.[15] The remainder of the regiment left Ussuri on September 14 and arrived at Khabarovsk September 16.[16] See map 3 for an overview of the situation in Russia on September 9, 1918.

While the major elements of the regiment were closing out the Ussuri campaign and moving into winter quarters, two companies continued to pursue the Bolsheviks. Maj. William C. Miller and a reinforced E Company left Khabarovsk on September 11 with two Japanese companies to capture Blagovestchensk in the Amur River valley. This group, the advance guard of the Japanese forces under the command of Major General Ymada, was charged with capturing the town.[17]

The pursuit was initially by train, but burned bridges and blocked tunnels delayed the advance. Foot marches were necessary. The cold took a heavy toll on the dismounted soldiers. The Japanese soldiers were particularly affected by the difficult conditions. During one twenty-five-mile march, Japanese troops were so exhausted, the Japanese commander ordered E Company to pass through his straggling men. E Company reached the end of this particular march, the village of Bureya on the Bureya River southeast of Blagovestchensk, an hour ahead of the Japanese soldiers. The American forces continued the pursuit, reaching Ushuman on September 20. There, C Company and eighty-three E Company recruits joined Miller on September 27. This last group had left Khabarovsk on September 16.[18] Otani, who was very pleased with the support he received from the Twenty-Seventh Infantry during the attack to Blagovestchensk, sent letters to Graves and Styer thanking them for their assistance.[19]

On September 22, General Ymada ordered an American detachment to Zeya on the Tega River to intercept enemy gunboats. Forty men traveled with 1st Lt. E. D. Doryland to Uhlmine Station by train. From there, the detachment marched northeastward to Kachbrin arriving three days later. Four boatloads of Japanese soldiers and two Japanese gunboats passed up the river clearing it before Doryland arrived. He camped that night on the riverbank. The next day, Japanese boats from Zeya passed by Doryland's position and reported the river clear. On September 27, the American detachment began its march back to Uhlmine Station, completing the fifty miles in thirteen and one-half hours over muddy roads in a snowstorm.[20]

General Ymada ordered C Company to Alexeyevsk on September 28. However, on October 7, C Company joined Miller with E Company to return to Khabarovsk. They reached Khabarovsk October 10.[21] See map 4 for the situation in Russia on October 7, 1918.

The Ussuri campaign was successful for the Allies in the sense that the partisan threat was pushed back so that the Allied force could exercise tighter control over that section of eastern Siberia. However, since at least the American force was not in Siberia to defeat the Bolsheviks or other partisans, the utility of the campaign cannot help but be questioned. From a purely military standpoint, the Allied force won even if the victory was eventually meaningless. Japanese and Cossack cavalry played major roles and provided hard-hitting, mobile forces that kept the partisan forces off-balance so that they could not establish an effective defense. The predominantly Japanese Allied force captured 2 armored trains, 3 locomotives, 100 freight cars, 7 automobiles, 1,500 rifles, and 1 artillery piece.[22]

The Twenty-Seventh Infantry undertook combat operations in poor weather. Two snowstorms and many periods of rain made the 1,100-mile campaign very difficult—especially considering the men were dressed in khaki, not winter uniforms.[23] The regiment showed it could move quickly when required to do so. However, the true test of its combat skills did not occur. Between August 24 and September 16, the Twenty-Seventh Infantry suffered no combat casualties.[24] The campaign was physically tiring but not combat in the same sense as that on the Western Front or even the Allied intervention in northern Russia. For example, within fifteen days of arriving at Archangel in northern Russia on September 4, 1918, the American forces principally composed of the 339th Infantry Regiment had sixty-nine dead.[25] In Siberia, the Japanese forces bore the brunt of the initial combat. Their casualties during the drive to Khabarovsk included seventy-seven soldiers killed.[26] While Styer and the Twenty-Seventh Infantry were prepared to fight, Graves was not. This difference in mission or attitude was stark between the AEF and its allies in Siberia. The difference in the AEF-Siberia's actions and the actions of the Americans in North Russia was also very apparent. The AEF would attempt to remain neutral in the conflict between the Russian factions while America's allies and especially the Japanese supporting the White Russian Cossacks would take a more active role in the civil war.

Thirty-First Infantry—Garrison and the Suchan Mines

After arriving at Vladivostok August 21, 1918, the Thirty-First Infantry Regiment established a garrison camp east of the city.[27] They arrived without their organic field transportation, so the regiment was not available for field service immediately. A later-arriving ship brought the regiment's transportation assets.[28] This tent camp in Gornastaya Valley served as the regiment's main base with detachments being sent out to guard various points along the railway. In September, the regiment moved the base camp from Gornastaya Valley to brick barracks in the edge of Vladivostok. The Russians had built these brick barracks after fighting the Japanese in the area in 1904–5.[29]

Other than posting guard elements at several places, little significant activity occurred between August and October. The regiment took its first casualties August 29 at Ugolnaya, twenty-five miles north of Vladivostok.[30] In September, M Company moved to the Suchan Mine area as part of the Allied Mine Guard under Lt. Col. S. C. Loring. F and G Companies moved to Spasskoe under Maj. F. B. Alderdice's command. Capt. Francis G. Bishop with L Company occupied Razdolnoe.[31] The mines in the Suchan Valley centered on the village of Suchan and were a source of coal. Bolsheviks took control of the mines in September 1917. Before that, the mines were run by the Russian minister of industry. After Bolshevik seizure, production dropped from 2,160,000 pounds daily to 720,000 pounds daily. The Allies decided to assume control of the mines in order to ensure a steady supply of coal.[32]

Loring's Allied Mine Guard for the Suchan Mines consisted of M Company (250 men), a Japanese company, a Chinese company, and a White Russian detachment (see Map 5, a sketch map showing the Thirty-First Infantry positions including the Suchan Mines area as of January 1919). This combined force departed Vladivostok on September 10. The AEF chief of staff, Col. O. P. Robinson, accompanied the group to report the political situation to Graves. Though expected, armed resistance was not encountered when the guard force arrived at Kanguaz, the Ugolnaya spur terminal, on the morning of September 11.[33]

It is fortunate the mine guard did not immediately enter combat since this conglomeration of cultures and national goals was certainly not a cohesive force, being made up of Americans, Japanese, Chinese, and Cossacks (about twenty soldiers—reduced from an earlier request for a company). M Company had not trained as a team either. When the company was alerted for duty on September 6, it consisted of only 104 personnel. By its departure from Vladivostok at 6:55 A.M., September 10, its size had grown to 250 soldiers. This increase was accomplished by absorbing officers and enlisted men who had just arrived in Siberia from America.[34]

Robinson had the mine guard assemble several inhabitants of Kanguaz so that he could tell them why the guard force was there. The local people seemed satisfied, so an American sergeant with ten men remained at Kanguaz to guard the telegraph station. The rest of the guard force then divided into four sections for subsequent rail movement through the mountains over a narrow gauge line. The forty-eight "versts" (one verst=0.67 miles) to Suchan required a combination of marching and rail to cover them. Guard details remained in several locations along the route:

Tigrovia—an American sergeant with ten men
Tahi—a Japanese sergeant with ten men
Fanza—an American officer with three squads, two Chinese officers with forty men, and a Japanese sergeant with twenty-seven men.[35]

The remainder of the troops arrived at Suchan at 7:15 P.M. on September 12. Since the guard force met no resistance, they used the local town hall for quarters. The former mine manager, Mr. Egroff (also spelled Egeroff in some documents), who had been removed by the Bolsheviks, was again placed in charge of mining operations by the Allied Mine Guard. The Japanese established a guard post at Mine No. 2 with the Americans at Mine No. 1. Most of the miners welcomed the return of Egroff to the mines. The local militia surrendered eight rifles at Mine No. 1, fifty-two at Mine No. 2, and seventeen at Fanza.[36]

Robinson spent a great deal of time explaining the guard force's mission to the local population. He strove to ensure the people understood that the Allies had no selfish plans but hoped to help them. To get his message across, Robinson issued the following proclamation.

TO THE CITIZENS OF THE SUCHAN MINE DISTRICT

I. The Allied Nations have come to Russia to help the Russian citizens and help win the war against Germany. In the prosecution of this Mission they have found it necessary to operate the mines temporarily, in order to increase the production of coal, thus making possible the distribution of supplies from one section to another, to keep the Russian people from starving and Russian women and children warm this winter. To increase the production of the Mines, the Allies wanted to get the man who was best acquainted with the mines, and have therefore prevailed upon Mr. Egroff to assume the management of the Mines during the temporary occupancy by the Allies. Mr. Egroff's orders for the operations of the Mines will be obeyed.

II. In view of the fact that troops are now here to protect the people against the Khunkhuzi there is no need for the citizens to have public rifles in their possession. In order to prevent misunderstandings due to differences in language, it is requested that all owners of private rifles present themselves to Mr. Egroff, who will issue a permit authorizing the owner to carry the rifle. This permit will then be presented to the Japanese and Americans commanders to be written in Japanese and English, in order that it may be shown to the guards.

III. Peaceable citizens do not keep machine-guns in their houses, as those weapons are only used in war. Therefore, any machine-gun in the vicinity should be turned in, and any one having any information of such should immediately report that fact.

IV. The Local government will continue to function.[37]

At roughly the same time Robinson made the proclamation above, Otani issued a proclamation to the Russian people. His September 6 announcement follows.

TO THE RUSSIAN PEOPLE—LOYAL TO THEIR FATHERLAND

The Operations of the Allied Armies on Russian territory have as their sole object the liberation of the friendly Czecho-Slovak troops from the power of forces organized from Austro-German prisoners, and at the same time to give assistance to Russia, now suffering indescribable calamities under a misguided Administration.

The Allies have, therefore, for their only enemy, the forces of Austro-German prisoners, and have no hostile intention, whatever, against the Russian people.

Having already concentrated sufficient forces, we are now advancing and pursuing the enemy without relaxation. We firmly believe that the day will soon come, when we shall be able to deliver Russia from the treacherous hands of the enemy, by annihilating the Austro-German prisoners. But in their retreat, these troops have destroyed all the means of communication. The destruction of the railroad makes the supplying of the neighboring vicinity with materials especially difficult and further delays the bringing of relief to the Russian people by the Allies.

Russian people who love your Country! Facilitate the operations of our Armies and render no assistance to the forces of Austro-German prisoners. Remember their *purpose and make* every effort to restore your country.[38]

When Robinson departed the Suchan Mines on September 15, he reported that no serious trouble was expected unless Egroff's desire for reprisals against people who previously caused him trouble provoked it.[39]

After Robinson's departure, concealed weapons continued to be the object of searches and confiscation. However, a good deal of judgment had to be used in this task. Hunting was a major activity in the region. Weapons obviously of primary use for hunting and not war were returned to their owners. This policy of searching for firearms did occasionally lead to excessive action. When the troops in Fanza searched private citizens' homes under the pretext of looking for weapons, Robinson cautioned the Japanese commander against abusing the Russian people.[40] The Americans and Russians had no problems other than a few threats and drunken fights. Unfortunately, Japanese-Russian relations were not as cordial due to the abusive actions of some of the Japanese soldiers toward the Russian citizens. Nonetheless, relations overall were friendly until February 1919.[41]

The continued searches of civilian homes by the Japanese provoked local hostility. Czechoslovakian soldiers had captured the last escaped German prisoners of war before the American and Japanese mine guard force arrived, so there were no Central Powers forces with which to contend. The only threat to the Allies was the Bolshevik influence that was already building in the area as the Allies arrived. In order to combat this support by confiscating weapons, the Japanese leadership conducted searches of private property. This then played into the hands of the Bolsheviks by angering the local populace. The civilians could witness any manner of rude or abusive behavior at the hands of the Japanese soldiers in their homes and their neighborhoods. Japanese brutality and lack of respect for Russian citizens guaranteed that the population would never rally en masse to the Allied side.[42]

AEF Headquarters: Arrival

After arriving at Vladivostok September 2, Graves met with Adm. Austin M. Knight, senior US Navy representative in the harbor with the USS *Brooklyn*,[43] and Otani. Graves was initially impressed with Otani and felt he was an excellent choice by the Japanese officials. Graves described Otani as "of kindly character, of temperate habits" and "manifestly fair and considerate" in his actions concerning the many Allied elements in Siberia.[44]

When Otani informed Graves that he was the commander of all Allied forces, Graves explained that the AEF had no orders to that effect. Graves also told Otani that his orders forbade him from placing American troops under the command of Allied officers. However, he desired to cooperate in any way possible. He only insisted that he be informed of the transfer of US troops and any change in their mission. Graves also informed Styer of the AEF's employment limitations.[45]

These limitations on AEF actions were crucial. At this time, Graves apparently thought he and the Japanese were in Siberia for the same reason, even though an August 9 War Department telegram had warned him of conflicting goals before he departed San Francisco. This warning pointed out that Japanese forces were striving to fragment power in Siberia rather than to assist the Russian people in establishing a strong government.[46] Graves's initial optimistic appraisal of Japanese intentions resulted in the continuation of operations by the Twenty-Seventh Infantry Regiment with the Japanese. He did not recall the Twenty-Seventh Infantry from its Ussuri campaign. In fact, when Otani asked Graves if he could continue to utilize the Twenty-Seventh Infantry Regiment once it was in Khabarovsk, Graves granted the request. Graves's reply stated, "I am very glad to have all of it or any part of it as you may desire, continue the advance with General Oi."[47]

There is no apparent reason for Graves to have ignored the War Department warning. He may have been only trying to be polite to Otani. He may have felt the threat of Central Powers prisoners of war so severe that joint operations were necessary. The situation was confused. No White Russian government that could truly claim to rule Siberia existed. The threat (whether Central Powers, Bolshevik, or other partisans) was not well defined. American troops were already in the field on an operation. Demanding their return might have added more confusion since the soldiers of the Twenty-Seventh Infantry might have then questioned their mission and actions. Regardless of the reason, the AEF commander allowed American soldiers to remain under Japanese operational control after he arrived. Graves would not do this again. This decision regarding command of American troops would help ensure that the AEF's operations remained true to their orders for the rest of the Siberian intervention; however, the decision also guaranteed that combined coalition operations would be difficult to implement.

Several administrative actions also demanded immediate attention. Quarters, transportation, and sanitation facilities had to be arranged to support the American, British, French, Czech, Chinese, Italian, Japanese, Serbian, Polish, and Russian forces in Vladivostok. The influx of soldiers and refugees swelled the city's population to over three times its normal size. Differences in culture and regulations also caused problems. Japanese, Chinese, Italian, and Russian officers thought nothing of putting 300 to 500 soldiers in a barracks that Americans would use to house only 150. When initially confronted with a rental fee of $8,000 per month for the AEF headquarters building, Graves refused and offered $750, an amount recommended by the mayor of Vladivostok. Guidance from Washington, DC, eventually reached the AEF so that Graves agreed to a fee of $6,000 per month.[48]

From August 15 to November 9, a variety of transport ships arrived in Vladivostok with the medical element of the AEF from the Philippines and San Francisco. An evacuation hospital with 400 beds, a field hospital with 216 beds, and regimental hospitals supported the soldiers in the AEF. Horse-drawn and motor ambulances were also available. A medical supply depot, veterinary element, and dental surgeons completed the medical support deployed to Siberia.[49]

The medical staff also set up two hospital trains using boxcars converted for medical support. The trains usually ran between Vladivostok and Khabarovsk, a distance of 480 miles. Medical supplies were plentiful. Sanitation was satisfactory after the American units arrived and cleaned the facilities allocated to them. The AEF set up two water-distilling plants to provide clean water. Influenza, venereal disease, diarrhea, dysentery, and pneumonia were the principal diseases that afflicted the AEF's soldiers.[50]

The lack of any form of functioning local civilian government meant that the military commanders had to take action in Vladivostok to run the city. Elements of the Czech Legion had seized the city the preceding June. Once the various Allied commands had arrived later in the summer, the senior officers agreed to allow General Nakajima from the Japanese army to command the garrison. A British major named Dunlop acted as the mayor. When Dunlop failed to impress the various commands favorably, the Czech lieutenant colonel Vuchterle replaced him. The Allies declared martial law so that they could ensure peace within the city that they relied upon as a base of operations.[51] In order to coordinate Allied actions, Otani organized several committees in cooperation with the other Allied commanders. The committees are listed in table 6 with a short explanation of their missions.

Allied commanders also met regularly (twice weekly initially, once per week later) to discuss common concerns. The committees did not have binding authority; however, the Allied commanders usually followed their recommendations as long as national policies were not violated.[52] The large number of soldiers with differing cultures and aims made maintaining control of events difficult. Graves was very concerned about the property supervised by these various committees when complaints arose that soldiers had stolen or confiscated property illegally. Military property not being consolidated in central locations complicated attempts to secure anything. Graves wanted any soldier or command taking property, such as from a warehouse, to file a receipt with the Japanese military garrison for Vladivostok. The Allies generally agreed, but the British and French did not want munitions included in the requirement because British money had originally purchased the ammunition. Regardless, Graves required the AEF to abide by his demand to safeguard and record the use of any confiscated Russian property.[53]

The AEF Intelligence Section continued to monitor the local press in order to assess the attitude of the population toward the American presence. An appraisal of the population living in the vicinity of Vladivostok after the AEF had been deployed for five months showed an interesting compilation of opinions. Peas-

Table 6. Allied Committees to Coordinate Operations

Committee	Mission
Materials	Supervise the care and disposition of war materials in the area
Barracks and Quarters	Supervise housing the Allied soldiers
Finance	Coordinate common expenses
Prisoners of War	Coordinate the care and safeguarding of prisoners of war
Purchasing	Coordinate purchases
Inter-Allied Railway	Arrange shipment and priorities for military supplies and troops
Sanitary	Ensure adequate sanitation measures were taken
Tariff	Coordinate a tariff schedule for rail movement of military personnel and supplies
Martial Law	Coordinate martial law administration for Vladivostok

From Graves, Report, "Operations to June 30, 1919," p. 7

ants tended to view the Americans in a positive light. Americans treated everyone with respect. American officers treated their soldiers well, unlike Russian officers. A typical working man viewed America as a good place to work with opportunities to learn and improve oneself after interacting with American soldiers for a few months. Physicians and merchants were described as generally being in favor of the American presence because of the needed influx of money. A clerk who was interviewed indicated that he did not trust the United States because Americans coveted money too much. Nonetheless, he noted that US policy "humored" everyone including the partisans. A Russian officer belittled American contributions to the victory in Western Europe, compared American officers to merchants who lacked military spirit, and concluded that the United States had prevented Japan from assisting the Russians in defeating the Bolsheviks. He also commented that the United States would never support a dictator but that Russia could not survive without one.[54] Differing opinions would affect the actions of the Russian people and the warring factions in the civil war. During most of the intervention, the AEF would try to remain neutral. This meant that the Bolsheviks and other partisans only had to be concerned about direct American intervention when they chose to attack the AEF.

The Allied operations near Ussuri and along the Amur River showed that initial Japanese estimates of enemy strength were incorrect. Otani convinced the Allies prior to the Ussuri campaign that fifteen thousand armed enemy soldiers occupied the Ussuri area with forty thousand more separating the Czechs west of Irkutsk and the Allies around Vladivostok. The ease with which the Allies captured Khabarovsk indicated that massive numbers of enemy troops did not exist. Also, the Czechs were in virtual complete control of the rail line between Irkutsk and Vladivostok by the time the AEF was in country. Certainly, forty thousand hostile soldiers did not separate the Czechs from the Allies. A few Central Power prisoners of war had joined various partisan groups but a huge, organized enemy army did not exist.[55] The poor communications infrastructure would plague all of the forces in Siberia throughout the intervention. Regardless of whether delivering food, water, arms, or information, no task was easily accomplished in the vast and often frozen stretches of early twentieth-century Siberia. The time delay transmitting information and instructions across the ocean further complicated the rapid reaction to the changing strategic environment.

The AEF estimate of total friendly Russian units in Siberia indicated a sizable force; however, five corps did not necessarily equal five corps on the Western Front of the military lexicon of today. The First, or Ural, Corps was headquartered in Chelyabinsk with about four thousand soldiers. The Second, or Siberian Steppe, Corps headquartered in Omsk and had approximately four thousand soldiers. Most of the soldiers in these first two corps were former czarist officers. The Central Siberian Corps was headquartered in Tomsk with an unknown strength. The Fourth Corps' size was also unknown and was located in the vicinity of Irkutsk. The Siberian Fifth Corps headquarters was at Khabarovsk, which would have put it the farthest east of the five corps. It was to have an infantry division as well as two divisions of Cossacks. However, the actual size of these divisions was not confirmed. Separate reports indicated that Cossack ataman Grigori Semenov, who also commanded the Fifth Corps, had over five thousand men including field artillery, motor transport, and an armored train at this time. Cossack ataman Ivan Kalmikov's forces were cavalry by and large. His only infantry were Cossacks waiting on horses for mounts. He also had four 6-inch howitzers, four Russian 3-inch field guns, six 75mm Argentinean mountain guns, and two 75mm Japanese mountain guns. Other White Russian forces also operated in Siberia with a variety of estimates as to size. Poles and Serbians reportedly joined the White Russian forces. Cossacks were present in a number of units scattered throughout the region and bore allegiance to a variety of leaders.[56]

From a strategic standpoint, the War Department considered the intervention in Russia as critical in preventing Germany from exploiting the resources available in Russia. The War Department reported that the area occupied by Germany contained one-half of the raw materials used by Europe and one-quarter of the food supply. This placed Germany in a strong position to continue the war. Japan clearly was interested in eliminating European presence and competition in Asia yet was friendly toward the Allies. The War Department considered the Czech Legion to be cut off from its line of retreat and in need of rescue. Germany's propaganda efforts seemed to be oriented on maintaining confusion within the Russian population and army in order to prevent a coherent defense against its aims of dominating Europe by dominating Russia.[57] Given subsequent events soon to occur on the Western Front, it is apparent that the War Department overstated the German ability to continue the war let alone dominate events in Russia. In a month, the fighting in Europe would end. This alone made much of the reasoning for the intervention and Allied actions relative to Germany's wartime capability meaningless. The AEF and other Allied forces would spend most of their efforts in achieving other national aims or simply attempting to stabilize a chaotic situation while political leaders contemplated changing the course that brought all of these forces to Siberia.

Two other significant events occurred during this time. Graves congratulated the Czechs on the recognition of their Czech-Slovak National Council as a belligerent government.[58] He also recognized that problems could arise between Japanese and American forces. German propaganda to cause such ill will was a particular concern. On September 18, he issued a memorandum to all AEF officers telling them not to discuss Japanese actions or policy. Russians complaining about Japanese conduct were to be told to contact the Japanese headquarters.[59] The American reputation of fairness, however, would result in many people bringing their complaints about the Japanese and their Cossack allies to American soldiers and leaders.

This initial period was relatively quiet. Both infantry regiments arrived and began to settle into a routine of operations. The AEF headquarters arrived and established its base of operations in Vladivostok. Even the Twenty-Seventh Infantry's actions in support of the Japanese forces were not true combat in the sense of combat as experienced on the Western Front. This lack of combat action was due to the confused situation in Siberia and due to the AEF mainly being concerned with establishing base facilities. The Japanese military had attacked an apparently hostile partisan force under the pretense of helping the Czech Legion, but no action on the scale of the war in Europe occurred. The Japanese attack supported by the other Allied elements in Siberia was a rapid success in a military sense. Graves apparently allowed this cooperation to continue initially because he believed that he and the Japanese officials had the same goals. Cooperation would demonstrate his desire to work with his allies. Time would change this almost peacetime atmosphere as future operations finally drew the AEF into conflict with its allies and the Bolsheviks.

Elsewhere in Russia

Except for the initial Japanese-led drive to clear the railroad of any armed partisans, Siberia was relatively calm during this time. However, this was not so elsewhere in Russia. The White and Red Armies found themselves in scattered groups with friend and foe seemingly in every direction in western Russia. There White Russian and Czech units fought against the growing Red Army. Several political groups with shifting alliances added to the confusion and danger. The Samara government of Social Revolutionaries tried but was unable to inspire popular support. Many White Russian military leaders considered the Social Revolutionaries too closely aligned in philosophy to the Bolsheviks to be trusted. The democratic intent of the government made them unpalatable to the Reds. The Siberian government in Omsk could not agree with how to support the Social Revolutionaries, who claimed to speak for all of Russia. Bolshevik atrocities and heavy-handed supply requisitioning, primarily by theft, caused peasants not to trust them, yet White Russian attempts to reinstate landowners who had previously kept the peasants as peasants prevented widespread popular support to the White movement.[60]

An attempt by representatives from both governments meeting in Ufa failed to produce an agreement. The Czechs had been pressuring the White Russian elements to provide aid. Unfortunately, the desires between the two groups were not easily reconciled. The inability to pick a militarist or democratic path in the end resulted in an unfocused effort to rule and an uncertain path, which the Bolsheviks exploited to the detriment of any hope of democracy for the Russian people. The Czechs tried to avoid a direct role in the brewing civil war because it was unclear whether the Social Revolutionaries could govern or whether other White Russians could be trusted to not reinstitute some form of undemocratic government. The ruthless horror of civil war would eventually prevent any voice of reason from inspiring enough of the Russian people to oppose the Bolsheviks. With the Czechs understandably more concerned about themselves than the Russian people, the only hope for democracy was an Allied intervention that would actively oppose the Bolsheviks and control the White Russians.[61]

This period would also see the Allied intervention in northern Russia begin in earnest. The factors motivating the intervention in northern Russia were the same as in Siberia. However, the conduct of American operations would be much different from that of the AEF-Siberia. Out of apparent concern of a German attack with the need for support to withstand it, Leon Trotsky sent a telegram on March 2, 1918, to the Murmansk soviet telling them to accept assistance from the Allies. British marines landed in April and increased in number to approximately five hundred in May. The British major general F. C. Poole with an expeditionary force of soldiers deemed unfit for the trenches of the Western Front arrived in June. A White Russian uprising on August 1 coincided with the arrival in Archangel of a force of 1,200 to 1,500 British, French, and American Marines, soldiers, and sailors.[62] This initial invasion force was small indeed; however, the Bolsheviks did not know that. Their retreat encouraged Poole to pursue them; however, he was unable to accomplish much. Allied naval forces consisting of warships like the British light cruiser HMS *Attentive* and the carrier HMS *Nairana*, as well as cargo ships and troop transports, convinced the local community that a large invasion was under way. Fifty American sailors from the USS *Olympia* commandeered a locomotive and gave chase to the retreating Bolsheviks until the Reds discovered the size and armament of the pursuit force.[63] The sailors decided to stop chasing a superior force.

Brig. Gen. Edmund Ironside, with the temporary rank of major general, would replace Poole and try to train a Russian force to face the Bolsheviks. Allied reinforcements would also provide him with sufficient combat power to make him believe he could drive south to link up with the Czechs and White Russian forces. These Allied reinforcements would include approximately 5,000 Americans in the reinforced 339th Infantry Regiment. Other reinforcements would include 6,000 British, 500 Canadians, between 900 and 1,700 French, and smaller groups of Polish, Italian, Estonian, Lithuanian, Serb, Finnish, Czech, and Chinese soldiers.[64] Ironside would take the fight to the Bolsheviks.

Initial Impressions

As the AEF and Russian Railway Service Corps elements settled in, the soldiers began to gain a better understanding of their environment. Vladivostok was a mixture of cultures and competing interests. American, British, Japanese, and Russian ships were anchored in the harbor while a mixture of Russian, Chinese, and Korean men and women intermingled with all of the nationalities represented by the Allied intervention. White and Red Russian sympathies were apparent. Other civilians disliked the White and Red elements but still wanted a new government with more freedom than had been available for the Russian peasant. The lead elements of the Czech Legion were on hand. Low hills surrounded the harbor. Restaurants were available for servicing the cultural mix and had small orchestras that could strike up *Stars and Stripes Forever* to honor a visiting American with little notice. Swimming was available for recreation with men and women segregated. Russian bathhouses provided a much needed source of a hot bath and shave. "Tough women" and "young girls" populated the streets and eating places. Chinese and Russian children might actually fight over the business associated with helping an American carry his baggage.[65]

Harbin was dusty and populated by a similar mixture of nationalities. Chinese soldiers patrolled in it. Thanks to the rail line, soldiers of all nationalities passed through Harbin. The Russian Railway Service Corps men, Red Cross workers, and every other national contingent intermixed in the rail yards, streets, shops, and restaurants. A member of the Russian Railway Service Corps might sit down one day for a conversation with a French officer claiming that he defeated six thousand Bolsheviks with only two thousand Frenchmen and have dinner with an army officer and two nurses the next while taking a train ride with Dr. Raymond Teusler, the head of the American Red Cross mission in Siberia on a different day. Riding on a Red Cross train could actually bring an American environment to a very foreign place as the railroad was used to move hospitals and everything else across thousands of miles.[66]

The Japanese army contingent was clearly a force to watch. The attitude of the Japanese soldiers alienated them from most other nationalities. Japan appeared to be intent on consolidating their hold on everything available from mining concessions to supplies. Japanese officers and soldiers on trains were known to be given seats in coach class but then to confiscate seats in first class. The Japanese army appeared to be very organized, but their actions did not win many friends.[67]

The September 21, 1918, intelligence report estimated the total hostile force in all of Siberia to be approximately 120,000. This same report indicated 15,000 to 40,000 enemy soldiers were near Ekaterinburg. An army of approximately 45,000 had seized Kazan. Another army of approximately 45,000 soldiers was moving along the Volga River from Ukrainia. Maj. David Barrows, the author of the report, believed that most of the enemy force was composed of released prisoners of war with some Bolsheviks and Tartars.[68] A subsequent report on October 6 based on messages from the Czech forces listed 7,000 Bolsheviks in the southern Ural Mountains and 12,000 in southern Siberia near Turkestan. On the Volga Front, there were 6,000 Magyars and Germans in a division, approximately 8,000 hostile soldiers near Nizhni-Tagil, a 3,500-man enemy brigade near Chasevnaya, and an army headquartered in Perm with 10,500 Russians and Cossacks fighting for the Reds. Approximately 50,000 hostile soldiers of one group or another were fighting the Czechs at various other locations.[69]

The concern about prisoners of war forming armies to fight the allies would persist until the strength of the Bolshevik or anti-imperial message became clear. Bolshevik and other partisan recruiting of working-class people and rural peasants would ultimately provide the soldiers to overcome the White Russian forces and make it clear that Allied intervention was not going to produce a new democratic nation that used Western ideas for governance. Garrison life would follow for several months as the AEF-Siberia soldiers waited for something to resolve the conflict among the Russian forces vying for dominance.

9
Garrison Life

The situation was relatively calm from October 1918 through March 1919. Few significant actions took place. Graves reported as early as October 31 that few troops were required in Siberia. In a letter to Gen. Peyton March, Graves noted that Japan already had sixty thousand soldiers stationed east of Lake Baikal. The presence of such a large number of soldiers was a source of discontent for the Russian people. Graves also noted the difficulty he had dealing with Russians allegedly friendly to the Allies. He pointed out that many Russian military officers claimed to have large followings in Siberia, but none of these officers could show proof of such strength. These various officers all requested funds and materiel in order to establish a stable government.[1]

After the armistice in November, conditions at home affected the AEF more and more. Understandably, morale suffered when the soldiers in Siberia did not go home as the soldiers in France did. Eventually the Women's Auxiliary of the Twenty-Seventh Infantry Regiment and soldier families demanded the return of the AEF. This led to President Wilson's decision to return drafted soldiers. New recruits deployed to Siberia as replacements.[2] On January 4, 1919, British soldiers at home on leave demonstrated against returning to France and going to Russia. The labor movements in Britain and France opposed the Russian intervention and threatened a general strike.[3] The civil unrest and agitation, however, did not result in a quick withdrawal of Allied forces. In fact, some of the agitation may even have encouraged a continued intervention by proving the fears of people who worried about the effect of noncapitalistic social fervor. Certainly the belief that labor unrest was a Bolshevik plot[4] made some people believe the intervention was necessary. Fear of the spread of Bolshevism would affect the decisions of the national leaders demanding the intervention as well as international relations long after World War I and this intervention ended. The lack of a clear mission and the continued conflict with the Allies in the intervention would continue throughout this period and result in conflict among supposed friends.

A number of difficult missions confronted the AEF including guarding prisoners, securing mines that were essential for the economy of eastern Siberia, and patrolling. Unrest and violence coexisted with peaceful activities. In December 1918 in Chita, someone attempted to assassinate the Cossack leader Ataman Grigori Semenov by throwing two explosive devices into a theater box seating area. Only one of the bombs exploded. This wounded a woman and a Serbian officer. Semenov received a leg wound. Five hundred people attended a celebration of his survival that was held in a cathedral in Chita on December 21.[5]

The sale of supplies to civilians was one item that was of interest to the AEF leadership. The American Red Cross was supposed to sell items to soldiers in uniform and members of the Russian Railway Service Corps. Accusations of large sales to civilians at this time were not found to be true. An occasional sale occurred due to an error, but generally the Red Cross workers abided by the regulations. The Japanese army and Semenov ran stores that sold to civilians for prices sometimes considered to be very high. Provisions for prisoners were often limited and resulted in starvation in several prisoner camps. Prisoners of war, Bolsheviks, and criminals were intermingled in some of the prison camps.[6]

The end of the war in Europe would eventually make some people doubt the purpose of the AEF and eventually result in the call for soldiers to be sent home. The end of the war also affected counterintelligence operations. During the war, the AEF Intelligence Section was concerned about pro-German sentiments among soldiers deployed to Siberia. The end of the war removed some of that pressure because Germany ceased being an enemy. In November 1918, several soldiers were being watched for just such views. These were older soldiers who apparently preferred Germany to France or England before the United States joined the Allies. Once the war ended the investigations ceased. Most of the counterintelligence effort focused on the influence of Bolshevism on the soldiers of the AEF. The close interaction with the civilian populace raised concerns that Bolshevik propaganda might affect the soldiers' attitudes toward operational requirements. The Intelligence Section reported that the Bolsheviks were conducting a campaign to exert an influence on the AEF's soldiers. As of February 1919, there still had been no indication of an attempt to inspire the American soldiers to mutiny or revolt. The propaganda effort appeared to be aimed at changing political beliefs alone. By and large the propaganda efforts failed with all but a few soldiers reacting negatively toward any attempt to change their political views.[7]

Garrison life would bring a variety of challenges for the infantry regiments and the men of the Russian Railway Service Corps. The Twenty-Seventh Infantry would find itself running a large prisoner of war camp in Krasnaya Rechks, guarding the railroad near Spasskoe, and coping with allies more brutal than the partisans in Khabarovsk. The soldiers of the Thirty-First Infantry would guard the mines near Suchan and towns in the area. The chaos in other parts of Russia would divert Allied efforts and fragment support to the White Russians. While all of this was occurring, the men of the Russian Railway Service Corps would continue their often lonely efforts to keep the trains moving.

Twenty-Seventh Infantry— Prisoners of War and Garrison Life

The majority of the Twenty-Seventh Infantry Regiment spent the winter of 1918–19 in Khabarovsk. However, one battalion occupied Spasskoe on the Vladivostok-Khabarovsk section of the Trans-Siberian Railroad. One company also supervised a prison camp containing two thousand Austro-Hungarian prisoners of war.[8] On November 4 the Twenty-Seventh Infantry's E Company took over the prisoner of war camp at Krasnaya Rechks (or Red River). Colonel Morrow was the camp commandant. Captain Larkins was the E Company commander. Capt. Benjamin Curdette, Medical Corps, assisted by two enlisted men composed the medical staff. John James and Harry W. Killpack, both second lieutenants, were the adjutant and supply officer, respectively.[9]

Krasnaya Rechks

Krasnaya Rechks was about sixteen versts, or about eleven miles, southeast of Khabarovsk. The wagon road that serviced the camp was in poor condition and was difficult to negotiate in the winter. Consequently, the railroad was the major transportation link. The camp was located about one and one-half versts from the railroad station.[10]

The compound had been garrisoned by a railroad regiment of the Russian army before being a prisoner of war camp. Brick one- and two-story buildings, frame warehouses, and stables were available. Even though sufficient buildings existed, including thirty-three warehouses, the poor state of repair and unsanitary environment made the camp a disreputable place. The camp had two compounds, each enclosed by a twelve-foot barbed wire fence and board fence. The space between the compounds was open, and prisoners freely passed between them. Large open ditches ran all over the camp. Water and sewage systems did not exist. Four kitchens supplied meals. The prisoners ate their meals in the barracks. Construction of a bathhouse and hospital had begun but had not been completed. The one bathhouse that did exist was outside both compounds. No wash house or recreation building existed.[11]

Approximately 1,550 of the 2,000 prisoners were officers. Various illnesses plagued 460 of the 2,000. Sick prisoners of war continued to live with their comrades, which served to spread disease. Lack of food was slowly starving the camp population. The Russian government paid the officers fifty to seventy-five rubles per month, depending on their rank, to provide an allowance to cover all expenses. The prisoners paid the prison officials sixty rubles per month for food. Danish and Swedish Red Cross officials provided the prisoners of war an additional ten rubles per month. Few prisoners of war had enough winter clothing.[12]

Prison officials did not have an accurate accounting of the prisoners of war. Four Russian colonels were stationed at the camp, and all four claimed to be in command. A local contractor supplied meals for the guards and prisoners of war but had not even installed a bakery. Two horses and two carts provided logistical transportation for the camp. The prisoners used one. The contractor who provided the mess facilities used the other.[13]

E Company immediately began to reorganize the camp by briefing the ten senior prisoners on the planned changes. The Americans promised construction of mess halls and better food, twenty-five dollars per month for officers below the rank of captain, and thirty-eight dollars per month for captains and above. Clothing and food costs would be deducted from these amounts. Thirteen camp companies, each with one captain, one first lieutenant, and one second lieutenant, were to be organized. The Americans guaranteed the construction of numerous facilities including a bathhouse; laundry; theater; hospital; electric light plant; water system for drinking, cooking, and bathing; tailor, shoe, carpenter, tin, and paint shops; and a club. Requirements for morning reports, sick reports, and duty rosters were set. Repair of buildings was also begun as well as construction of a railroad spur to the camp. The prisoners of war were grateful and very happy to be under American supervision.[14]

Prisoners drew tools from Russian warehouses near the railroad line and were the labor to construct the facilities promised. Open fires on concrete floors were necessary until heating boilers could be repaired. Within a week of E Company taking over the camp, a bathhouse with barber and laundry was in operation. Mess hall improvements meant that prisoners of war would not have to eat in their four- to eight-man barracks cubicles. Hot and cold water was piped to the kitchens and mess halls. E Company with its prisoner workforce built tables and benches and painted buildings. The prisoners tore down the board fence to provide building materials and a better view of the prison compound.[15]

Water and electric lighting systems were operational within a few weeks. Shops for tinsmiths, tailors, carpenters, blacksmiths, plumbers, shoemakers, and electricians were established. A new club provided four reading rooms. The prison theater had box and balcony seats, orchestra pit, dressing rooms, and scenery. A school opened, and the barracks were cleaned and painted. The prisoners staffed two orchestras, one Austrian and one Hungarian, with thirty-seven and forty-six pieces, respectively. Two choirs began with forty and fifty members, respectively.

The Americans set up a telephone system to connect the various prison sections. They also strung a telegraph line connecting the camp to Khabarovsk and Vladivostok. With the improving conditions, the prisoners were able to construct a railroad spur leading up the hill to the camp location. The camp was even able to absorb a group of 442 Cossacks who mutinied against Cossack ataman Ivan Kalmikov in January 1919 with little negative impact.[16] A little American ingenuity and compassion made a dramatic change for the better at the prison camp.

Providing supplies was a perpetual problem because of the poor economic state of all of Siberia. The winter climate further complicated acquisition and transportation of supplies. Wood for heating and fresh vegetables had to be procured locally. Russian officials were more of a hindrance than a help. Their incompetence was a challenge for the Americans and prisoners of war to overcome. Thanks to the energetic action of the American guard force, and especially the supply officer, the residents of the camp obtained the supplies needed. Regardless of the hardships, the prisoners at the camp were never cold or hungry.[17]

As spring approached, the prisoners prepared flower gardens. Plants grown in hothouses were transplanted to the gardens when the weather permitted. Tennis courts, a football field, and a general sports field were outlined for use in good weather. The prisoners prepared a map of the area including a "plaster relief map" constructed to scale. The Japanese government subsequently purchased this three-dimensional map.[18]

Without a doubt, E Company performed splendidly. When the Americans took over the camp, it was in a wretched state. Sanitation was nonexistent. An influenza epidemic that incapacitated 1,800 prisoners of war had just swept the camp. But under E Company's supervision, the camp became a model facility. Knowledge of the American's humane treatment of the prisoners spread all over Siberia. The goodwill felt by the Austro-Hungarian prisoners of war toward the Americans manifested itself later when the Twenty-Seventh Infantry was stationed at Verkhne-Udinsk, two thousand miles from Khabarovsk. There one thousand Austro-Hungarian prisoners of war under Semenov's care volunteered to fight for the Americans of the Twenty-Seventh Infantry. They asked for no pay or clothing but only the chance to repay those who had helped their countrymen. This reaction by a group of men who did not directly experience the humane treatment at the prisoner of war camp makes a strong case for the fair and equitable treatment of other human beings. The benefit of treating people well may not be apparent in the short term, but it also may become apparent when least expected.

The gratitude felt is best summarized by the words of Lt. Col. Ferdinand Reder, senior prisoner of war. His letter to the regimental commander concerning E Company's performance ended as given below. "After all those years, we felt raised to the dignity of manhood again, and we began to love the life to which we had been restored. And, now we have returned to our dear ones at home, we would like all the world to know that we owe our lives, our health and happiness, our power for good in this world, to the noble American Officers of the Twenty-Seventh Foot Regiment, to the great American nation."[19]

Spasskoe

The First Battalion, Twenty-Seventh Infantry Regiment, occupied Yefgenyefka in November 1918, a town on the rail line about two hundred miles north of Vladivostok. The American soldiers, however, confused Yefgenyefka with the actual village of Spasskoe about two miles from the railroad. The Americans referred to both towns as Spasskoe.[20] See map 6 for a summary of the situation in Russia on November 25, 1918.

The three groups of brick buildings in Spasskoe were divided between the American, Japanese, and Russian units occupying the town. F and G Companies of the Thirty-First Infantry Regiment were in the town when the Twenty-Seventh Infantry's First Battalion arrived. The two Thirty-First Infantry Companies were originally stationed in Spasskoe to relieve elements of the Twenty-Seventh Infantry guarding the railroad. This enabled the entire Twenty-Seventh Infantry to participate in the Ussuri campaign. The Russian garrison was by and large composed of officers attending aviation, engineer, and other schools in Spasskoe. American-Russian relations were cordial with frequent visits and parties through the late spring and summer of 1919.[21]

When the First Battalion arrived in the week after the World War I armistice, the soldiers found the Japanese battalion already in the town. Living conditions for the Americans were not good. The barracks were poorly ventilated, heated, and lighted. A kitchen was on the end of each floor in the barracks. Latrines drained into open cesspools. Wood-burning stoves provided heat. The town had narrow winding streets, and animals wandered loose. The local citizens used an open market place to exchange goods such as dried meats, salted fish, wild rabbit, pheasants, poultry, butter, eggs (wrapped in straw), stags, wild boar, and even a tiger. Three-horse sleighs provided the local populace transportation in the snow. Vodka houses and cafes served as places for soldiers to relax and even talk to young women when not on duty. A barracks of German and Austrian prisoners of war even mustered an orchestra that would play evening concerts including popular American songs. This off-duty entertainment helped break the tedium of life in poorly ventilated and constructed barracks that housed the American soldiers.[22]

The German and Austrian prisoners of war saw a major change in their confinement when the Americans arrived. The Americans rounded up the prisoners who were wandering around the city; however, the prisoners then learned that American rations were better than anything they were finding in the town. The food was so good several Russians attempted to pose as Germans so that the Americans would imprison them. This situation then resulted in the Americans granting basically a parole to the prisoners. A pass carried by the prisoners identified them as such so that as they checked out during the day they could later identify themselves to a sentry when they returned.[23]

When the snow melted in periodic thaws in the fall, the ground around Spasskoe would be spongy. The ground near the rail line stayed dry and was a favorite place for people to walk. One American soldier just after seeing people gather for an afternoon walk saw children playing with a human skull. The harsh reality of living through a civil war had already hardened these children to death and human remains.[24]

The Allied garrison received reinforcements from an unexpected source. During the winter, a Chinese company arrived and volunteered to help the Americans fight. The Chinese had arrived late at night and surprised the American garrison by bugle calls to wake up the next morning. The officer in charge volunteered to fight anyone that the Americans chose to fight. Even though the Americans at that time were not fighting anyone, the Chinese were ready to help. The soldiers of the AEF did not expect to get in a fight, but they would later learn that fighting was unavoidable. The Chinese may have understood the reality of the conditions in Siberia better than the Americans. The arrival of the Chinese meant that four nations then had garrisons in this single town.[25] However, life for the AEF remained uneventful until spring.

Khabarovsk

The Twenty-Seventh Infantry's Second and Third Battalions remained in Khabarovsk. Training was emphasized in order to prepare the soldiers for their duties in Siberia. Initially, the situation was quiet, and the Americans were on cordial terms with Kalmikov's Cossacks in the city. However, Kalmikov's brutality changed this.[26]

Kalmikov began his rise to power in the spring of 1918 when the Ussuri Cossacks' fourth council meeting elected him ataman. This group also passed a resolution authorizing him to seek a loan from the Allies so spring planting could begin. The Japanese provided the loan with a promise from the Cossacks not to join the Bolsheviks. Military equipment followed. However, when Kalmikov realized that many of his potential supporters were Bolsheviks, he fled to the Japanese consul in Vladivostok. The Japanese then provided more money to combine with that taken by Kalmikov for the Cossack planting that enabled him to move his base of operations to Manchuria and recruit his band. The Cossacks under the command of Semenov and Kalmikov were a source of discord and conflict throughout the intervention. Semenov spent much of the intervention out of contact with the Americans, but Kalmikov operated in the vicinity of the AEF's subordinate elements. The Japanese provided most of their materiel support beyond the supplies confiscated by the Cossacks from the civilian population. The Cossack lack of discipline and their cruelty drove Russian civilians away from support for the Allied intervention.[27]

Kalmikov and his band of eight hundred Cossacks arrived in Khabarovsk thanks to his support of the Japanese in the Ussuri campaign between July and September 1918. When the first Japanese soldiers entered Khabarovsk on September 5 and 6, Kalmikov also arrived and established the city as a base of power. He then began his campaign of terror.[28]

Arrests and executions of "well-to-do citizens" were common as was seizure of their property. All this was done under the guise of fighting Bolshevism. Kalmikov succeeded in his tactics by terrifying the local population.[29]

On November 15, twenty women appealed to the Twenty-Seventh Infantry headquarters to save their husbands who were being held by Kalmikov for execution. The women again asked for help November 16 and 17. When an American officer questioned the Cossacks, they told him not to be concerned about their activities. Two women then went to the Twenty-Seventh Infantry headquarters on November 18 and reported that their husbands had been killed. The women then led several American officers to eleven unburied bodies of men who had been shot. One of the dead had on no underwear and five no shoes. Reporting this incident and others to the Japanese did little to restrain Kalmikov. Cossacks burned the bodies at approximately 4:45 P.M. on November 18 near the execution site. Kalmikov executed civilians and his own soldiers at will.[30] The AEF's war diaries are filled with reports of Cossack atrocities. Personal accounts of the intervention are also. However, protests by Graves and other Americans consistently failed to deter Cossack brutality. These tactics hardened the feelings on both sides in the civil war and did much to prevent popular support from reaching a level to help the White Russians defeat the Bolsheviks.

Kalmikov's cruelty to his troops included a group of former Bolshevik soldiers called the "Model Hundred." Whips, fists, and the threat of execution were liberally used to instill discipline in the men. This system was again applied to a volunteer Cossack group in December 1918. This second group, however, rioted and mutinied when subjected to such abuse. The officers were arrested, but Kalmikov's soldiers were not satisfied. Grievances reported to the Twenty-Seventh Infantry included enforced enlistment, whippings, unnecessary executions, poor food and clothing, no pay, cruel and drunk officers, and executions as well as mutilations of civilians.[31]

On the night of January 27–28, 1919, around 700 of Kalmikov's men decided they could take this treatment no longer and deserted. Approximately 300 hid in nearby towns. Thirty asked the Chinese garrison to protect them. The remaining mutineers, 398, marched as a group with their equipment to the Twenty-Seventh Infantry's headquarters and surrendered. They brought 4 cannons, 3 machine guns, and 350 animals. The Japanese estimated Kalmikov still had 400 Cossacks. The Americans estimated he had 250 men, 2 6-inch cannon, 2 3-inch cannon, and 4 smaller cannon that he could still use.[32]

The Twenty-Seventh Infantry's leadership decided to hold the mutineers as prisoners, informed the Japanese, and reported the incident to Graves in Vladivostok. Graves approved the Americans holding the mutineers and decided the regiment would not surrender the men to anyone to whom the prisoners objected.[33] This decision took a significant amount of moral courage. Cossack brutality was clear now to the Americans. Even though the Americans' Japanese allies supported the Cossacks, there was a limit to the injustices that the American leadership would accept. The soldiers of the AEF were known for their even-handed treatment of prisoners and civilians even if they were unable to stop the unjustified inhumanity of certain of their allies.

The Japanese suggested a joint American-Japanese guard be placed over the deserters, but Styer, in command at Khabarovsk, refused. On January 30, Gen. Shigemoto Oi demanded to know in a memorandum to Styer why the Americans were interfering with Kalmikov's disciplining his soldiers. Graves told Styer to refer the Japanese to him. Styer told Graves that releasing the deserters would result in their murder, so Graves then told Styer not to release any of the prisoners without his permission.[34]

In order to safeguard the prisoners, the Twenty-Seventh Infantry escorted them to the Krasnaya-Rechks prison camp on February 1. Additional desertions after the initial mutiny raised the total number of Cossacks under American protection to 442. The Cossacks remained separated from the Austro-Hungarian prisoners of war until the release of the last of the Cossacks in March 1919.[35] Styer was particularly concerned about the welfare of the Cossacks if released because during the mutiny they had wounded a Cossack colonel, who subsequently died of his wounds.[36] The punishment that would result from killing an officer did not promise to be easy.

Graves maintained the position that Styer had "simply disarmed a band of men to prevent bloodshed." Graves's policy was that the men should be released as they desired—not as Kalmikov or anyone else desired. This policy of releasing the Cossacks individually or in small groups was successful. Only thirty-five Cossacks were still in American custody by March 15.[37]

Japanese and Cossack propaganda stirred up ill will between the Americans and the local population. This propaganda alleged the Americans instigated the mutiny. However, the Volna Special Cossack Assembly February 12, 1919, deposed

Kalmikov as ataman due to his cruel misconduct.[38] The Cossacks themselves were now becoming tired of the atrocities and disgraceful actions.

Continued Japanese anti-American propaganda and their defense of Kalmikov prompted Styer to send a letter on March 25 to Oi, the Japanese commander in Khabarovsk. Styer said that Kalmikov's troops were not considered Allied soldiers by the Americans. He protested the undisciplined, disorganized nature of Kalmikov's troops (he was not the ataman but still exerted some control over his former soldiers). Styer objected to the Japanese supporting Kalmikov, while accepting no responsibility for their actions. Graves sent a copy of the letter to Otani with a note supporting Styer and asking for Otani's assistance in controlling the Cossacks. Otani continued to claim no responsibility for Kalmikov's band but agreed to assist the Americans by speaking to Kalmikov about Graves and Styer's concerns. Once Kalmikov departed Khabarovsk, the situation calmed and Cossack statements attacking him appeared in local newspapers.[39]

Another issue related to the mutiny was the equipment turned in to the Americans when the mutineers surrendered. This equipment included horses, weapons, and other items. The Japanese requested the equipment be given to them since Japan had originally provided it to the Cossacks. When the Japanese satisfactorily identified the material as that provided to Kalmikov, Styer returned it to them on April 8, 1919.[40]

Bolshevik currency was another problem in Khabarovsk at this time. The widespread circulation of Bolshevik printed money had basically surpassed that of Russian imperial rubles. Within Khabarovsk, a bank had to stamp the Bolshevik paper money for it to be used in business transactions. However, outside the city that was not the case. In fact, the AEF Intelligence Section reported that north of Khabarovsk, the Bolshevik paper money was the primary currency in exchange. Anyone using imperial rubles typically received their change in Bolshevik paper. However, this may have been an attempt to hoard rubles and get rid of Bolshevik paper.[41]

This Bolshevik paper money seemed to be a means of propaganda. As the Bolsheviks retreated from the Allied advance, they passed out large amounts of their currency. This garnered them goodwill from the common people, who lacked money. The lack of other paper money in circulation resulted in this Bolshevik paper money becoming the common currency. Many people favored the Bolsheviks over any other Russian government or any of the Allies thanks to having some form of money to use to pay for goods and services.[42] The Bolsheviks continued to win the support of the Russian peasants throughout the intervention and subsequent civil war.

The Japanese army also had special currency to use in Siberia. This paper money had "Imperial Japanese Province" printed on it. However, at least one Japanese officer realized that this phrase caused a great deal of resentment on the part of the local populace. Russian merchants did not want to accept the money but often had no choice when dealing with the Japanese soldiers.[43]

The economic condition of the local populace was also poor. Sugar, tea, salt, soap, candles, and clothing were in short supply. Chinese merchants appeared to control the availability of such staples. Allowable purchase amounts were small. For example, sugar was rarely available in amounts exceeding one-half of a pound at a time. A low-quality tea was available for purchase in single pound packages. The lack of salt to purchase had the effect of making it very difficult for people to cure fish for winter storage. Shoes were a principal clothing item that was not widely available. Poor people believed that the arrival of the American force would improve their economic situation. The expectation was that the Americans would bring sufficient quantities of supplies so that the civilians could purchase such staples. The local poor did not seek charity but rather sought some means of purchasing food to stave off their fears of starving in the winter.[44] The Americans were not equipped to meet this expectation to the level envisioned by some of the local populace.

Thirty-First Infantry—Garrison and Mine Guard

Little activity occurred during this time in the Thirty-First Infantry's area of responsibility. Replacements continued to arrive so that regimental strength increased from 1,952 on October 31, 1918, to 3,589 on December 31. Patrolling was a constant activity. The planned assassination of the civilian mine supervisor in Suchan almost resulted in the death of Lieutenant Colonel Loring, who was the American in command of the mine guard. Apparently Loring resembled the mine supervisor and came under fire while riding his horse. Fortunately the assassin missed.[45]

By January 31, 1919, elements of the regiment were deployed as shown in table 7.

January, February, and March 1919 were difficult months. The winter weather took a severe toll on the soldiers. Several Thirty-First Infantry soldiers lost an arm or leg due to frostbite. However, in general, sufficient food, fuel, and warm clothing were available. Officers and enlisted personnel arrivals and promotions caused changes of command in the companies and brought new soldiers to the theater. It was becoming clear that mobility was a problem. More cavalry would have been useful. The horses brought from the Philippines handled the dramatic climate change with little difficulty. Footwear was a concern with hobnailed shoes and moccasins not performing well in the harsh conditions. The fur-lined gloves were bulky and inhibited the use of other equipment.[46]

Table 7. Thirty-First Infantry Regiment Locations, January 31, 1919

Unit	Location
Headquarters, Machine Gun Company, Supply Company, E Company, H Company	East of Vladivostok
A and B Companies	Gornastaya Valley
C and D Companies	Diomedes
I Company	Churkin (with detachments at Pervaya Rechka and Russian Island)
K Company	Base and line of communications
F and G Companies	Spasskoe
L Company	Razdolnoe
M Company	Suchan
Legation Guard Detachment	Harbin

From Paul, *Regimental History*, p. 16

Company B moved to Harbin in February. The political and economic situation in Siberia was expected to bring guerilla warfare if not revolution in the spring with Adm. Alexander Kolchak's government as the principal target. Partisans fired on southbound trains on March 14 and 17.[47] On March 23, H Company moved to Suchan to replace M Company as part of the mine guard. However, both companies remained there.[48]

The Chinese company in the Allied Mine Guard moved to Tigrovia before winter. The Americans it replaced moved to Fanza. Lt. Col. L. L. Pendleton replaced Loring February 12 as the commander of the mine guard. Trouble in the area began shortly thereafter.[49]

Bolshevik attempts to organize support in the Suchan area during the middle of February resulted in the Russian general Smirnoff, a Kolchak supporter, moving into the valley with seven hundred soldiers. He occupied Frolovka and Novitskaya in order to suppress Bolshevik agitation. Kolchak's attempt to draft local citizens in March caused great discontent. Many of the miners told to report for military service resisted the call. A large number of mine workers quit the mines and left the area. Coal production fell. Two foremen were murdered. Two Japanese soldiers were also killed. The murderers mutilated the Japanese bodies.[50]

Exempting the miners from the draft failed to stop the discontent. Peasants had begun to organize resistance. Those miners still working demanded a pay increase, and problems continued into the next phase of Allied operations.[51] Such unrest was typical of the result of the continued Bolshevik propaganda and the inability of the White Russian government to establish firm control and security for the occupants of post–World War I Russia.

Events Overall

While the Americans in Siberia established garrison-like operations, life was not so calm in the remainder of Russia. In January 1919, the Bolsheviks moved into the Caucasus oil fields. This led to an increase in violence between White and Red Russian forces. Gen. Anton Denikin led a White Russian counterattack to drive out the Reds. When White Russian general Lavr Kornilov was killed in his command post the previous April, Denikin had assumed command of the White Russian forces in southern Russia. Continued Bolshevik attacks toward Odessa resulted in the French forces there evacuating in early April, leaving Denikin without much-needed military support from the Allies.[52]

A substantial Allied intervention force had landed in Odessa in December 1918. Initially, 6,000 French, 2,000 Greek, and 4,000 Poles landed. This force eventually grew to two French and two Greek divisions. The combined Allied force reached approximately 40,000. Another 7,500 French and Greek soldiers deployed to the Crimea. This combined force landed with the intent to allow for the restoration of order. However, the Allied leaders soon discovered that Denikin was elsewhere fighting the Reds and few organized White Russian elements were in the area.[53]

The intervention in northern Russia continued and also included a significantly higher level of combat by the American forces. Approximately fourteen thousand Bolsheviks faced the combined Allied force in northern Russia.[54] Here there was no American general officer to insulate the lower-ranking officers and men from the influence of America's allies, who wanted to fight the Bolsheviks to eliminate their rising to power. The intensity of combat during this time was very different from that experienced in Siberia because Graves insisted on a stance neutral to the warring Russian parties.

For example, a company of approximately three hundred American infantrymen under the command of Capt. Robert Boyd, as part of a force that also had three hundred other Allied troops such as a company of Royal Scots and Canadians, spent November 11, 1918, in a fierce battle at Toulgas in northern Russia. The Allies fought from log bunkers and peasant homes while Bolshevik infantry attacked with gunboats on the Dvina River providing indirect fire support. The Americans were two hundred miles south of Archangel. Bolsheviks had surrounded the town. Canadians manned the two artillery pieces of the small Allied force. The weather was brutal. The ground froze at night and thawed during the day.[55]

When the Bolsheviks captured the Allied hospital building in town, an orderly tried to distract Melochofski, the Bolshevik leader, from murdering the wounded by offering him food. However, the murderous intent of the Red soldiers was not stopped until Melochofski's mistress, apparently a beautiful but tough young woman, entered the building and announced that she would personally kill anyone who harmed the wounded. Melochofski then countermanded his previous decision to kill the wounded. The survivors also reported that later in the day Melochofski returned to the little hospital mortally wounded so that his mistress could care for him until his death.[56]

A surprise attack upon the position rear forced the Canadian artillerymen to turn their howitzers around and fire directly into the charging ranks of Bolshevik infantry. The Canadian point-blank fire and American machine guns ripped great holes in the massed Red infantry, stopping the attack. The fighting was rough with artillery fire, sometimes shattering a blockhouse and killing those inside. Nonetheless, the Bolshevik attacks across open ground left a heavy trail of death and injury. A counterattack by the Royal Scots recovered the wounded protected by the young Russian woman.[57]

The battle ebb and flow finally broke the way of the Allies when an American counterattack afforded the opportunity to blow up the Bolshevik ammunition reserves and the freezing river forced the Bolshevik gunboats to retreat out of range. After these events, the surviving Red infantry retreated. Many soldiers died of exposure in the forest. The Americans destroyed several houses to clear fields of fire and wondered why they were sitting in Russia fighting Bolsheviks when they had expected to go to the Western Front to fight Germany.[58]

Siberia Overall

The Russian Railway Service Corps men were provided support throughout the railway network and were not under the command of the two infantry regiments. Therefore, their experiences would cut across both regiments' areas of operations as well as many of those of the Allies in the theater. An account of one train as told by 2nd Lt. William C. Jones provides an example of the types of challenges faced by the AEF, the Russian Railway Service Corps, and the other soldiers and civilians fighting, working, and trying to stay alive in Siberia during this time. Jones recorded that a trainload of Bolshevik prisoners passed through Myandohe on November 7, 1918. Czechs guarded the train and told Jones and others not to give the prisoners any food. Fortunately for the prisoners a few local people were able to sneak some food to the Russians, who were in poor condition. Japanese and White Russian soldiers guarded the rail stations.[59]

This same train went eastward to Harbin, where the local authorities refused to allow it to stop and off-load. Consequently the train returned westward and once again passed through Myandohe in January. The Czech guards relented somewhat in their attitude because Jones recorded that many Russian Railway Service Corps officers had purchased food for the prisoners as the train returned westward. In one town, the Russian Railway Service Corps officers arranged for a priest and doctor to examine the prisoners. However, such help was limited due to conflicting loyalties and the generally difficult conditions of life in Manchuria and Siberia.[60]

Besides observing the poor treatment of prisoners, Jones also witnessed just how different the culture was in Siberia when compared to that in the United States. In addition to the train traffic, caravans of horse- and camel-drawn wagons passed through the area carrying goods for sale. Small groups of people would travel by caravan instead of the train. The local Mongolian people were friendly and welcomed the Russian Railway Service Corps officers into their homes. After several months in Myandohe, Jones returned to Harbin for another assignment. Up to this point the Russian Railway Service Corps officers had no clear line of authority and provided advice to anyone who would accept it.[61]

The Japanese continued to engage in combat with groups in Siberia opposed to their presence. The Tanaka Battalion attempted to destroy partisans operating near Skramskoe, Ternoski, and Yufta. When the Japanese command lost contact with the battalion, an infantry regiment marched to the same area. This relief force engaged a partisan force of approximately two thousand men that retreated from the area leaving no Russian casualties. Only four wounded Japanese soldiers from the Tanaka Battalion were alive when relieved on February 26, 1919.[62]

This garrison period was relatively uneventful for the soldiers of the AEF-Siberia even if the violence of the civil war continued to wrack the political and social structure of Russia elsewhere. No large-scale American maneuvers took place in Siberia even while Americans and other Allied soldiers were fighting a brutal war in northern Russia. The American soldiers in Siberia energetically carried out their assigned tasks while remaining wary. Trouble was brewing. As the AEF worked more and more with its allies, differences in goals and techniques, such as the use of torture, arose. This laid the foundation for the subsequent animosity among the Allied forces. Additionally, Bolshevik strength grew while White Russian forces remained fragmented. The continued conflict forced the Allies to devise a plan to safeguard the railroad for the benefit of their own forces and the region. This railway guard mission followed.

10
Railway Guard and the Twenty-Seventh Infantry

The requirement for continuous railway operations as a means of transportation and communication made cooperation between the United States and the Allies essential. Conferences were held between the intervening nations' representatives to divide responsibility for operation of the railroad. Roland B. Morris, US Ambassador to Japan, represented American interests at these conferences. The representatives decided to form a "Special Inter-Allied Committee" to supervise the Chinese Eastern and Trans-Siberian Railroads. Each power with military forces in Siberia had a representative on the committee. The chairman was Russian.[1]

The Allies formed two special boards. The Technical Board was composed of railroad experts from the nations with military units in Siberia and was charged with technical and economic management. John F. Stevens, the US railway expert with the Russian Railway Service Corps, was elected the board president in early March 1919. The second board was the Military Transportation Board, which coordinated military rail transportation.[2] The various boards were an attempt to coordinate Allied operations in these areas.

After discussion among the various representatives, on April 14 the commanders agreed to divide the rail line into sectors to be guarded by military forces. The sectors for each nation are provided in table 8. The assignments would then drive the physical location of AEF units, which would affect the Allied forces and threats having an impact on operations. The lack of contiguous sectors also made the massing of forces difficult for the AEF. Fortunately there was no attempt to consolidate more than a battalion for large unit action. The railroad remained the critical piece of infrastructure necessary for military operations and civilian economic activity.

On April 14, Graves issued orders for AEF elements to assume their designated guard posts. On April 21, he published a proclamation to the Russian people in which he explained his views concerning the necessity for AEF soldiers to guard the railway. He pointed out that guarding the railway was in the best interests of the Russian people regardless of their political affiliation. He also pointed out

Table 8. Railway Guard Sectors April 1919

Nationality	Sector
American	1. Vladivostok to Nikolsk-Ussuri with the Suchan Mine branch line—144 miles 2. Spasskoe-Udinsk to Ussuri—70 miles 3. Verkhne-Udinsk to Baikal City—265 miles (This sector was later enlarged to include Verkhne-Udinsk to Mysovaya, which added 102 miles to the length giving a total sector size of 316 miles.)
Japanese	1. Nikolsk-Ussuri to Spasskoe—61 miles 2. Guberovo to Verkhne-Udinsk and from Manchuria Station to Karimskaya—2,200 miles
Chinese	1. Ussuri to Guberovo—60 miles 2. Nikolsk-Ussuri to Manchuria Station. This included the Chanchun line—1,165 miles
Russian	Mysovaya to Baikal City
Czech	Baikal City to Omsk

From Graves, Report, "Operations to June 30, 1919," pp. 15–17

that the Allies as a group had decided that the guard mission was necessary. The AEF's purpose was to "protect the railroad and railway property and insure the operation of passenger and freight trains" in the AEF's sector "without obstruction or interruption." Graves promised to treat everyone equally regardless of "nationality, religion, or politics." He also stated "interference with traffic will not be tolerated." The lack of an anti-Bolshevik statement upset Kolchak supporters.[3] See map 7 for the situation in Russia on April 7, 1919.

By now the operations of the base areas had taken on a reasonably settled state. Albert W. Palmer, an incoming YMCA secretary and former pastor, would describe his arrival in Vladivostok with great enthusiasm. Reaching the port was a welcome break from the monotony of an ocean voyage. The lack of space on deck precluded any games requiring physical activity. Only cards and dice were available to pass the time.[4]

Fog could obscure the entrance into the harbor at Vladivostok, while Chinese fishing junks would mingle with modern military warships and transports. Fortifications, warehouses, and the docks surrounded the waterway. The city enveloped the harbor. In the summer, the surrounding hills were green with vegetation. Palmer also discovered that pro-Bolshevik propaganda was circulating among the

American troops. There was no way to prevent the subversive element of propaganda from having some sort of impact. The Americans and other Allied soldiers worked and relaxed among the local citizens. Some of them were loyal to the White Russians while others supported the Reds. Maj. Sidney Graves, Graves's son, accompanied a committee from the Allies to Olga Bay and Tethue, which are north of Vladivostok, in order to ascertain the local population's feelings. They met with a number of people including local Bolshevik organizations. Most of the Russians were friendly toward the Americans but not toward the Japanese or the Kolchak government. It was clear from that visit that many people simply wanted the Allies to leave.[5]

The Americans and the other military forces were not constantly under fire. Consequently the AEF leadership and supporting organizations such as the YMCA, YWCA, and American Red Cross strove to provide entertainment that would not harm the morals of the young men. The July 4, 1919, celebration in Vladivostok included three American young women who arrived from Japan in order to provide such entertainment for a month. They sang and served ice cream. Patriotic speeches emphasized the meaning of the day. Local vendors joined in the festivities to capitalize on the opportunity to make money.[6]

The deployment of the AEF units resulted in combat occurring between the Americans and the Bolsheviks. The White Russians and Allies principally controlled towns and villages. The railroad linked these power centers. Partisans occupied rural areas. Since the railroad supported the White Russians, the partisans opposing the White Russians felt they had to interdict it. American attempts to protect the railroad, whether to help the Russian people survive or aid the Allies, forced the AEF into conflict with the partisans who did not support the White Russian effort. Combat and American casualties were inevitable. The Twenty-Seventh Infantry would fight partisans at Kraefski, Shmakovka, and Uspenka and Cossacks at Iman. A dispute about rifles almost exploded into a major conflict with their supposed Cossack allies. While the Twenty-Seventh Infantry continued to guard the railroad and tried to remain true to its orders, the Russian Railway Service Corps would manage the rail network and gradually have to begin the long trek to the east to escape the White Russian collapse.

Twenty-Seventh Infantry: Bolshevik and Cossack Troubles

Graves's original orders concerning the railway guard mission sent the Third Battalion to Verkhne-Udinsk near Lake Baikal. A and B Companies had arrived there from Spasskoe in late March. By May 15, the entire battalion was at Verkhne-Udinsk. In late May and early June, the Second Battalion moved from Khabarovsk to the Spasskoe area. The two Thirty-First Infantry companies that had been in

Figure 1. Maj. Gen. William S. Graves, Vladivostok, Siberia, November 23, 1918. National Archives and Records Administration.

Figure 2. Company B, Twenty-Seventh Infantry, waiting to unload supplies from Russian boxcars, railroad yards at Khabarovsk, Siberia. November 15, 1918. This type of car was used in Siberia for movement of troops. National Archives and Records Administration.

Figure 3. Service Company Trains having hard going between Nikitofka and Runovka, Siberia, Twenty-Seventh Infantry, AEF-Siberia, 1918. Combined Arms Research Library (CARL), Archives/Special Collections, Fort Leavenworth, Kansas.

Figure 4. American troops en route to Ussuri. Scene is near Spasskoe. AEF-Siberia, 1918. Combined Arms Research Library (CARL), Archives/Special Collections, Fort Leavenworth, Kansas.

Figure 5. Detail of Company M, Thirty-First Infantry, stationed at Fanza, Siberia, out to investigate an outbreak of Bolshevik, November 26, 1918. Lt. J. W. Resing in charge. National Archives and Records Administration.

Figure 6. Thirty-First Infantry on practice hike, medical wagons in foreground, looking northwest from Vladivostok. National Archives and Records Administration.

Figure 7. Peace Parade, Allied nations, led by US Troops, Thirty-First Infantry, Vladivostok, Siberia, November 15, 1918. National Archives and Records Administration.

Figure 8. Pano of Vladivostok, Siberia. National Archives and Records Administration.

Figure 9. USS *Brooklyn* taking her place alongside the British cruiser HMS *Suffolk*, Vladivostok Harbor, December 23, 1918. *Brooklyn* was the flagship of the Asiatic Fleet and carried Rear Adm. William L. Rogers. National Archives and Records Administration.

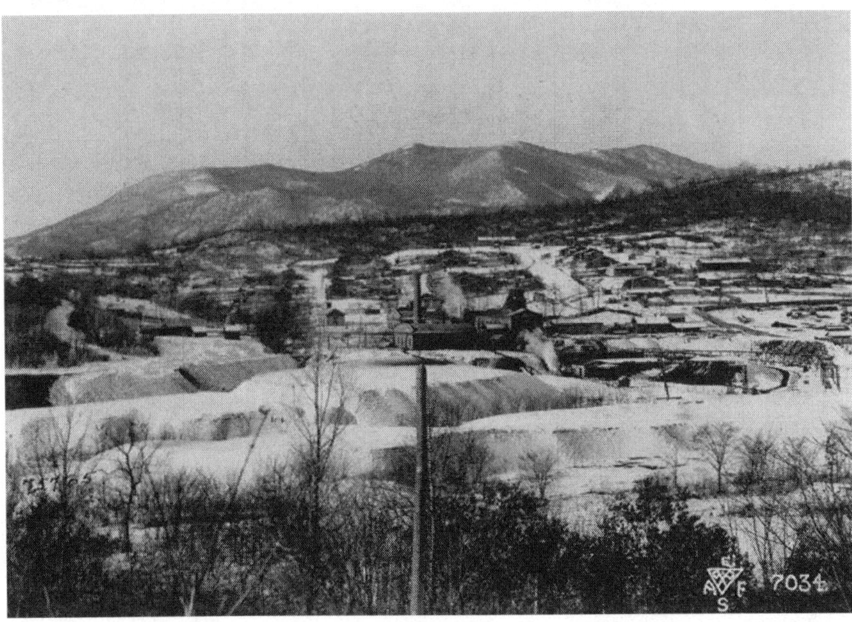

Figure 10. Village of Suchan and Mine #1, Siberia, looking south from reservoir, near headquarters, Company M, Thirty-First Infantry. November 28, 1918. Screenings or steamship coal piled in foreground. National Archives and Records Administration.

Figure 11. General Graves and staff and Ataman Seminoff and aides. National Archives and Records Administration.

Figure 12. Col. George H. Emerson, Russian Railroad Service Corps, and John Stevens, chairman, American Railroad Commission to Russia, on steps of Mr. Stevens's car in yards at Vladivostok, Siberia. National Archives and Records Administration.

Figure 13. Trans-Siberian Railroad station at Nikolsk, American and Japanese soldiers in the foreground, December 1, 1918. National Archives and Records Administration.

Figure 14. American Red Cross Train No. 3, carrying food, clothing, and medical supplies to the front. American soldiers are guarding the train. National Archives and Records Administration.

Figure 15. Approaching one of the series of tunnels that line the railroad along Lake Baikal, Siberia. National Archives and Records Administration.

Figure 16. General Gaida, commander of the Czech troops, of the North Ural Front, at his desk, Ekaterinburg, Russia, 1918. Gaida is seated in the room of the house at Ekaterinburg that the czar occupied when he was kept prisoner by the Bolsheviks. National Archives and Records Administration.

Figure 17. Czech armored train, 1918. In this manner the Czech camouflaged their train and captured many stations from the Bolsheviki. National Archives and Records Administration.

Figure 18. Machine gun nest on wheels. An armored car of the Russian armored train *The Avenger*; the car behind is headquarters car for the staff of the department of armored train. National Archives and Records Administration.

Spasskoe departed once the Second Battalion concentrated there. In late May, C and D Companies moved out of Spasskoe to a small village to the north. E and F Companies followed C and D in June, which left only H Company in Spasskoe.[7]

Relations with all parties involved in the civil war in Russia remained tense. On May 21, 1919, a large Bolshevik force surrounded the small American force in Sviyagino. The initial report indicated that 3,500 Bolsheviks had surrounded the town. This prompted a plan to launch two rifle companies in twelve railway cars to rescue the Americans. A second report disclosed that the detachment faced a Bolshevik force of approximately 150 cavalry and 400 infantry soldiers. The Bolsheviks sent an officer into the town to discuss their plan with the American lieutenant in command. A promise of no hostile action by the Bolsheviks reduced the level of concern. The Bolsheviks sent four telegrams and left. No American reinforcements went to Sviyagino.[8]

Relations with local Russian authorities such as Cossack ataman Grigori Semenov in the Verkhne-Udinsk area were difficult throughout May. A group of Cossacks captured three American soldiers on May 18 and paraded them through town. While initially refusing to release the soldiers, a threat of their recovery by force by the Twenty-Seventh Infantry convinced the Cossacks to release the American soldiers to their command. On May 28, a private named Karas from the American military police killed a Cossack named Corporal Krakoff. Four drunken Cossacks including Krakoff assaulted American soldiers in a boarding house. Three American military police attempted to break up the fight. The Cossacks pulled their revolvers, so the Americans pulled their M1911 automatics. Karas and his fellow military policemen won the battle after Karas killed Krakoff. The Americans captured the remaining Cossacks.[9]

This incident far from quelled the ill will between the erstwhile allies. Instead, the Cossacks began a series of attacks upon the American soldiers and Russian railroad workers. A dispute over which side owned a railroad car resulted in a Cossack armored train aiming its guns at a train operated by the Russian Railway Service Corps. American soldiers were aboard as guards. No one fired but clearly that was only a matter of time. The Cossacks while initially refusing did eventually remove the armored train named "Merciless" from Verkhne-Udinsk. Japanese support of the Cossacks delayed agreement to move the Merciless.[10]

Kraefski

In June, two squads from C Company were guarding the Kraefski railroad station twelve miles north of Sviyagino. At least one hundred Bolshevik fighters surrounded the Americans. The American sergeant in charge of the detachment decided resistance was futile and allowed the Bolsheviks to remove the telephone equipment from the station. The partisan leader spoke excellent English and even asked the Americans for Bull Durham tobacco. He was carrying an American pistol that he twirled on his finger. A girlfriend of the Bolshevik leader told the Americans in Sviyagino that he had been a sergeant in the Thirty-First Infantry Regiment who deserted from Vladivostok several months before. In the Red Army he progressed in rank to a point that he was responsible for three villages.[11]

Repositioning units to execute the railroad guard missions prescribed by Graves included a platoon from F Company under 2nd Lt. Wilson A. Rich occupying Kraefski. Rich's platoon was reduced to three squads when a force was organized by Maj. Ralph Wallace to search out Bolsheviks who had been interfering with the railroad. Wallace was reacting to the guard detachment allowing the Bolsheviks to steal telephone equipment while they watched.[12]

Near midnight the night of June 11–12, a woman tried to speak with a sentry but ran off before an interpreter could be found to explain what she was saying. Lieutenant Rich assumed the woman was trying to warn the detachment, so he prepared for action. Due to a shortage of ammunition, he instructed his men not to shoot unless they could see at least one-half of an attacker's body. Before daylight, Rich had his men reposition from the sheet metal warehouse they had been sleeping in to a trench along the railroad embankment. He had one BAR, but the gunner had never fired the weapon. This particular soldier was the only man besides Rich who knew how to operate the weapon. Rich told the BAR gunner to stay by his side and only fire when ordered to do so.[13]

On the morning of June 12, the Twenty-Seventh Infantry openly fought with Bolshevik forces for the first time. At 3:30 a.m., a band of an estimated 110 to 185 Bolsheviks and Chinese bandits attacked Rich's detachment. The attackers emerged from a group of trees approximately eight hundred yards from the Americans and moved in a skirmish line through waist-high grass toward the Americans. The Chinese bandits were on the left flank of the main attacking element. The hostile attackers spread out in a skirmish line and advanced on the Americans who they apparently hoped to catch unaware of their approach. The cries of "Forward!" in Russian could be heard by the waiting American soldiers.[14]

When five hundred to six hundred yards from the American position, the Bolsheviks stopped, knelt, and fired at the sheet metal warehouse where the Americans had slept. Fortunately, the men in the shallow trench were protected from the initial volley. Rich did not return the shots. One American described the fuselage as sounding like "hailstones on a tin roof" as the bullets slammed into the building's sheet metal sides. Clearly had the soldiers remained in the warehouse, this might have been a major disaster with this understrength platoon being destroyed by a much larger force. The Bolsheviks apparently did not realize their error regarding the location of the Americans.[15]

After firing, the Bolsheviks became extremely overconfident. The lack of opposition apparently convinced them that victory was within their grasp. They rose from their firing positions and charged at the warehouse. Rich calmly waited while the Bolsheviks yelled and screamed while they ran at the empty building. He ordered his men to hold their fire until the Bolsheviks were two hundred yards from their position. When Rich decided that the Bolsheviks had come close enough, the platoon remnant rose from the bottom of the trench and opened fire. The American barrage smashed the Bolshevik charge as the surprised partisans were blown to the ground or dived for cover. The Chinese bandits had managed to reach a log pile where they could have provided enfilade fire into the American position from four hundred yards away. However, just as the Chinese began to peer over the logs hiding them, AEF soldiers shot two of them in the head. This deflated the spirit of the Chinese attackers, which resulted in their fleeing the battlefield without causing any harm.[16] American marksmanship made its impact felt.

A spirited firefight continued between the Americans and Bolsheviks. The Americans left the prepared trench because the tall grass hid the enemy troops. Boxcars, an embankment, and shacks provided cover for Rich's men to continue the exchange and steadily maneuver forward to destroy the attacking force that outnumbered them. Bolshevik casualties continued to grow as the Americans' accurate fire took its bloody toll. A cook, who was accidentally left over one hundred yards in front of the main position, climbed onto a shed and opened fire on the Bolshevik right flank reportedly hitting eight enemy troops. The Bolsheviks finally broke when the BAR gunner could stand the excitement no longer. He emptied his twenty rounds into the Bolshevik position all at once. The heavy fire of the BAR sounded like a machine gun and crushed the Bolshevik will to continue. The Bolsheviks retreated. The battle had lasted about thirty minutes.[17]

Casualties were relatively light. While on a reconnaissance patrol, two Americans were captured the night before the attack and held for twenty days; they were released in a prisoner exchange. While searching for wounded and dead Bolsheviks after the battle, one American sergeant was killed by a wounded Bolshevik. One American was killed in the battle. Rich's men found eleven enemy dead and two wounded men in their search of the area after the fight.[18]

After the battle, the local citizens flocked to the area to see what had happened. Whether due to accident or skilled marksmanship, the two Chinese bandits killed by head wounds attracted much attention by the civilians. The local citizens were impressed with the marksmanship of the American soldiers. When Rich had his men start digging graves for the Bolshevik dead, the AEF soldiers collected money to hire several Chinese citizens to bury the enemy dead instead.[19] The American soldiers had no desire to carry out manual labor, and the civilians were apparently happy to have the money.

Shmakovka

On June 8, Bolshevik partisans burned the railroad bridge at Shmakovka. Two railroad officials were captured but released later.[20] The attackers stole telephone instruments from the railroad station.[21] This was a direct attack on the railroad's ability to function and support military and civilian operations.

Lt. Christian Gross and twenty-five men of F Company departed Yefgenyefka for Shmakovka to reestablish order. They traveled for three hours on a train engine and gondola coal car to reach Shmakovka. Periodic stops and questioning of local citizens en route produced no useful information.[22]

Upon arriving at Shmakovka, Gross discovered the bridge had been destroyed by fire and dynamite—what did not burn had been blown up. The Americans put a gang of Korean laborers to work rebuilding the bridge, and they questioned the local inhabitants. Later that night, another detachment of Americans arrived to check on Gross since there was no way for Gross to contact his superiors. The kidnapped railroad officials returned near midnight. Gross spent the remainder of the night questioning them. The following morning he returned to Yefgenyefka and made his report.[23] Colonel Morrow deemed the incident at Shmakovka as sufficient justification for an attack and issued instructions for an expedition to destroy the Bolsheviks that had been interfering with the railroad and telegraph communications. This force moved by train to Shmakovka shortly before dark and camped.[24]

Uspenka

Intelligence reports previously indicated that Uspenka was a Bolshevik headquarters and base of supply. Therefore, the first objective was to seize that town. To accomplish this mission, the provisional company discussed earlier that included part of Rich's platoon was available. The march was a difficult one. Wagons carried supplies. The march routine included ten-minute rest periods every hour. Rough roads, marshy ground, and swarming insects made the march an unpleasant task. The maps available were poor and indicated a much easier march than the one encountered.[25]

The American force spent the night at the Shmakovka Obitel, an Orthodox monastery, after the thirty-mile march. The monks had led a quiet life of agriculture and horse breeding until a Bolshevik band raided them the previous month. The Bolsheviks stole most of the monks' food and horses. Hay served as mattresses for the Americans when they arrived. Reconnaissance the next day disclosed a swamp separating the Americans from the Bolshevik stronghold. The Americans could find no passage through the swamp, so the company used a road to detour around the swamp. At 2:30 P.M. the afternoon of June 11, the American soldiers saw several armed men running across a field and up a hill in the distance. As the Americans advanced, they discovered thirty dummies to the right of their advance. The Bolshevik ruse failed to draw fire from the Americans. Gross led eight men forward as an advance guard. The Bolsheviks could be seen now as the American main body remained under cover while Gross continued to advance.[26]

When the advance guard was about two hundred yards from the enemy, they saw several Bolshevik partisans preparing to engage them. Gross did not hesitate. He immediately charged the enemy. The furious Bolshevik fire drowned out the patrol's shots and wounded two Americans before the advance guard could do more than to drop to the ground. The enemy fire halted the patrol except for Gross, who decided that staying in their location was pointless. Since lying on the ground was getting them killed, he decided that the best thing to do was to charge the partisans. He did not stop until he was inside the enemy position. With no hand grenades, because none had been shipped to the AEF, Gross quickly shot a Bolshevik, who was in the same place he landed. Two soldiers from the advanced guard rolled over to shield one of their wounded comrades, whose yells for help were attracting Bolshevik attention.[27]

Gross found himself in a tight spot. He faced several armed partisans who had just seen him run up the hill at them and then he jumped into their trench and shot one of their own. For a moment, Gross and the partisans stared at each other and then everyone started firing. Gross's close-range marksmanship was better than his opponents' ability to shoot. Two of the partisans decided that discretion was the better part of valor and jumped out of the position to escape. Gross killed at least one more partisan who tried to shoot it out with him. Confusion now spread among the partisans who were surprised by Gross's charge. Gross later wrote that he was "bewildered and unconscious" when he made his one-man attack. Thinking their lieutenant was dead, the advance guard withdrew to rejoin the main body leaving Gross inside the enemy position eventually out of ammunition for his rifle but still on his feet with his .45-caliber Colt automatic pistol in his hand.[28]

Meanwhile, the American main body advanced from its covered position to rescue the patrol and fight the Bolsheviks. Gross tried to attract their attention. Since he was presumed dead, every time he showed himself to wave for help, the American soldiers started shooting at him. The main body's attack forced the partisans to withdraw. When the soldiers came close enough for Gross to recognize the voice of one of his fellow lieutenants, he called out to him, giving details of their deployment to Siberia. The lieutenant crawled up to Gross's position where the two friends were happy to see each other. The American main body found two members of the advance guard wounded. Two enemy soldiers were killed with several wounded and captured.[29]

Uspenka was still three miles away. The next day the Americans attacked. Bolshevik prisoners and civilians provided the Americans with a rough layout of the defenses in the town. A friendly peasant drove a wagon to the bridge leading into town and stopped there as a distraction to the Bolshevik guards. The Americans fired hourly signal rockets as a diversion. Two squads of Americans charged into town down the main street. One squad attacked along each flank with two additional squads following the main attack as a reserve. The American automatic rifle fire routed the defenders. No Americans were wounded or killed. They captured four Russian wagons filled with supplies. The American force remained in the town to prevent the Bolsheviks from returning.[30]

G Company with a machine-gun detachment set out with a Japanese force to hunt Bolshevik partisans on the night of July 17–18. This was the final AEF operation against the Bolsheviks in the area during the summer. The combined American-Japanese group operated east of Spasskoe but failed to engage any enemy elements. G Company returned to Spasskoe after a few days. The machine-gun detachment remained with the Japanese unit until August 8.[31]

Meanwhile, relations with the White Russian Cossacks went steadily downhill. Cossack armored trains roamed the rails. Railroad officials were terrorized. Cossacks tortured and executed civilians at a whim. Semenov's and Kalmikov's troops were subject to no authority other than their own. The Russian people were generally friendly toward the Americans but could not understand why the AEF units protected the railroad and allowed the brutal Cossacks free passage. The Cossacks hated the American soldiers because they interfered with the Cossacks' raping and pillaging. This placed the AEF troops in a difficult position. On one hand they were trying to prevent the Bolsheviks from attacking Semenov's and Kalmikov's forces; at the same time these Cossacks were obstructing American efforts to enforce justice.[32]

Iman

One deserter from the AEF had gained the particular enmity of the Americans because he had led Bolsheviks in attacks on American positions. This man, known as "Karachun," had been a member of K Company, Thirty-First Infantry. Capt. Lindsey P. Johns of the Twenty-Seventh Infantry received orders to capture Karachun. To do this, he took Corp. Benjamin Sperling of K Company, Thirty-First Infantry, as an interpreter and went to Iman. Sperling knew Karachun prior to his desertion.[33]

Iman contained a varied group of American allies (or supposed allies). Kalmikov and Kolchak had followers in the town. Japanese and Chinese troops also garrisoned Iman. On August 31, 1919, Johns and Sperling went to the Japanese and Chinese headquarters to obtain assistance and were well received. At the Cossack headquarters, they were treated cordially until they stated they hoped to use Cossack and Kolchak secret agents to trap Karachun. The Cossacks demanded written passports authorizing the Americans to travel in the Russian sector. When none could be produced, the Cossacks arrested Johns and Sperling. The Cossacks imprisoned both Americans, did not allow them to communicate, and demanded that the American government officially recognize Kalmikov.[34]

Johns managed to escape that night. He ran to the Chinese garrison and demanded a message be sent to his headquarters. Cossack soldiers recaptured him there. The Chinese did not send the message.[35]

However, on his third night in captivity, Johns escaped again. This time he had more luck with the Chinese garrison. They put him on a rail handcar with two Chinese soldiers as an escort. He reached the American sector at Ussuri and then hurried to Spasskoe to report the incident. However, a civilian had already reported the capture.[36]

The leadership and soldiers of the Twenty-Seventh Infantry did not appreciate the conduct of the Cossacks and their Japanese allies. A rescue force of 8 officers and 150 men moved by train through the American sector from Spasskoe toward Iman. The Russian train engineer that took the American unit was nicknamed Casey Jones by the Americans because of his friendly attitude toward them. At 3:00 A.M., the train charged into the Iman station.[37]

When the train stopped, 158 determined Americans leapt off the train and raced through the town to set up positions covering any hostile movement. Within ten minutes, the American soldiers controlled Iman. They fired three shots in the capture of the town. The first shot killed a Chinese peddler's horse. The peddler was wearing Cossack pants, which prompted the shot. The Americans paid for the horse. The other two shots were accidentally fired by recruits. One almost shot himself in the chin when he dropped his rifle and it fired. Needless to say, the Japanese and Cossacks were startled by the American assault. The Japanese garrison intervened between the American and Cossacks to prevent bloodshed. The Americans then discovered that the Cossacks had taken Sperling to Khabarovsk the night before. The American force took three Cossacks hostage and returned to Spasskoe. Two days later, the Cossacks returned Sperling. Four Cossack officers had repeatedly whipped his face and back until he fainted. The situation remained tense between the AEF and Cossacks after this incident prompting the AEF headquarters to issue a warning to all units to be alert for future hostile action.[38]

In September, except for guard detachments along the rail line, the regiment moved eight miles west of Verkhne-Udinsk to Beresovka. Preparations for winter began immediately.[39] Concern over Cossack actions forced the regiment to concentrate at Spasskoe in October. When the situation calmed, E Company moved to Ussuri. H Company occupied Shmakovka. G Company occupied Sviyagina.[40]

Rifles

The US government decided to support Kolchak's forces by supplying rifles in several shipments. One contract with Kolchak for 245,000 rifles from Remington continued even though the Provisional Government never paid for it. The US State Department encouraged a number of military equipment suppliers to honor contracts by allowing the supplies to go to White Russian forces even though the Russians did not pay for them. One summary indicates that $50 million worth of military supplies went to White Russian forces without the direct consent of Congress thanks to the efforts of the Wilson administration. The story of one of these shipments that included 45,000 rifles on a train guarded by forty-five men of the Thirty-First Infantry under the command of 1st Lt. Albert E. Ryan follows.[41] As the train entered the Twenty-Seventh Infantry sector, the operation ceased being routine.

Ryan left Vladivostok at 1:00 a.m. October 14, 1919. He had planned to leave the previous afternoon, but mechanical delays, wrecked trains, and local hostility slowed his journey. Ryan lost one railway car because the Russian rail personnel declared it unserviceable. He had to bluff his way past a Japanese train when those soldiers were trying to use their bayonets to force the Russian rail officials to let them pass. The weather was cold, and snow was falling. While on the way to Harbin, he had to stop and return the engine to look for a soldier who had left the train while it was stopped at the Imayampo station. Stops en route provided the Americans opportunities to bathe and purchase food. On October 18 at 6:30 p.m. the train reached Harbin. Ryan noted that Americans were not well liked there. The Americans left Harbin at 1:50 p.m. on October 19 and arrived at Manchuria Station at 7:00 p.m. on October 22. When Ryan ordered a one-hour stop to purchase food at Olydiania the following day, the Russian lieutenant on board with the guard force threatened to have Japanese or Russian troops arrest the Americans. Ryan ignored him and took a two-and-one-half hour rest.[42]

At 5:00 a.m. October 24, Ryan arrived at Chita and stopped in order to purchase beef. At 10:00 a.m., the Russian lieutenant presented a telegram to Ryan that the Russian claimed to have just received from his headquarters. The telegram authorized the Russian to give fifteen thousand rifles to Semenov. Since Ryan's orders were to deliver the entire trainload to Kolchak's army, he refused to part with the fifteen thousand rifles unless orders from AEF headquarters to do so arrived. Threats to take the rifles by force did not dissuade Ryan from his stance.[43]

Furious telegram traffic between (now) Colonel Morrow, Graves, Semenov, and the Japanese and Russian representatives confirmed Ryan's orders. Morrow, Graves, and even the Japanese delegate supported Ryan's decision.[44]

Ryan now prepared for a fight. He constructed fighting positions under the train cars and barricaded the track to prevent the theft of any cars. Russian reinforcements then began to arrive. A Russian armored train pulled alongside the American train at 2:45 a.m. on October 25. Later a Russian company with four machine guns approached the station at 10:00 a.m. but did not attack. At 1:25 that afternoon, the Russian lieutenant who had tried to seize the rifles returned to the station and told Ryan the matter was settled. Semenov had agreed to allow the train to continue on its way.[45] Ryan refused to take down his barricades until the Russian armored train pulled away. By 5:00 p.m., it had. At 10:15 that evening, Ryan finally left Chita. He credited his success to a firm stand from the start and the help of the local American consul and an American Russian Railway Service Corps engineer with the train. On October 27, Ryan transferred the rifles to Kolchak's forces at Irkutsk.[46] Ryan's determined obedience to orders was commendable. His refusal to cave in to illegal demands showed the Cossacks that the AEF would not be intimidated.

The Japanese later told Graves that Semenov had received the rifles. No doubt Graves was concerned about Semenov having a large number of weapons because of the risk of an attack by Semenov's forces on the Americans. The Cossacks had more field artillery than the AEF, so any weapon transfer potentially could swing a future conflict between Semenov and the Americans. Months later when the AEF was near to leaving Siberia, a Russian approached Graves to tell him that a train car on an obscure siding contained several thousand rifles being guarded by the Japanese. A series of communiqués between the American and Japanese headquarters resulted in Graves sending a detachment of soldiers to retrieve them. The soldiers found 5,900 rifles in their original crates and returned them to US control.[47]

The Russian Railway Service Corps Perseveres

While the AEF-Siberia soldiers were guarding their segments of the railway, the Russian Railway Service Corps continued to advise and try to coordinate rail service throughout the area. They worked in sectors of the railway guarded by Americans but also on the line guarded by other national contingents, if guarded by anyone at all. Their independent spirit and devotion to preserving this critical transportation mode made them a small group of Americans who affected every element of military action and support for the population. The story of one of these railroad men illustrates some of the challenges they faced.

Lt. William Jones of the Russian Railway Service Corps noted in his diary that on May 25, 1919, Col. George Emerson distributed assignments on the Chinese

Eastern Railway because the Russian Railway Service Corps was to take over its operation. However, the Russians he encountered seemed not to understand or always accept that the Russian Railway Service Corps would be in charge. On June 4, Jones left Harbin on a French military train en route to Omsk. The area initially west of Harbin was very fertile but gave way to a large desert. Jones saw few people along their route. As the train neared Chita and Russian territory, they encountered a terminal with a number of Semenov's men and armored train engines. Jones considered Semenov's men to be poor soldiers who abused their power to punish anyone they chose for any offense.[48]

After passing through Chita on June 9, Jones observed few inhabitants but many rivers and creeks. He felt the area resembled northern Minnesota. All along the route Jones and the other members of the train crew and passengers would run into small groups of Russian Railway Service Corps men at lonely stations, sometimes operating in groups of two or three. The chance to say hello to men he knew was a welcome change to being surrounded by the difficult environment. At Verkhne-Udinsk on June 10, the train reached the Twenty-Seventh Infantry Regiment's camp. West of the camp, Japanese soldiers were protecting Semenov, who had previously been ordered to leave Verkhne-Udinsk. The trip around Lake Baikal was a beautiful scene with snowcapped mountains framing the lake as day turned to night making the lake's surface transform into a mirror that reflected the deep purple hue of the mountains. The final glow from sunset did not disappear until almost midnight.[49]

The train arrived at Irkutsk on June 11. There Jones saw British soldiers training White Russians as part of Kolchak's forces. Irkutsk contained many large churches. Streets were a combination of cobblestone and dirt. Sidewalks lined some streets and were built of concrete or wood. There were few Chinese people in Irkutsk, the population principally being Russian. Food, especially fish, seemed to be plentiful thanks to Lake Baikal being so close. Austro-Hungarian and German prisoners of war also formed part of the population. The situation of the Russian people was clearly a dangerous one with Bolsheviks and White Russians fighting to the west and Japanese and Cossacks like Semenov all around. There was little hope for the civilians.[50]

The situation on the ground seemed to become more and more chaotic as the train moved westward. Czechs and even Bolsheviks at times controlled portions of the rail line. In Krasnoyarsk, Czech and Italian soldiers were maintaining order and were well disciplined. By June 11, Jones reached Novonikolayevsk. Refugees had swelled the population of approximately eighty thousand to one over two hundred thousand. Many of these refugees were crowded around the rail yard hoping for some form of help from anyone who might provide it. The YMCA had a station in town. Jones saw many Czech soldiers and was told that fifteen thousand Polish soldiers, as well as a large contingent of White Russian soldiers, were on site. However, the Russian soldiers undergoing training looked like "ignorant Siberian peasant boys."[51]

On July 14, Jones left for Omsk, arriving there the next day. He estimated the population of Omsk to be six hundred thousand people. Refugees crowded the rail depots. City streets were partially paved. Sidewalks were cement or wood. Some city parks had orchestras for entertainment. The Red Cross and YMCA both had stations in the city. Transportation ranged from horseback to automobiles.[52]

While in Omsk, Jones heard many reports of advancing Bolsheviks and retreating White Russians under Kolchak. Typhus and dysentery were major problems with whole trains coming through devoted to evacuating such cases. He felt that the White Russian army was ineffective and that only the presence of the Czechs provided any hope for Kolchak. The Cossack and Czech conflict was building and leading to a problem for the White Russian cause.[53]

During this same time, other Russian Railway Service Corps men continued to try to organize the Russian and Chinese railroads and keep the rail lifeline working while trying to help elsewhere as they were able. For example, another railroad man named Fred Roberts reported that, in Harbin, cholera was a major problem on August 6, 1919. Roberts found himself helping distill water in September after there were 1,700 dead from cholera by August 16. Several Russian Railway Service Corps men were evacuated to ships in order to return to the United States but died en route. Even with all of the confusion, a reinforcing group of Russian Railway Service Corps men arrived on August 26.[54]

Jones and the other Russian Railway Service Corps men with him assisted in operating the Omsk station while they were there. Life continued to be hard. On August 27, Jones was a pallbearer for Capt. Francis Desmon Conner of the American Red Cross. Conner had been "in charge of the anti-typhus delousing train for six months" before typhus and pneumonia killed him. His work had generated much goodwill so that Russian, Polish, and Czech attendees were at the cemetery to honor his service.[55]

As the fall approached, many men in the Russian Railway Service Corps had served beyond their original appointment and were allowed to leave. This then afforded men who stayed an opportunity to be promoted. The obvious difficulties experienced by the White Russians made it wise to question the wisdom of remaining. As the Bolsheviks approached, the Czechs began to move eastward and Russian soldiers began to desert in larger numbers. Poor relations between the Americans and Japanese added concern and uncertainty to the overall situation for the Russian Railway Service Corps and others in the area. Running the railroad became more and more problematic as the Reds relentlessly attacked eastward, and the White Russians evaporated. The Russian Railway Service Corps and other trainmen sent train after train streaming toward the east with the safety of distance being on everyone's mind. The few reinforcements moving westward by train to try to make a stand in Omsk had difficulty reaching the city because of all of the trains fleeing eastward. In early November, Great Britain even sent a few railroad men and other civilian employees such as translators to take the place of the Russian Railway Service Corps men in Omsk out of concern that the American railroad men would soon leave.[56]

Once the Russian Railway Service Corps personnel left Omsk, control over train dispatch fell to the military power with the most influence with the Russian government. Even though an American train with the Russian Railway Service Corps detachment, American consul general Ernest Harris, US agricultural experts, and the Red Cross left Omsk ten hours before British general Alfred Knox on November 7, Knox's train and six additional trains passed the Americans during the night. French general Maurice Janin was supposed to be controlling train movement, but in reality the White Russian government was running the line as it saw fit. The rest of the movement east was sporadic as elements of the White Russian government also sought escape. Gradually in spurts of movement on temporarily clear track the various Allied contingents worked their way eastward. The Russian Railway Service Corps men along the route joined the last trains with Americans as they passed through station after station.[57]

On December 11, 1919, Jones and the Americans traveling with him passed through Irkutsk. Along their route they had seen Polish soldiers that could not find enough rail transport for their evacuation; therefore, some were moving on foot. Many civilians were doing the same. After sharing trains with Czechs, Russians, and Japanese, Jones and his compatriots reached Vladivostok and safety on January 28, 1920. He left Vladivostok on February 5 on a ship bound for Japan and then San Franscisco.[58]

The difficulties faced by the soldiers of the Twenty-Seventh Infantry Regiment and the men of the Russian Railway Service Corps were indicative of the situation throughout Siberia. The Thirty-First Infantry Regiment also faced challenges within its sectors of the rail line. In one case in particular, the soldiers of the Thirty-First Infantry would endure massive casualties but still hold their ground after the fight.

11
Railway Guard and the Thirty-First Infantry

The Thirty-First Infantry Regiment generally spent this time trying to preserve law and order in its assigned area of operations. American forces took casualties but forced their attackers to pay an even higher price. H Company arrived at the Suchan mines on March 23 to replace M Company, but the unrest in the area resulted in both companies remaining. Due to concerted action by the Thirty-First Infantry and other Allied units, the pattern of Bolshevik robbing, looting, and violence eventually decreased. Colonel G. H. Williams arrived on June 10 and took command of the American forces at the mine. He called for a meeting with the partisan leaders in order to reduce the likelihood of armed conflict. The partisan leaders appeared friendly; however, this positive attitude soon evaporated. The American provost marshal arrested a Russian named Samusenka, who was wanted for robbery in Vladivostok. The partisans demanded his release, but the Americans refused.[1]

America's allies continued to press operations against the Bolsheviks. Increased Bolshevik attacks on American troops would change the AEF's neutral stance. The AEF Intelligence Section provided a secondhand report of British support of a Russian seaborne landing of infantry at America Bay in April 1919. The intelligence officer of the USS *Albany* reported that the HMS *Kent* escorted two boats loaded with approximately five hundred Russian soldiers. On April 16, approximately one hundred of the Russian soldiers landed at Nahodka Bay at 2:30 A.M. The small flotilla then landed the remaining four hundred soldiers at a village to the north and further into America Bay. The crew of the *Kent* fired 6-inch shells in support of the landing at the village. When the Russian soldiers moved toward Vladimir-Alexandrovskoye, the *Kent* again opened fire to suppress any Bolshevik opposition. The naval gunfire of around sixty rounds demoralized the Bolshevik opposition in the area. The *Kent* intelligence officer told the *Albany* intelligence officer that the crew of the *Kent* was disappointed that they did not have the opportunity to fire more. Misidentification of a group of Bolsheviks as government soldiers prevented the *Kent* from engaging a large number of Bolsheviks retreating up a hillside.[2]

Bolshevik activity resulted in the American rifle companies attacking to clear their areas of operations of partisans. Company actions cleared the areas to the north and west of Shkotovo with a few American wounded and an unknown number of Bolshevik casualties. Continued patrolling kept the area relatively clear of Bolshevik forces after a series of minor firefights.[3] American units continued to have problems with their allies due to the original AEF orders not to take sides in the civil war. The Thirty-First Infantry would protect the Suchan mines until no longer practicable. Actions would include American offensive and defensive operations near Novitskaya, Romanovka, Suchan, and Shkotovo. The actions would occur against the backdrop of intrigue continuing among America's allies in Vladivostok and Harbin.

Operations in the Suchan Area

Graves decided to send Lt. Col. Robert Eichelberger to the Suchan Mines area on April 21 after the HMS *Kent* began operations near there. Reports of damages to villages in the area prompted the need for an investigation. Eichelberger was accompanied by two lieutenants and one enlisted soldier, who acted as his interpreter. During the trip by road, Eichelberger encountered a number of refugees fleeing the area. Most were women and children. Upon arriving at Piryatin, White Russian officers he met accused him of being a Bolshevik and tried to confiscate the group's weapons. Eichelberger refused to comply with the demand of the Russians to disarm. The Russians then arrested the Americans and escorted them to a schoolhouse for holding. Eichelberger believed that the guards would allow him to escape so that they could then kill the Americans, so he returned to the Russian headquarters and demanded a Russian officer escort when the Americans left. The attitude of the Russians had changed a bit by this point. They refused Eichelberger's demand for an escort but stated he could leave the following morning. The Americans departed in daylight and reached an American unit nearby. Several peasants thanked Eichelberger because the Russians had told them that the village was to be destroyed. Eichelberger's presence apparently disrupted the Russian plans to burn the village. Only one building was destroyed.[4]

Novitskaya

Hostilities between the American mine guard force near Suchan and Bolshevik partisans occurred on June 22, 1919. Bolsheviks captured an American lieutenant and four enlisted men that day while the Americans were fishing on the Suchan River south of town. The Bolsheviks then held the five men in Novitskaya. When the Bolsheviks refused to release the five prisoners, M Company (two platoons) attacked. Williams, who was then in charge of the Allied Mine Guard, accompanied M Company.[5]

Upon reaching Novitskaya, Lt. Albert S. Ward, Williams's adjutant, and Private Craig of H Company rode into the town ahead of the main body. Bolshevik gunfire downed both. Craig died immediately. M Company advanced into the town, reaching Ward to rescue him. Ward died after being found. An estimated 150 Bolsheviks occupied the town.[6]

M Company continued the attack into Novitskaya and suffered two more men killed and two wounded. The company did not find the five American prisoners because the Bolsheviks had moved the prisoners to Kazanka before M Company attacked. The Bolsheviks eventually exchanged the five Americans for one of their leaders, named Samusenka, who was imprisoned earlier for stealing money at Vladivostok and was still being held at Suchan. Bolshevik losses were unknown.[7]

Partisans attacked the American camp at Suchan the night of June 24. That same night other hostile activity occurred. The Bolshevik partisans continued their attacks against the Americans. Attacks damaged cable line power houses and destroyed bridges and telephone lines. These attacks against the communications infrastructure severed the links between Suchan and Shkotovo. Partisans blew up a bridge to the east of Fanza and a telegraph office west of Fanza on June 23. Lt. F. C. Shepard reported telegraph stations at Sarkotnay and Taseno also destroyed on June 23. Shepard took four squads to investigate rifle fire and explosions heard in the direction of Fanza. In Kishmisi, he found the Chinese military detachment had been attacked while they were eating by a Bolshevik force that killed two and wounded five of the Chinese soldiers. Chinese rifle fire drove off the estimated forty to fifty Bolsheviks. When the train from Kanguaz arrived with three American soldiers as guards, Shepard instructed the train crew to return the way they had come, and he reinforced the American guard force with two additional soldiers.[8] These incidents indicated a growing level of violence; however, the worst incident occurred on June 25 at Romanovka.

Romanovka

A security detachment from A Company[9] was guarding the railroad at Romanovka, a "fairly large village" with a rail line that separated the village itself from a cliff. Two recently arrived lieutenants were with the guard force that was camped in a small valley near the railroad one mile outside the town. This site provided easy access to a water supply and put the guard detachment near the bridge it had to guard. The force tapped a nearby telephone line for communications.[10]

The Americans pitched their tents in a square and placed sentries on the surrounding hills. The camp was basically in a bowl. Second Lieutenant Lawrence Butler arrived the night of June 24 to replace the current platoon leader. Eichelberger and Major Graves passed through the area that same day en route to Suchan. Both noted the danger that the unit faced. Butler recognized the dangerous position and planned to shift the camp to a safer location on higher ground the next day. The night of June 24 to 25 passed quietly. However, a sentry, who had not been relieved, left his post a few minutes after first light and began walking toward the camp. That was the opportunity the three hundred Bolsheviks hiding near the camp wanted. They attacked by firing from the overlooking ridgelines down into camp position in the low ground.[11]

The Americans never had a chance. Many were killed while they slept.[12] Others fought in their underwear or while wrapped in their blankets. The struggle between the Bolsheviks and Americans lasted several hours due to the courageous resistance of the surviving American soldiers. Butler rallied the survivors and refused to retreat. Even though suffering a gunshot to the face that shattered his lower jaw and ripped off his lips in the initial moments of the attack and then a gunshot to the leg, the young lieutenant continued to rally his men and lead the fight. His injury was so severe he was not able to speak to give orders during the battle. Butler's heroic conduct inspired the men of the platoon to fight on even when half of the platoon was killed or wounded early in the fight. When a survivor, Corp. Louis Heinzman, escaped in order to find reinforcements for the American force, the Bolsheviks withdrew. During the fighting, the girlfriend of Sgt. Almus E. Beck rendered first aid to the wounded including carrying water to them while under fire. She was not wounded as she bravely ran between the wounded and the position's water bag; however, the water bag was punctured numerous times during the battle. Beck married the young lady from Poland, who had been a nurse with a White Russian unit nearby.[13]

Heinzman evaded capture, even though wounded, and succeeded in flagging down a train that then backed down the track to the nearest guard force. This rescue force arrived at Romanovka four hours after the battle. They found nineteen dead with twenty-five wounded. Five of the wounded subsequently died. The twelve dead Bolsheviks included the village cobbler, who had sold milk to the same Americans he later killed. The American soldiers recognized five of the Bolsheviks as local citizens. Some of the local citizens were no longer willing to allow the Americans to remain. Butler and Heinzman received the Distinguished Service Cross for their gallantry. Beck's girlfriend was recommended for a medal but did not receive one. Butler showed that he retained his determination and strong spirit by tying a handkerchief around his head in the hospital as a substitute lower lip so he could smoke a cigarette.[14] This battle was a tragedy for the soldiers of the AEF and the greatest loss of life in a single firefight experienced by the Americans in Siberia. Nonetheless, even with the mistakes, the soldiers were not overrun. They held their ground at the end of the fight.

Suchan

Continued partisan activity concerned AEF Headquarters. Consequently, it ordered a provisional battalion be sent from Shkotovo to Suchan to reinforce M Company. This provisional battalion was under the command of Maj. W. H. Joiner. Components of the battalion included C Company, D Company, one platoon from the Regimental Machine Gun Company, and three 37mm guns that arrived at Kanguaz on June 23.[15]

One C Company platoon remained at Kanguaz to guard surplus equipment and ammunition. The M Company squad already on site remained there under the command of the C Company platoon. The provisional battalion moved into the Suchan Valley and was attacked by partisans at Sitsa on June 24. The battalion's fire kept the partisans at a safe distance. Sniping continued as the battalion moved toward Suchan on June 25 and 26, but no American casualties were incurred.[16]

Supplying the mine guards was a continuous challenge. The American supply system shipped meat and bread daily from Vladivostok for the various rail line detachments between Vladivostok and Suchan and for the mine guard. Canned corn beef and roast beef emergency rations were also issued. The M Company squad at Kanguaz had a mission to transfer the supplies from the train from Vladivostok to the narrow gauge cars used to carry supplies to the mines.[17]

Damage to cable car power houses caused a supply problem. This forced supplies hauled overland to traverse thirty miles of narrow, poorly constructed roads—an inviting target to partisan attack. Destruction of the railroad bridges between Kanguaz and Shkotovo on June 26 forced the mine guards to look to the sea for help.[18]

America Bay was about twenty-six miles from Suchan. The supply route ran through Vladimiro-Alexandrovskaya and the Suchan Valley. In order to secure the route, the mine guard decided to clear the partisans from Novitskaya, Kazanka, and any positions to the south. However, partisans attacked Suchan July 1. Outposts defeated the attack.[19]

As of July 1, the leadership of the Thirty-First Infantry believed the Bolshevik strength in the Suchan Valley area totaled approximately 2,000. Bolshevik companies ranged in size from 100 to 150 armed men. These enemy companies were distributed with one company each at Vladimiro-Alexandrovskaya, Yekaterinovka, Unashi, Piryatina, Novitskaya, Nikolaevka, scattered between Yurievka, Kazanka, and Sergaevka. An estimated four companies were at Kazanka and two at Frolovka. The Kazanka contingent was considered the best available for the Bolsheviks. Armed with high-powered rifles, each partisan had 50 to 150 rounds of ammunition. The Bolshevik fighters in the southern part of the valley were armed with modern rifles and ammunition. The Americans believed that several Koreans were with this partisan force. The Bolsheviks in Frolovka and Sergaevka by contrast were the weakest, being poorly armed and only having three to five rounds of ammunition per man. The number of Koreans in the Bolshevik forces was a surprise. The Bolshevik force at Vladimiro had forty Russian and sixty Korean fighters. Sixty Koreans were in each company at Piryatina and Nikolaevka. Many of the Bolsheviks were criminals fleeing prosecution.[20]

On July 2, Colonel Williams with C Company (less guard detachments), a machine-gun section, a 37mm gun section, and a Japanese company headed toward Novitskaya. C Company platoons were organized with seven squads. Two of these squads were automatic rifle squads, while the other five were standard rifle squads. Automatic rifle squads contained two automatic rifles and four riflemen. Platoons often maneuvered with automatic rifle squads on the flanks using the corporals leading those squads to maintain contact with adjacent units. Approximately one-half of the enlisted men were experienced soldiers. However, training on the automatic rifle was limited since the regiment received the BARs after arriving in Siberia. Commissioned officers were a mixture of officer training camp programs, graduates of the US Military Academy, and former enlisted men. Soldiers carried two additional bandoliers of ammunition. Recent combat experience had resulted in American forces defeating hostile groups of larger size. Morale was high. H and D Companies defended Suchan. Williams attacked Novitskaya from the west and south. The Americans quickly captured the town and forty prisoners. The partisans fled to the north. C Company with wounded and prisoners returned to Suchan. The remainder of Williams's force moved toward Kazanka.[21] The American forces were clearly now taking the fight to their elusive Bolshevik enemy. The level of violence was increasing, and the AEF was now assuming a more combative and less neutral posture.

C and D Companies, the other machine-gun section, and the remaining 37mm gun left Suchan for Kazanka on July 3. Kazanka was the headquarters of the Bolshevik forces in the Suchan Mine area. The machine gun and 37mm gun were transported by mules. The terrain around Kazanka provided several advantages to the defenders. Kazanka was on the southwestern side of a low mountain range. The Suchan River passed the town approximately eight hundred yards away. The river was forty feet wide and five feet deep with steep four-foot banks. A wheat field separated the town from the river. A small building, surrounded by trees and positioned between the river and the town, was approximately one hundred yards from the river. Brush and trees lined the banks. The local population was decidedly pro-Bolshevik, which limited any ability to gain intelligence on enemy locations and intent.[22]

When the advanced guard neared the town, the defenders opened fire. This resulted in the American forces deploying to the flanks and advancing to clear the positions. Fire and maneuver by squads kept the momentum of the attack moving forward. The attack began when the range was 850 yards or more to the partisans. Much of the initial American fire actually went over the heads of the partisans as the Americans adjusted to the range. An attempt by one platoon in the rear of the line to fire overhead as part of the force advanced resulted in friendly fire striking within the ranks of the advancing infantry. Nonetheless, the attack persevered.[23]

As the attack progressed, the enemy fire slackened. The continued pressure from the American infantry convinced the partisans that they needed to withdraw from Kazanka, passing through the wheat field and crossing the river. C Company's Fourth Platoon pursued the retreating partisans, who fled northward. After two squads cleared a fording site and the far bank, the platoon crossed and took up a position to observe the enemy withdrawal. The platoon's soldiers could see the 37mm gun firing on the Bolsheviks, but the rounds fell short. After crossing the river, the American attack halted as much from fatigue after the five-hour attack on little sleep as any orders directing that the advance stop.[24]

After approximately a twenty-minute break in action, the advance began again. Fire and maneuver by squads resumed but halted once effective Bolshevik fire began anew on the right flank. A sergeant with an automatic rifleman and one additional soldier moved by way of the riverbed to that flank. The sergeant believed he saw movement in treetops and had the BAR open fire at seventy-five yards distance. Partisans began falling out of the trees. The small American automatic rifle team killed and wounded several. Those able to do so found escape and concealment in the wheat field. The advance then continued into the town. The Americans cleared the buildings and confirmed that the partisans had hurriedly evacuated Kazanka. The pursuit continued to clear a ridge outside of town on the eastern side in order to ensure that movement within the town would be safe. The American soldiers helped fight several fires that had started in buildings in Kazanka. Prisoner interrogations revealed that the partisans believed that the BARs were machine guns and that they were amazed at the number of machine guns used by the Americans and the way they maneuvered. The prisoners also were surprised that the Americans took time to extinguish fires burning in an obviously hostile town. At approximately 4:00 p.m. the combined American and Japanese force departed Kazanka to return to Suchan. American casualties were one dead and two wounded. Meanwhile, H Company defeated another attack on Suchan.[25]

D and M Companies, a machine-gun platoon, three 37mm guns, and a Japanese company under Major Joiner's command left Suchan for America Bay on July 5. Small groups of partisans harassed the force as it marched. Partisan fire wounded six Americans near Piryatina. Patrols, machine-gun fire, and 37mm gun fire prevented two subsequent ambushes. During the afternoon, Vladimiro-Alexandrovskaya was taken with little difficulty. By July 5, American casualties in this operation to secure the Suchan valley had resulted in six dead and thirteen wounded. Bolshevik dead totaled fifty-nine with nineteen known wounded.[26]

The cruiser USS *Albany*, two Russian ships, and a British ship arrived in America Bay with supplies on July 6. A landing force of one hundred soldiers from G Company and one hundred Russian soldiers accompanied the ships. The supplies were stockpiled at Vladimiro-Alexandrovskaya. One section from M Company remained there to guard the supplies that could not be loaded in wagons for the return trip. On July 9, the mine guard force began its return march to Suchan. The advance guard of the American force drove off a small partisan force as the Americans reached Piryatina. H Company marched to Vladimiro-Alexandrovskaya on July 10 to escort the remaining sixty wagon-loads of supplies to Suchan. No additional fighting occurred.[27]

During the latter part of July, approximately 1,400 Japanese troops entered the Suchan valley area. They had no contact with partisan forces until they were joined by Russian troops from Nikolsk. The American hospital at Suchan treated the wounded.[28]

By July 23 the situation had calmed sufficiently for the American units from the Shkotovo area to return there. On July 24, this group left Suchan and entered Fanza. It arrived at Kanguaz on July 25. C Company remained at Kanguaz. D Company, the machine-gun platoon, and the 37mm gun squad at Kanguaz marched to Suchan July 26. Other AEF elements in Kanguaz returned to their parent units.[29]

The period July 25 to August 7 was quiet in most areas but not all. Patrols kept a watch on the area. The overseas deployment after the World War I armistice was beginning to hurt morale. To lessen morale problems, the YMCA provided movies for entertainment. The Americans improved their rations by trading excess syrup, canned beef, and bacon rations for eggs and vegetables. Platoons reorganized and received new missions as complete units rather than being parceled out in smaller elements. These measures improved morale.[30]

Combined operations with Russian forces kept the Thirty-First Infantry engaged in operations beyond patrolling. B Company received orders to assist a Russian force of 300 soldiers and two artillery pieces in executing a landing at Tethue. Partisans were manufacturing weapons at machine shops associated with mines in the vicinity of Tethue and Olga Bay. The White Russian intent was to effect landings near both partisan bases in order to occupy the towns and destroy this manufacturing capability. B Company was to land on July 30 with the Russians and then to depart via ship once the Russians were securely ashore. USS *New Orleans* would transport the 175 soldiers of B Company and two Russian transports would carry the Russian soldiers. K Company received a similar mission to conduct a landing with a force of 250 Russians also on July 30 in the vicinity of Olga. Once the landing was in place, K Company also would re-embark and return to Vladivostok. HMS *Carlisle* supported K Company at Olga. Two Russian transports carried the Russians.[31]

In execution of the landing at Tethue, sailors and marines from the *New Orleans* joined with the B Company soldiers to assist the Russians. The executive officer of the *New Orleans* commanded the American naval forces assigned to the landing force. While the original plan called for 300 soldiers, the *New Orleans* intelligence officer reported that only 215 Russians actually deployed. The B Company soldiers moved forward to seize a ridgeline that overlooked the landing area. The naval detachment formed a skirmish line on both sides of a railway bed and moved forward to ensure that that area was clear of any hostile forces. These actions occurred to establish a safe beachhead for the landing of the Russian main body.[32]

The naval landing party captured two Chinese men before the Russian main body landed. One of the men asked to be allowed to board a ship in order to avoid the fighting that he believed would soon occur. The other man told the American command group that approximately one hundred partisans were in a nearby town with an armored train. The partisans were planning to move to the mines at Tethue.[33]

The Russian main body landed but seemed reluctant to move ashore and march to the mines. During the three hours estimated for the landing, the Americans began to encounter a small number of partisans. Both sides fired several rounds. At least one partisan fell as if wounded. The Americans also observed a number of civilian houses with white flags flying apparently in an attempt not to be targeted. The landing force spent the night near the bay. On August 1, the American and Russian forces began moving toward the Tethue mines. Marines cleared a village along the route in an attempt to speed up the movement. Civilian reports from women whose husbands were not home indicated that the partisans had already left on their armored train. Reports also disclosed that partisans were moving toward the mines from throughout the area.[34]

During the lunch halt, partisans engaged the Americans at long range. The Russians began firing at the suspected partisan position and then began searching the nearby village for hostile elements of the population. Several men tried to escape but could not outrun the Russian fire. A few died because they begged for food at the wrong time. The evening was relatively quiet. Continuing the march the next day, the Americans encountered a number of houses flying white flags. Local civilians expressed concern that if the White Russian soldiers returned without the Americans the White Russian troops would abuse the civilians, especially the women. The naval party returned to the *New Orleans* on August 1. The B Company soldiers returned on August 2. The Americans noted that the Russian soldiers were by and large conscripts with low morale.[35]

A partisan ultimatum to Williams sparked the next combat action. A local citizen told Williams on August 6 that the partisan band in the area forbade the Americans to bring any additional beef cattle to Suchan, which did not make Williams very happy. Therefore, he detailed Capt. O. R. Rhoads to take a force to destroy the partisans. Rhoads selected Second Platoon, H Company for the task.[36]

Lieutenant Leslie commanded the Second Platoon. Since he had only thirty-six fit soldiers, M Company provided a few reinforcements. Lieutenant Resing of M Company was detailed as a guide. The total force was composed of three officers and approximately forty enlisted men.[37]

On the evening of August 7, Rhoads led his force from Suchan to the Novo Litovskaya valley. The platoon rested until daylight then passed through the valley seeking information on the partisans. Rhoads stopped at Novo Litovskaya in the late afternoon to purchase eggs. He had discovered no information concerning the partisans. Just after Rhoads left the village to march toward the Eastern Bay beach, a local citizen confidentially told him the partisans were ten miles away on the Novo Litovskaya River mouth into the Eastern Bay. Rhoads continued in that direction until his point element sighted the partisans.[38]

The partisans were on a flat piece of ground about fifty yards wide along the river edge close to the river mouth. The river broadened here, so it resembled a bay. The mouth contracted as the river met the Eastern Bay. The actual river mouth was about three feet deep and fifteen feet wide. The partisans were between a log hut and the water's edge. Rhoads's force was about five hundred yards from the river mouth when it spotted the partisans.[39]

The Americans were able to deploy without alerting the partisans. Rhoads sent one automatic rifle team to cover the left flank and two such teams to cover the right flank. One squad was detailed as a reserve. The remainder of the force moved one squad at a time to within twenty feet of the riverbank, which was fifty yards from the water line.[40] These maneuvers allowed the Americans to surround the partisans. The Americans had three directions cut off with the river behind the partisans.

Rhoads, through his interpreter, called upon the partisans to surrender. They answered with rifle fire and attempted to escape or take cover. Some ran for the log cabin. Other partisans jumped in the river and swam away. Another group tried to run around the American flanks. A few partisans slipped between the American platoon and right flank automatic rifle teams but were later killed or captured. At the cabin, BAR fire wounded two partisans and suppressed their fire long enough for two Americans to charge through the door and capture the two now wounded partisans. The battle started at 6:00 p.m. and lasted ten minutes. The quick victory decimated the Bolshevik force. Of the thirty partisans, six were captured (two severely wounded), seventeen were killed, five drowned or were killed in the river, and two escaped. No Americans were injured. Rhoads sent a small detachment to pursue the surviving partisans. The Americans discovered that this group was newly formed and was training along the riverbank. The recruits were from the local area and some of the Americans recognized them from the villages. Promises of a job and money had encouraged several to join the partisan band. Rhoads confiscated a Chinese junk to transport the platoon, prisoners, and captured weapons. He left the small craft secured to the shore at Vladimiro-Alexandrovskaya near America Bay. The US government had to pay the owners of the junk one hundred dollars. The platoon returned to Suchan on August 11.[41]

Rhoads's force rested in Vladimiro-Alexandrovskaya on August 10 while en route to Suchan, where relations with the Japanese detachment were not good. The M Company detachment was still in the town to act as a point of contact for supply operations through America Bay. The Japanese signal officer told the American sergeant in charge of the detachment that he had to pay for all messages with money or food. The sergeant refused. The Japanese detachment commander was discourteous to Rhoads. The provocations were so severe, one of the Second Platoon's squads wanted to kill several Japanese soldiers who had tried to injure Rhoads.[42]

After returning to Suchan, Rhoads again received orders to prepare an expedition to attack the partisans. However, before he could set out, AEF headquarters directed that all Americans leave the Suchan mine area. On August 14, AEF headquarters ordered the Americans to meet the USAT *Merritt* in America Bay on August 18. The destruction of the rail line and the inability to keep it open in the face of partisan interdiction made retaining AEF soldiers to protect the mines pointless. There was now no transportation for the coal.[43]

The First Platoon, H Company, departed Suchan the morning of August 15, using wagons gathered from the area. The last Americans, except for a burial detail guard (a platoon from H Company), left at 6:00 A.M. on August 17. In all, five wagon trains moved the Americans. Rough weather prevented the *Merritt* from unloading the burial detail on board until August 18, even though it arrived August 16. Unfortunately, the platoon left at Suchan had exhumed and then reburied the American dead when the burial detail failed to arrive. When this H Company platoon reached the bay, an M Company platoon went back to Suchan with the burial detail to exhume the bodies again. This group brought the bodies to America Bay.[44]

The *Merritt* completed loading on August 19 and sailed at 9:30 P.M. that evening. The transport arrived at Vladivostok at 10:00 A.M. on August 20. American participation in the Allied Mine Guard was finished. However, other operations would be conducted in the Suchan area even if guarding the mine had ceased.[45]

In August and September, Russian engineers completed repairs to the railroad and asked for protection. The Thirty-First Infantry element in the Shkotovo sector was ordered to extend its sector to include the Suchan area. C Company moved to Fanza and Sitsa. I Company occupied Kanguaz, Tigrovia, and Tahe. The troops carried supplies and ammunition to last an estimated three months. H Company (composed of only one hundred soldiers) reinforced the Fanza garrison on December 5. Thirty of these soldiers occupied Baritznaya. Forty occupied Kishmish.[46]

The sector was relatively quiet from August 8 until December 10. Partisan bands occupied Kazanka and Frolovka. On December 10, 24, 25, and 31, elements of these bands attacked C Company detachments at Sitsa and near Fanza, but no Americans were wounded.[47]

Outposts and patrols were used to protect the detachments from surprise. Patrolling was active just before daylight. Partisan contact, when made, often occurred at that time. Small detachments usually occupied a building that had a squad room and a kitchen with a breastwork constructed around the building for defense. These small American detachments practiced drills, so everyone knew how to exit the buildings quickly and occupy fighting positions.[48] The situation remained virtually unchanged until the next phase of the expedition to Siberia.

Shkotovo

Attacks on passenger trains in the vicinity of Ugolnaya became a source of concern in April. Small partisan bands would fire at passenger trains moving at night. This resulted in the Thirty-First Infantry establishing a sector headquarters at Shkotovo. E Company occupied the town on April 24 and actively patrolled the area.[49]

Partisan activity continued to increase into May. Consequently, the Thirty-First Infantry organized A, C, D, and I Companies into a provisional battalion May 18, with its headquarters at Shkotovo. A 37mm gun platoon and a machine-gun platoon were also assigned. This provisional battalion provided guard detachments spread along the railroad line to secure area.[50]

Companies operated north of Shkotovo during the period May 21–25, fighting several minor engagements. Casualties were few, but the Bolsheviks withdrew from the rail line. Reconnaissance patrols continued after this time to monitor any resurgence of partisan activity.[51]

Partisan activity did, in fact, resume. This activity was centered on the Ugolnaya-Suchan railroad between Shkotovo and Kanguaz. The AEF had to reinforce and shift assets to counter this increased activity. The machine-gun platoon in Shkotovo moved to Kanguaz in early June but later returned to Shkotovo. Another machine-gun platoon was moved from Vladivostok to Shkotovo June 25. This platoon soon moved to Romanovka.[52]

On June 26, 1919, Maj. W. H. Joiner began a deployment from Shkotovo to Suchan by train with D Company, C Company (minus nine squads), a platoon from M Company, a machine-gun platoon, and a 37mm platoon. The lead element under the command of 1st Lt. Olaf P. Winningstad came under fire by about twenty Bolsheviks in the vicinity of Sitsa as they passed through with a load of railroad ties. One American, Private Yorick, was wounded in the leg. A platoon from C Company, already at Sitsa guarding the railroad station and bridge, began firing at the Bolsheviks. Both sides exchanged fire for several hours until the advance guard of Joiner's command arrived and added its fire including a machine gun to that of the C Company platoon. The Bolsheviks abandoned their position. Private Low from a reinforcing squad out of D Company that also moved to Sitsa was severely wounded in the abdomen. A subsequent patrol to the Bolshevik position counted nineteen dead enemy partisans. During this operation, besides recognizing Winningstad, Joiner singled out two soldiers for special praise. PFC John C. McCaffrey acted as a train engineer when he noted the center of a hastily built bridge beginning to sink. McCaffrey recognized the problem and ran the train across before the collapse of the bridge endangered the train. Joiner also recognized Corp. Jacob Czyaz for his leadership of his machine-gun squad. The C Company commander reported that Czyaz's squad alone killed eleven of the Bolsheviks.[53]

Operations through the remainder of the summer consisted of continued patrolling and skirmishing with partisan elements. Major Graves led several patrols to clear the area of partisans. On July 2, he set out for Suchan with two C Company platoons and two machine guns but came under sporadic partisan rifle fire during the movement. This element had to occupy a hill outside Suchan to stop the sporadic sniping after they arrived. M Company and a Japanese company left Suchan and moved toward Novitskaya. Snipers wounded a lieutenant but were finally driven off using 37mm fire. All elements returned to Suchan.[54]

On July 3 Joiner led D Company, two platoons of C Company, a 37mm gun crew, and two machine guns and marched to Kanguaz. Joiner reached Kanguaz without being detected and captured a guard element. He then led this combined force in attacking the town to destroy the Bolshevik headquarters located there. The surprise attack routed the Bolshevik force and produced a large number of documents for analysis in the abandoned enemy headquarters.[55]

On July 5, M Company, D Company without one platoon, a machine-gun platoon, two 37mm gun sections, and a Japanese company left Suchan with the aim of occupying Vladimiro-Alexandrovskaya on the way to America Bay. Sniping during the movement did not slow the advance until the force reached Unashi where the hostile firing increased. Four Americans were wounded. Fire from the 37mm guns and the machine guns and maneuver by the Americans cleared the ridge and allowed the advance to continue. On July 6 a patrol from this element reached America Bay and linked up with American and Russian soldiers from the USS *Albany* and HMS *Carlisle* that had escorted several Chinese junks with a months' rations for the Suchan area soldiers.[56]

Table 9. Shkotovo Sector

Element	Location
Provisional Battalion Headquarters with signal, medical, and quartermaster detachments	Shkotovo
A Company	Shkotovo
C Company	Kanguaz
D Company	Shkotovo
E Company	Romanovka
I Company	Novo Nezhino
K Company	Ugolnaya

From Major Thomas S. Arms, "Siberia Expedition—The Shkotovo Sector, 31st Infantry, from September 1919 until the Withdrawal of the Expedition" (U.S. Army Command and General Staff School, Fort Leavenworth, KS, Individual Research Paper No. 84, 1931), p. 3

K Company, consisting of about 100 men, temporarily withdrew from the sector to go to Tethue on board the British cruiser *Carlisle*. B Company (175 men) was withdrawn from the Harbin delegation and went to Olga aboard the USS *New Orleans*. Russian troops aided both forces that landed on July 31. The partisans reported in the two areas were not there and no resistance was encountered.[57]

In September, the Shkotovo sector forces were arrayed as shown in table 9. Company size elements occupied most of the positions.

All companies by this time were filled out to approximately 250 soldiers. With summer operations completed, the American units established tent camps on dominating ground outside nearby villages and towns except in Shkotovo. Trenches with four- to five-foot berms provided defensive cover for the camps. The situation in Shkotovo was different because there the Americans occupied brick, former Russian army buildings. Kolchak's and AEF units were housed in several groups of buildings. The Russian garrison, referred to as a regiment, numbered approximately 1,000 soldiers. Even though this Russian unit formally was under Kolchak's command, in reality Kolchak's government exercised little direct control over its actions.[58]

The sector was quiet until mid-October. Cold weather forced AEF units to reposition to better quarters. Tents were inadequate in the changing temperature. K Company moved to Razdolnoe. One D Company platoon replaced K Company at Ugolnaya. Boxcars were taken off their wheels and used as quarters. Soldiers piled dirt around the boxcars for added protection. One E Company platoon stayed at Romanovka occupying two adjoining houses. The soldiers constructed a six- to seven-foot earth wall around the houses. One I Company platoon stayed at Novo

Nezhino fortifying two houses in the same manner as those at Romanovka. The rest of I Company moved to Shkotovo. As winter approached, the AEF expanded the Shkotovo sector to include the Suchan area and made contact with the Japanese mine guard once new quarters were constructed by Russian engineers. A level of risk was inherent in this decision due to a marauding band of Russian deserters who were pillaging villages throughout the area. All of these new buildings constructed were one story with a large room, kitchen, and storage area as well as being built on ground that commanded the surrounding area. It took the Russian construction crews ten days to finish the new buildings.[59]

During October and November, many drafted men returned to the United States. Replacements arriving at Shkotovo required a great deal of training and were a burden to the command there. One officer reported that the replacements he saw had never fired a rifle before arriving in Siberia. By January 1920, roughly 80 percent of the original AEF-Siberia had returned to the United States.[60] The negative impact is not surprising. Replacements always face a certain level of negative reaction until the unit accepts and integrates them. However, this low level of training certainly put effective operations at great risk.

As December approached, the partisan bands grew in size. Their recruiting efforts were very successful and bred confidence in their ability to attack the Americans. Lack of distinctive uniforms made distinguishing them from local citizens virtually impossible. Patrols to locate and identify the roving bands threatening the area met with little success.[61] On December 4, H Company under Rhoads's command moved from Vladivostok to Shkotovo to reinforce the garrison. Maj. Thomas Arms, commanding the provisional battalion, then sent H Company to Fanza to reinforce C Company.[62] See map 8 for the situation in Russia on December 15, 1919.

Christmas 1919 was not a quiet one for the Americans in Shkotovo. A patrol of four soldiers began their patrol about one hour before sunrise in Sitsa. When they were moving along the rail line about one mile from the barracks, the group heard voices that they initially assumed to be a group of laborers. When the corporal leading the group commanded the approaching group to halt in Russian, the opposing machine-gun company quickly deployed. The American patrol was already on the ground in the snow. The American patrol immediately began firing with its rifles and then BAR. The BAR operator was so intent on engaging the Russians that he failed to notice the remainder of the American patrol when they all retreated. Fortunately the Russians retreated at the same time, and the automatic rifleman was able to rejoin the patrol while en route to the barracks. A larger group of Americans returned to the site of the firefight and found blood in the snow but no bodies. No Americans were injured. The Americans intercepted a Bolshevik report several days later and learned that five Russians were wounded in the fight.[63]

At approximately 1:00 A.M. December 28, Americans heard several shots in the Russian barracks. Thinking it was a typical drunken brawl, no one worried. However, at 2:00 A.M., the Russian garrison commander arrived at the American headquarters and was very excited. At least one-half of the eight-hundred-man Russian garrison had deserted. Four or five Russian officers had been murdered.[64]

The American garrison, about four hundred strong, was alerted. The American headquarters dispatched elements to secure the town and guard supply stores. The deserting soldiers apparently fled to join the Bolsheviks. This large-scale desertion was indicative of the inability of the sitting government to maintain a sense of security. Kolchak's government was about to lose control.[65] His capital, Omsk, had fallen to the Reds on November 15.[66]

The mutiny destroyed the Russian garrison. The officers moved all their families into one building and took turns walking guard around it. Requests for American soldiers to act as guards were denied by AEF headquarters in Vladivostok. However, an American squad took up a position inside the building to maintain liaison with the Russian garrison. American rifle companies moved into Shkotovo to secure key facilities. At the railroad station, the Americans found eight Japanese soldiers who had arrived in the town ten days earlier now bound and gagged in preparation for their execution. The American efforts to secure key facilities resulted in the Russians fleeing the area without killing their captives.[67] No major changes occurred until early January. The degree of fear that must have permeated the group is not hard to imagine. The Russian government was coming apart. When an army's officers feel that they must personally protect their families, clearly security is failing.

Vladivostok and Harbin

The headquarters of the regiment remained at Vladivostok throughout this period. During January 1919, the Harbin Legation Guard size increased to seventy men. On May 26, G Company left Spasskoe after relief by the Twenty-Seventh Infantry. G Company moved to Vladivostok and replaced K Company as the base guard company. K Company moved to Ugolnaya.[68] In October, Col. Fred W. Bugbee replaced Colonel Sargent as the regiment commander.[69]

Vladivostok was relatively quiet until November 16. The disintegration of Kolchak's government led the Czech general Rudolph Gaida to believe he could successfully revolt against Kolchak and establish his own government in Vladivostok. Gaida had misjudged his popularity and the level of support he could muster. The revolt failed.[70] Cossacks loyal to Kolchak shot down Gaida's supporters in the streets. The Czech Legion, Gaida's old unit, remained neutral. M Company, Thirty-First Infantry, cleared everyone out of the railroad yard and stood guard. Gaida's men were surrounded by his opponents. Japanese and American troops guarded the city outside the ring of White Russians surrounding Gaida. He had no chance. His men surrendered. Many were executed, but several found protection by surrendering at AEF headquarters.[71] Gaida promised to leave Siberia within three days.[72]

The rail line now gained in importance as it was the only means of moving large numbers of people to the safety of the east. While the occasional reinforcements and logistical support would move west, the focus of most people and organizations was to escape the fighting, which meant moving east. A description of how difficult that turned out to be follows.

12
Riding the Rails

Railway travel continued to be a challenge but also was required for anyone trying to move from one place to another in Siberia. Firsthand accounts of travel on the railroad show the difficulty of travel and the importance of the railway while the civil war continued, and the violence increased. The partisan forces throughout Russia began having more success. As the Bolsheviks began to win the civil war, the Allies began to rely on the railway as a long line of retreat toward Vladivostok. At the same time, the Allied forces in southern Russia and those in northern Russia began to collapse after hard fighting. Vladivostok remained the beacon drawing all sides whether for safety or victory in Siberia. The story of a YMCA employee provides a glimpse into life on the railway as experienced by some of the people that relied upon for transportation and as a supply lifeline. The AEF-Siberia soldiers protected the railway so that these other organizations could use it. The Russian Railway Service Corps assisted Russian civilians in maintaining and operating the railroad.

Americans on the Railway

Albert Palmer spent his summer of 1919 assisting the YMCA as it provided services for American soldiers. His travels by train provide a glimpse into the difficulties faced as Russia continued to tear itself to pieces. He noted the difficulty of buying a ticket to travel because engineers were not always available. The trains would stop for twenty minutes or more in stations, so that passengers could take a break to purchase food.[1]

Palmer lamented the constant discussion of sex. He much preferred the movies and lectures and books provided by the YMCA. Palmer was very upset by the constant focus on women in conversations. However, even this talk did not prevent Palmer from recording his observations of the landscape. The grass and foliage attracted his praise.[2]

The Russian people by this time often feared the arrival of Americans and would run away when an American unit approached. Sometimes entire villages would evacuate to avoid the fighting while leaving only farm animals and old women to greet American soldiers. The AEF soldiers would sometimes confiscate such abandoned property for food, but they also left payment.[3] Previously the AEF soldiers had tried to be neutral in the civil war, but American operations in response to Bolshevik attacks made it clear that the presence of the AEF meant combat and the increased level of violence now included American units.

Palmer spent much of his time while traveling in speaking with AEF soldiers. They often complained about things that they could not control. Stories from home about soldiers being imprisoned for minor offenses caused concern. Other soldiers complained about having trouble with their wives who felt abandoned or whom they feared might be enjoying their absence with the freedom to see other men. Soldiers also told stories of their compatriots who had acquired second wives, maybe even children, during their long stay in Siberia.[4]

Americans served in all sorts of places throughout Siberia that summer. Palmer ran into an American nurse with the Red Cross, who was escorting four hundred children of Russian parents who supported the White Russians as they fled the advance of the Bolshevik army. In Buchedu, he met an American Red Cross doctor who worked in a hospital there and was greeted at the railroad station by a Russian Railway Service Corps officer's wife who was from Kansas. While walking through one town in Manchuria, Palmer discovered a woman with her two American-born children who had accompanied her on a visit to her Russian homeland. She had been living in Saint Louis and was now trying to get to Harbin to join her husband and return to the United States. Through all of his travels Palmer encountered refugees from all over Russia and also China as well as soldiers from every nation participating in the Allied intervention as they all sought to escape their current location and reach almost any other place.[5]

Palmer reached the Twenty-Seventh Infantry Regiment's camp at Verkhne-Udinsk during his rail adventure. The cleanliness of the camp impressed him along with its athletic fields, drill field, theater, and YMCA facility. Colonel Morrow, the regimental commander, also impressed him as being a good commander though they had a major disagreement about topics for discussion. Morrow advised Palmer not to waste his time preaching against soldiers having sex because that was a hopeless cause. The soldiers would stop listening to the rest of his message if Palmer made that argument. This did not sit well with the former Protestant minister who was determined to carry out his mission. The two men disagreed on the futility of preaching abstinence. However, both men agreed that prostitution was a problem to be resolved. Palmer was very pleased to learn that Morrow and their resident YMCA secretary had arranged a time for showing movies so that soldiers did not have time to walk home any young ladies invited to attend and still return to camp by the curfew hour. This scheduling of movies then helped reduce prostitution because the entertainment value of the movies was so high that the soldiers and local women wanted to go to the theater even if this affected the time for other activities afterward.[6]

Palmer began his return to Vladivostok on August 27. He had to change trains a number of times as he saw firsthand the agony of people trying to escape eastward to stay ahead of the advancing Bolsheviks while Kolchak's government and army began collapsing. In Irkutsk, he met young women Red Cross workers seeking the safety of an American unit. He also encountered a YMCA secretary who had been serving with the Czechs. Palmer related that the Czech soldiers called the YMCA their "American Uncle" because of the support provided in the preceding year. Russian, French, Czech, and other nationalities of soldiers had trains and train cars that they slowly worked into line to move eastward. Palmer had to change trains several times during his journey in order to keep moving eastward to reach Vladivostok in time for his scheduled departure by ship.[7]

Albert Palmer's roundabout trip ended safely, and he departed Vladivostok on the *Hozan Maru* sailing for Japan on September 10. He managed to stay healthy and avoid the cholera epidemic that had swept through Harbin and reached Vladivostok shortly before his return from the railroad trip. Palmer reported that the death rate in Harbin had reached five hundred per day before the Russian Red Cross would accept help from the American Red Cross. Upon arriving in Vladivostok, he saw warnings against eating in local restaurants and against eating any uncooked vegetables and fruit.[8]

During roughly the same time as Albert Palmer was traveling by rail for the YMCA, Corp. Jesse A. Anderson was part of the guard force on Red Cross Train Number 15. The guard force consisted of 2nd Lt. Paul W. Gerdes and ten enlisted men. The train had forty cars loaded with medical supplies, canned food, potatoes, blankets, and other equipment. While on the Chinese Eastern Railroad in Manchuria, the train used Chinese crews. Once in Russia, the crews were Russian. Three Chinese cooks fed everyone on the train. The guard force traveled in a boxcar. One passenger car was part of the train for the officers and any civilians who joined such as a representative from the International Harvester Company and one from the White Sewing Machine Company.[9]

Anderson noted the varied nationalities of people traveling the railway just as Palmer. Anderson also observed that, near Lake Baikal, the train passed through thirty-seven tunnels in five hours. He could see deer and bears in the distance as the train traversed the countryside. Wheat farms were evident as were timber mills.

Czech soldiers and refugees were in abundance. One Red Cross dentist moving with the Czechs reported having pulled 1,200 teeth the previous week. The guard force had to use mosquito nets for protection at night.[10]

The slow rate of travel and the existence of scattered Red Cross facilities providing service for everyone filled the pages of Anderson's diary. As most any American male soldier would do, he noted the names of a number of nurses, American and Canadian Red Cross, and female American Red Cross civilian employees he met during his journey. Upon his return to Vladivostok, he had to be deloused and receive a shot to ward off cholera. He also noted that disease could kill even those who were trying to bring relief to the soldiers in Siberia and the Russian civilians. Upon returning to Vladivostok he recorded that one American civilian who had been traveling with them had survived typhus and made it back to Vladivostok. Earlier while in Tomsk on August 15, Anderson noted that a nurse had died of the disease. Anderson had originally left Vladivostok on June 4. He reached Chelyabinsk on July 6 and Ekaterinburg on July 13. Anderson arrived back in Vladivostok on September 4.[11]

By September 13, 1919, the Allied forces in Siberia were drawing down significantly. The AEF cabled a report to the War Department on September 13 that the Italian mission would only have two or three officers assigned within three months. The French battalion that had been conducting operations was en route to Tientsen, China, with a few soldiers remaining on General Janin's staff. Britain's Middlesex battalion had departed. The Hampshires was either on the way to Vladivostok or already there. The report indicated that the Japanese strength was forty-five thousand with the expectation that one division would soon depart for Japan. However, the civilian presence in Siberia had increased with the number of stores established by Japanese civilians in Vladivostok doubling between December 1918 and September 1919. Graves recommended on September 26, 1919, that Japanese and American forces leave Siberia. In October 1919, the Intelligence Section concluded that the Bolsheviks were originally in favor of American intervention as a restraint against atrocities by the Japanese and their White Russian allies. However, American protection of the railroad indirectly supported the Kolchak regime, which made the United Sates their enemy.[12]

The railroad was the key transportation mode available in Siberia for trade, military operations, and personal safety in escaping the Reds or Whites depending on the side someone chose. The railway guard mission for the AEF was characterized by small unit actions and brought the AEF soldiers into direct conflict with the Bolsheviks since the railroad was the link between White Russian urban power centers. However, the AEF did not actively attempt to fight the Bolsheviks or other partisans except as required to keep the railway open. The AEF's policy to remain neutral and treat everyone in a humane way resulted in conflict between the AEF and its allies. This discord among the Allies continued throughout the intervention until the AEF departed Siberia. Regardless of events in Siberia, the civil war and misery faced by the Russian people continued unabated.

Allied Failures

Morale of the French soldiers was not high in the south Russian intervention force. With the war in Europe over and the large casualties experienced there, few French soldiers were enthusiastic about risking their lives to support the White Russians. Bolshevik propaganda encouraged the French soldiers to question the reasons that they were in Russia. The Allied force had moved north the previous February. However, attacks by Red forces succeeded in pushing back the French troops. By March 10, the Bolsheviks had cleared Kherson of French and Greek soldiers. Attempts to disrupt Bolshevik committee meetings succeeded in killing and capturing some of the Red leadership, but did not stop the effect of propaganda on the morale of the Allied soldiers in the south. Word of the unrest and lack of progress convinced the French leadership in Paris to conclude that withdrawing was the only choice. The French in Odessa received the order to withdraw on April 2 with the last French ship leaving on April 6.[13]

Events in the Crimea would follow a similar pattern in a few months. The White Russians in the Crimea were doomed to struggle forward with little help. By the end of April, the French had fled since the White Russians were unable or unwilling to stand and fight. After this, the only aid provided by the French to the White Russians in the south relied on naval forces.[14]

British intervention had occurred in the Caucasus with an eye on the oil resources available in the region. The recent independence of Georgia, Azerbaijan, and Armenia had attracted British interest. However, by the summer of 1919 British interest was focused on Ireland, India, and Egypt rather than the Caucasus oil fields. Most British forces departed during that summer with the final elements not departing until July 1920.[15]

The north Russian intervention also ended during this time with the British leaving Archangel on September 27 and Murmansk on October 12, 1919. British forces withdrew from Siberia in November 1919. British and Indian soldiers had also been in the Trans-Caspian region on the eastern side of the Caspian Sea. Most such forces left this area in the summer of 1919.[16]

The history of atrocities by White Russian forces continued during this time outside Siberia, as well. Denikin's attacks into the Ukraine in August and September included an anti-Semitic pogrom with murder, rape, torture, and robbery, characterizing the Whites' attitude toward many Jews. The assumption that Jews collectively supported the Bolsheviks heightened the anti-Semitism that had existed in Russia before. The White Russian forces were captive to their long-held beliefs about Jews that grew to a fever pitch after the revolution.[17]

Kolchak's regime continued to fail in motivating the peasantry to support it. His forces demanded recruits when the peasants only wanted to be left alone. Taxes on the peasants provided needed resources, but the government provided little in exchange. The Bolsheviks operating in Siberia had lost enough battles early on that the peasants did not remember the Red version of confiscated food and money. Consequently many peasants were indifferent to the Reds and hostile to the White Russians. Kolchak also failed to use sufficient force to crush the Red insurgency early. He never appreciated the Bolshevik ability to recover from their losses. Combined with the ill treatment of the peasantry, a growing partisan threat would eventually destroy Kolchak's attempt to rule.[18]

The combined Allied force in northern Russia continued its battles against the Bolsheviks while their brethren in the AEF-Siberia guarded the railroad and gradually came into conflict with Bolshevik partisans and its own allies. In northern Russia operations were similar to the battle at Bolshie Ozerki during the period March 31 to April 2, 1919. Uncoordinated attacks by British, White Russian, and American soldiers earlier in March had failed to push the Bolsheviks out of the town. Waist-deep snow exhausted the attackers so that they could not overcome the defenses. After destroying the village with artillery, the Allies set to constructing log blockhouse fortifications outside the ruins. Approximately two thousand Allied soldiers now faced about seven thousand Bolsheviks.[19]

The Bolsheviks attacked in force starting at about 3:30 a.m. on April 1. The Reds had already cut the telephone lines as they maneuvered to surround several of the blockhouses. Artillery in the direct fire mode had been necessary to fight off the attacks the previous day. The attack on April 1 was larger in size and concentrated on the forward Allied positions. Bolshevik losses were high, prompting some of the Bolsheviks to lose faith and desert to the Allies. An Allied counterattack the following day suffered the same result as the Red attack. The difficult terrain made the speed needed to cross the open areas impossible to achieve. Exhaustion from wading through the snow and casualties limited fire and maneuver.[20]

Both forces were ill equipped to deal with the difficult terrain and temperatures. The Red infantry were predominantly from southern Russia and not accustomed to the harsh conditions in the north. The Shackleton boots worn by the Allied soldiers would get wet when the snow melted during the day. This then resulted in a large number of frostbite cases. Both sides experienced excessive casualties from frostbite alone. The defense carried the day in and around Bolshie Ozerki. While both sides could claim tactical victory in defensive battles, the Bolsheviks won in an operational sense. The Allies were unable to force their way to the south in order to link up with White Russian or Czech forces.[21] The exterior lines of the Allied and White Russian effort did not enable them to crush the Bolshevik resistance. Had an Allied linkup occurred, the history of the Russian civil war might have turned out very differently.

The Allied powers tired of the effort in north Russia and took steps to evacuate. Public pressure in the United States made the decision to withdraw from the war against the Reds an obvious one to take. American troops began to move back to Archangel in April in order to prepare to depart. By the end of May, almost all of the American infantry had withdrawn to the city. Four thousand British soldiers arrived May 27 to relieve the Americans. By June 28, the 339th Infantry Regiment, supporting 310th Engineer Battalion, and other American elements had boarded the British ships and set sail.[22]

The British would remain a little longer but would leave within a few months. Russian units they had trained were unreliable in action. Some even mutinied and deserted. Support in Great Britain did not last, and British troop withdrawals from northern Russia began on September 10 and were completed by September 26.[23]

Shortages of supplies and no hope for relief doomed the few White Russian battalions left in northern Russia. They succeeded in holding out against Bolshevik attacks for several months; however, resistance could not last forever. On February 19, 1920, the last of the White Russian leaders left Archangel for Norway. Red infantry occupied Archangel on February 21 and Murmansk on February 23.[24]

The plight of other Allied forces trying to retreat from battles in the west and reach safety in Siberia was also a difficult one. A YMCA representative with a Polish division that was part of these other Allies moving eastward provides a description of the terror, danger, and confusion that plagued everyone seeking to make their escape. L. C. Convis recorded the collapse of Russian military discipline and the desperation of the Allied forces to move toward Vladivostok in November 1919. The officers leading Kolchak's disintegrating army often tried to position their units so that an Allied contingent separated them from the advancing Reds. Russian officers would sell weapons and ammunition to the highest bidder, but transportation was the true mark of riches. Buying a horse or a sled was virtually impossible. Vodka was the best money to use because everyone would take it for anything.[25]

Convis described how the Polish troops could not move past the Czech units that controlled the railroad. The Red Army caught up to the Poles who fought back. White Russian units would rally and fight alongside the Polish units. YMCA representatives continued to provide support throughout the battles. Empty trains abandoned because of a lack of fuel blocked the rail line. Refugees clogged the trains and roads, begging for help and struggling to escape to the east. Many refugees did not seem to know their destination. They only knew they had to get somewhere.[26]

People on the roads used sleds and horses. Others walked on the tracks. Many carried small packs, and most only had bread to eat. Terrified horses tried to break free seemingly sensing the terror that people feared. Convis's description of the carnage at one gully is indicative of the horror faced by this human flood. He noted that several hundred sleds were jammed into this small space trying to work around a wreck. Women, children, and horses were screaming for help while men pushed and shoved each other and their possessions to try to reach safety on the far side. A group of Cossacks approached and demanded to be let through. When no one complied, the Cossacks showed their anger with the way forward clogged by people. The Cossacks rode into the snow and fired into the people and animals who had blocked their movement. Convis estimated that somewhere between thirty-five and forty people died while the Cossacks laughed at their handiwork.[27]

Families became separated and sometimes never regained contact. For one British woman, crossing a bridge meant that she had to spend two hours walking over dead bodies carrying her baby to safety while her husband looked for a sled. Another man who had been escaping in a car left his wife and children in it so he could try to find food. He did not find the car until a week later, and the car was over 130 miles from its previous location. Their possessions had been rifled, and he never found his wife and children. Russian "sanitary trains" were filled with wounded, injured, and sick, who were often abandoned to die while suffering from their ailments and the cold. Men near dying were stripped naked and stacked in piles on the tops of railcars in the cold to hasten their deaths.[28]

Whites and Reds attacked anyone who blocked their paths or had something they wanted. A complete breakdown of discipline precluded an effective defense by the White Russians against the Reds. Civilians and soldiers alike suffered and died horribly. In one town, Convis recorded that bodies and parts of bodies remained unburied, scattered around homes and even hanging from trees and telegraph poles. Coal and wood were hard to find to fuel the trains. The cold would freeze water tanks. Railroad crews had to melt snow to fill engine boilers.[29]

Convis and the Poles continued to struggle to the east, bargaining with the Czechs to trade locomotives for the right to pass their women and children through to safety. He eventually abandoned his YMCA railcar and with several other people continued his journey on several sleds. For Convis, leaving the soldiers he had supported was difficult, but he was not part of the fighting element and everyone staying with the trains had to be ready to do just that. After a struggle of several miles he and his group reached another rail station, Klukvinaiya. There he was able to find a YMCA railcar that had been supporting the Czechs. This group made room for Convis and his party so they could once again start eastward by train.[30]

In late January, Convis reached Mingatua. The trains continued to struggle toward the east, which resulted in his arriving at Irkutsk on February 6. By now Kolchak was dead, and the Reds occupied Irkutsk. Fortunately for him, the Reds were not out to kill Americans and most of the Allied soldiers and civilians were able to find a ride on a train to continue to move to safety. Convis's train left Irkutsk on February 10. Once outside Irkutsk, Convis's trip settled down to a simple ride through the Siberian countryside so that he eventually reached safety in Vladivostok and was evacuated.[31]

A couple of weeks prior to this, the AEF-Siberia Intelligence Section received a report from the Polish division intelligence officer that many of the Poles had surrendered. The Polish division was cut off, and four regiments and one cavalry regiment had surrendered. A call for complete surrender and turning in of their weapons was rebuffed. The Polish government called for a large attack of Polish forces along the Poland-Russia border. Volunteers in the Polish division wanted to surrender, while the regular army members of the division wanted to fight their way eastward. The expectation was that much of the division would surrender with soldiers opposing surrender trying to make their escape eastward to Vladivostok. The cold weather and the recent practice of killing their own wounded accounted for many of the losses. The AEF-Siberia Intelligence Section blamed Czech interference in the escape of the Poles as one factor leading to the Polish division being surrounded.[32] Eichelberger reported that the Polish division was surrounded near Krasnoyarsk on January 11 and surrendered. He listed the division strength as fifteen thousand men.[33]

The disjointed nature of the intervention is clear from the accounts of the Allied forces fighting outside Siberia and escaping through Siberia to reach Vladivostok. The lack of synchronization of effort meant that the Allies could not play a decisive role in the resolution of the civil war. The differing national goals precluded even simple cooperation at times because there was no central command and control of all Allied military forces let alone a headquarters to assist any Russian group vying for power. Chaos was the result and many people, soldiers, civilian government employees, and Russian civilians suffered as a consequence.

The tragedy playing out along the Tran-Siberian Railroad was indicative of the collapse of the White Russian cause and consequently the end of the Allied intervention. This final conclusion to the effort to reinvigorate an Eastern Front and accomplish the other varied and sometimes conflicting goals of the Allies was obviously near. Soldiers and civilians struggled to reach Vladivostok and perceived safety. The intervention was doomed. The Allied leaders simply had to admit it.

13
The Final Days

Pressure to bring the AEF home continued to build in Congress and from the soldiers' families. World War I ended with the armistice in November 1918. Russia was coming no closer to democracy through the AEF's presence. The situation in Washington, DC, was also not encouraging. Wilson's participation in the Paris Peace Conference after the war was a terrible strain. His battle against opponents of the League of Nations Covenant added to the burden. The stress resulted in Wilson suffering a stroke October 2, 1919. Even though now physically and mentally unfit, he refused to relinquish his office. His unwillingness to compromise with political opponents regarding the League of Nations Covenant doomed its ratification. The political leadership of the nation was involved in a bitter struggle to win the 1920 election.[1] The United States was tired of conflict overseas. The War Department sent a message to Graves on December 31, 1919, telling him to prepare to leave. Graves then issued orders to his units to begin concentrating and moving to Vladivostok.[2] Though not engaged in the horror of open and constant combat, these preparations to depart had to give heart to the Bolsheviks and dishearten the White Russians. With the Americans gone, no party that had tried to be neutral in the conflict would remain. Only Japan would maintain a force of any size in Siberia except those Russians locked in the bitter struggle of civil war.

While AEF headquarters was making its plans, the guard detachments continued operations. The White Russian situation continued to deteriorate. By October 1919, Kolchak was clearly losing his grip on controlling his forces. Red successes were steadily gaining ground and pushing his forces backward. The White Russian deprivations generated plenty of peasant soldiers for the advancing Reds. On November 14, the Red Army captured Omsk. As the end became clear, the Czech leadership expressed its disgust with the actions of the White Russian atrocities and requested evacuation from Siberia. This made it clear that Kolchak had little hope of remaining in power. By December 15, the Czechs controlled train fuel allocations such that only their trains could move. On January 4, 1920, Kolchak abdicated and passed leadership to Denikin. Kolchak's own personal guard force had already deserted to the Bolsheviks. He appointed Cossack ataman Grigori Semenov the commander of all Russian military forces in Irkutsk Province and east of Lake Baikal. By boarding a train flying the flags of the Allied nations, he hoped to escape capture.[3]

Kolchak's attempt to escape worked for a few days. Upon entering Irkutsk on January 15, he and the former premier V. Pepelyaev found themselves at the mercy of the Irkutsk Bolsheviks, who were bargaining for his release to them. The Czech Sixth Regiment that had been escorting Kolchak eastward was confronted by a Bolshevik demand to turn over Kolchak or the Bolsheviks would attack. Kolchak had no support. He had previously threatened to attack the Czechs when they stopped his trains from moving. The Czechs handed over Kolchak and gold reserves from the Russian government to the Bolsheviks so they could continue toward Vladivostok. With only perfunctory questioning and after a short imprisonment, the Bolsheviks marched Kolchak and Pepelyaev to the edge of the river on February 7, 1920. Kolchak marched resolutely toward his death, apparently determined to present a dignified memory. The Bolshevik guards had to drag a weeping and frightened Pepelyaev. A priest was on hand to console the two prisoners, but this did little to calm Pepelyaev's obvious terror and emphasized the demeanor of Kolchak. A carefully positioned hole in the ice allowed both bodies to fall into the Angara River after the Chekist firing squad performed its duty in two ragged volleys. The bodies vanished in the swiftly moving water. The Bolsheviks executed Kolchak in Irkutsk, the same town in which he was married.[4] Against this backdrop of continuing chaos, the Twenty-Seventh Infantry and Thirty-First Infantry soldiers continued to do their duty.

Twenty-Seventh Infantry: Poor Allied Relations and Withdrawal

A large Bolshevik force was reported to be in Mukheeno about twelve miles from Verkhne-Udinsk on January 3, 1920. To prevent an attack on Verkhne-Udinsk, Lt. Col. Alvin C. Gillam led a 250-man force to attack the village. American scouts were fired upon when they neared Mukheeno, but the Reds quickly sent a message to Gillam stating that they would not resist his entry into the town.[5]

Gillam met the Bolsheviks and discussed their intentions. The Bolsheviks stated they were friendly toward the Americans. Their objective was to fight the White Russian general Levitsky's forces in the area. This White Russian unit was committing atrocities throughout the vicinity. After the Bolsheviks promised not to interfere with the American forces, Gillam and his troops returned to Verkhne-Udinsk on January 5.[6] Remaining neutral in this Russian dispute over who would lead the country prevented another fight from occurring here.

A serious incident occurred a few days later and illustrated the poor state of relations between the AEF and the Cossacks. An M Company platoon under the command of 2nd Lt. Paul W. Kendall was stationed at Posolkaya, about ninety versts from Verkhne-Udinsk. The local stationmaster was not friendly to the American guard force. Many local residents had previously left town fearing that trouble would occur soon. Kendall's Third Platoon had two officers and forty-two enlisted men to oppose any armed threats. The detachment was housed in boxcars located on sidings at the railyard.[7]

Semenov's armored train, the Destroyer, pulled into the station at 12:45 A.M. on January 10. After taking on wood and water[8] and the stationmaster conferring with the crew,[9] the train moved up the track to a position alongside boxcars used by Kendall's platoon as quarters. The Destroyer and the soldiers on board were armed with one 3-inch Japanese field gun, one 1-pounder cannon, four machine guns, sixty rifles, and a large supply of hand grenades. Cossack general Nicholas Bogomolitz, six officers, and sixty-six enlisted men were on the train.[10]

At 1:00 A.M., the Destroyer opened fire. Forty feet separated the Cossack and American cars. The Americans leaped from their cars and returned the fire. Fortunately, the Cossack aim was not good. While the two forces blazed away at each other, American sergeant Carl Robbins climbed onto the Destroyer's engine. Even though severely wounded, he was able to throw a hand grenade into the engine cab. The Cossack fire killed the young American, but the hand grenade severely damaged the armored train. Kendall led the platoon into the attack firing a BAR. His ammunition bearer, Pvt. John R. Montgomery, was shot to death at his side. Pvt. Homer D. Tommio tried to board the train but the defenders pushed him back. While lying beside the track and before he could get up to charge the train again, a car ran over his foot.[11]

The Destroyer moved about fifty yards down the track after a few minutes and stopped. The mutual exchange of fire continued. The Americans poured rifle fire and threw hand grenades against the train. The Destroyer again moved—this time about one hundred yards. Firing continued unabated as the American infantry courageously fought against the armored train with only small arms, refusing to be cowed by the Cossacks behind their steel plating. At 1:45 A.M., the train left the station moving toward Selenga.[12]

As The Destroyer moved away from the American cars, Kendall's force did not retreat. The Americans maneuvered along both sides of the track keeping up a steady rate of fire against the Cossacks. After the train cleared the station and moved out of range, the Americans ceased firing. Robbins's grenade forced the

Destroyer to stop at Temlue, twelve versts away. General Bogomolitz then telephoned Kendall and asked if the Cossacks could return and surrender.[13]

Meanwhile, Kendall had called the American detachment at Selenga and notified them of the firefight. The commander there loaded a part of his force on a train and started toward Posolkaya. This force soon reached Temlue and received Bogomolitz's surrender. Five Cossacks had been killed, one wounded. American casualties were two killed and one wounded. Kendall, Robbins, Montgomery, Tommio, and 2nd Lt. John C. Stinell received the Distinguished Service Cross for their bravery under fire.[14] The Americans released the captive Cossacks to Semenov after he promised they would stand trial.[15]

Companies stationed in the Spasskoe and Ussuri areas left for Vladivostok in six echelons. The first echelon left Ussuri January 8. The sixth echelon left Spasskoe on January 13. Only difficulty in finding enough railcars slowed their departure.[16]

Loading details worked day and night in Vladivostok in very cold weather to embark these units aboard ship. By January 14, all Spasskoe-Ussuri sector troops were in Vladivostok. All were on the USAT *Great Northern* by January 16. On January 17, the Second Battalion, C Company, D Company, Headquarters Detachment, Machine Gun Detachment, and a Supply Company Detachment sailed for Manila. The ship arrived at Manila January 26 after a three-day layover in Nagasaki, Japan. The troops occupied Camp Thomas H. Barry in the Manila port area.[17]

The troops in the Lake Baikal area moved to Vladivostok in eight echelons. American and British Red Cross workers accompanied them. On January 16, the first echelon left Verkhne-Udinsk with the last leaving January 29. The Twenty-Seventh Infantry required 380 railroad cars to transport all personnel and equipment. The temperature in the open was -62.5° when the regiment began its movement. The echelons arrived between February 1 and 25. This was a difficult move because of the distance involved and the violent conditions throughout Siberia. The American echelons contained extra cars with wood supplies. Troops carried ninety days rations and forage. The regiment ensured that the trains carried all US Army, Red Cross, and YMCA personnel seeking evacuation, even delaying its departure to afford a Red Cross train to join its echelons for safety.[18]

On March 10, the remaining Twenty-Seventh Infantry units departed Vladivostok on the USAT *Thomas*. They arrived in Manila on March 17. The last of the regiment joined the earlier arrivals in Camp Barry.[19] The Twenty-Seventh Infantry took a Russian bear to the Philippines as a mascot. When the bear became too large for the soldiers to handle, they donated it to the Municipal Zoo in Manila. Two returned deserters also left Siberia with their former comrades. Some of the regiment's soldiers wanted to kill the deserters for having joined the Bolsheviks. The deserters were locked up in cages below deck to protect them from their former comrades. The transition from the cold of Siberia to the heat of the tropics was difficult for the Twenty-Seventh Infantry Regiment's soldiers initially. The pet bear experienced the same acclimatization difficulty, so that the zookeepers had to dig a large hole for the bear to use to escape the summer heat[20] (see map 9 for the situation in Russia on March 22, 1920).

Thirty-First Infantry: Revolution and Withdrawal

The Thirty-First Infantry units in the Shkotovo area received orders to move to Vladivostok on January 3, 1920. H Company moved to Shkotovo on January 5. All troops left Kanguaz on January 7. The last two companies moving from Kanguaz to Shkotovo had difficulty using the railroad. Bolsheviks destroyed two railroad bridges between Romanovka and Novo Nezhino. The Americans were forced to "requisition" over one hundred local wagons on sleds to move. Twelve miles of track were destroyed. The troops in the area were all concentrated at Shkotovo by January 10.[21]

Engines to move the entire body of troops were then difficult to find. Only one engine near Ugolnaya was eventually obtained. Russian railroad officials protested its seizure, but a four-man guard detail guaranteed its security. The Americans used the engine for seven days. By January 18, all troops from the Shkotovo sector moved to Vladivostok.[22]

The Razdolnoe sector units (D, F, K, and M Companies) were the rear guard for the Twenty-Seventh Infantry units evacuating Verkhne-Udinsk. Prior to the evacuation, little violence had occurred in this area. However, the departure of American troops brought on an increase in Bolshevik activity.[23]

Kolchak's troops deserted to the Reds as his regime collapsed. Japanese forces continued to battle Bolshevik elements in many areas and remained allied to the White Russian forces. The Americans continued to strive to remain neutral.[24]

Revolution continued to wrack Siberia during the closing months of the AEF's intervention. A, C, I, and L Companies continued to patrol Vladivostok to maintain order. Between January 25 and February 3, a coalition of Social Democrats, Social Revolutionists, and Bolsheviks overthrew Kolchak's supporters in the Amur area. On January 31, a group of 3,100 troops of this new government occupied Vladivostok. This group was opposed to continued Allied intervention.[25]

The delegates of this group had visited Vladivostok earlier on January 27. The Vladivostok Russian commander refused to meet with them. Japanese general Shigemoto Oi's attitude convinced the delegates who had arrived from Nikolsk that Japan wanted to stall for time and send reinforcements to Siberia. Therefore, seizing Vladivostok was the only way to end the Allied intervention and extend governmental control.[26]

Between February 15 and April 1, the Thirty-First Infantry departed Siberia on the transport ships *Crook*, *Dix*, *South Bend*, and *Great Northern*. The Second Provisional Battalion consisting of A, C, E, H, and I Companies departed first and arrived at Manila on March 5. Each echelon stayed at Camp Barry temporarily before moving to Fort McKinley. Regimental headquarters reached Manila on April 6. F, K, L, and M Companies with the AEF staff arrived at Manila on April 8 aboard the *Great Northern*. The entire regiment was assembled at Fort William McKinley April 17. Graves became the Fort McKinley commander.[27]

America's Siberian intervention ended, but peace was not close in Siberia or the rest of Russia.

The Civil War Grinds On

The American departure did not end the civil war or the suffering of the Russian people. Baron Peter Wrangel continued the White Russian effort in the Crimea when he took command of forces there in April 1920. His soldiers were demoralized after a string of defeats. However, Soviet preoccupation elsewhere provided a respite to prepare as well as a time for hope to take root. British mediation with the Bolsheviks produced no solid agreement, but no Soviet final drive to crush Wrangel's force materialized. Wrangel instilled discipline and punished officers for acts that had previously alienated the Russian people so often. He even succeeded in defeating Red forces in several engagements even though outnumbered. The French continued to provide supplies even though the British seemed only intent to end the war.[28]

Bolshevik-Polish fighting also helped take some of the pressure off Wrangel when that began in April. The Bolsheviks were much more concerned about Poland than they were about the remaining White Russian soldiers in southern Russia. With the Crimea a poor base and needing to motivate his army, Wrangel decided to attack. On June 6, Wrangel seized Melitopol near the Crimea. Wrangel paused and then continued the attack into the southern Ukraine. His intention to carry out land reform by allowing peasants to retain land they had seized as long as they paid back one-fifth of the harvest each year to the government failed to motivate the peasants to join his cause. Many felt that they had already earned the right to take the land and did not owe the government anything for having done so. Even dissatisfaction with the Bolsheviks in the area previously was not motivation enough to add much support to the White Russians.[29]

Wrangel then tried an attack into the Kuban area along the Sea of Azov. While initially successful, the attack by his Cossack allies lacked the energy needed to prevent the recovery of the superior Bolshevik force. Counterattacks drove the

White Russian Cossacks back to the Crimea even though successful recruiting among Cossacks in the area more than replaced in numbers the losses incurred. Even with the increase in numbers, the attack clearly was a failure.[30]

Wrangel was obviously a threat to Red control over all of Russia. The Bolsheviks assembled an army of 137,000 to eliminate Wrangel's estimated 35,000 troops. On October 28, 1920, the Reds attacked, crossing the Perekop Isthmus and entering the Crimea. The Perekop city trenches withstood the Bolshevik crushing blows until November 7. An amphibious assault across the Gulf of Sivash by the Reds allowed them to take Wrangel's forces in the rear and on its eastern flank. Wrangel had no choice but to withdraw under fire and occupy a new defensive position to the southeast at Ushun on November 8. The Bolsheviks pursued and continued to attack the new position relentlessly. On November 11, Ushun fell. An estimated 145,683 White Russian soldiers, family members, and civilians made their escape and settled elsewhere in Europe. Wrangel had fought well, but his efforts were too little, too late.[31]

Organized White Russian resistance ended with Wrangel's defeat. The Allies had already departed. A few attempts by other White Russian leaders to establish a new front ultimately failed. One such attempt lasted until July 1921 in Mongolia. The Czech Legion ceased following any instructions from French general Maurice Janin and sought to save itself with the rear guard leaving Vladivostok on June 1, 1920. The last Czech envoy departed Vladivostok the next day. Japan would retain forces in parts of eastern Siberia until October 25, 1922. British authorities feared that the American departure would result in Japan trying to dominate Siberia, which would leave the railroad vulnerable to attack. The presence of the AEF had interfered with Japanese attempts to control events in Siberia. The Japanese departure removed the last real check on the expansion of Bolshevik power so that by January 1923, virtually all of Siberia was under Bolshevik control.[32]

Even after escaping Russia, the White Russians would not always find peace. Wrangel moved to Brussels, Belgium, after founding the World Organization of Russian War Veterans. He died, apparently of natural causes, in April 1928. However, Gen. A. P. Kutepov, a successor to Wrangel, was snatched from a Paris street by two men on January 26, 1930. One estimate is that the Communists still viewed him as a threat and either killed or kidnapped him, taking the body to a ship waiting off shore. Kutepov's successor as the leader of the White Russians in exile was Gen. E. K. Miller, who had fought at Archangel and now also lived in Paris. On September 22, 1937, after leaving his office to confer with two Germans about the possibility of an alliance with the Nazi Party, Miller also disappeared. A large wooden case loaded onto a Soviet freighter may have been his body.[33]

A Cossack attempt to establish their own state in northern Italy by Gen. P. N. Krasnov failed thanks to the success of the Allies in World War II. The British handed over a number of Cossack prisoners to the Soviets. *Pravda* carried an announcement of Krasnov's and others' executions in January 1947. Semenov remained in Manchuria in support of the Japanese.[34]

Semenov visited the United States in April 1922 and met with then-major Robert L. Eichelberger (many officers held temporary ranks during the war higher than their permanent ranks to which they reverted afterward). During the conversation, Semenov told Eichelberger that the Japanese officers with whom he spoke were convinced that Japan and the United States would eventually be at war. Japan intended to control Sakhalin Island and eastern Siberia. American naval forces would be at a great disadvantage due to the distance to the United States from Asia. Japan could easily seize the Philippine Islands. Japanese troops in China were essential in order to ensure a steady flow of food and other resources to Japan. Semenov also felt that establishing a stable government in Siberia was not possible because of all of the unrest in the region. Semenov returned to Siberia after this visit and remained a Japanese ally. When the Soviets overran Manchuria near the end of World War II, they captured and hanged him.[35]

The YMCA continued to try to support the Russian people and look for a way to continue operations. The Soviet government was pleased to accept aid for prisoners but continued to mistrust the YMCA's true purpose. In the end, the White Russians and Reds had distrusted the YMCA's intent and perceived interference in the civil war, but the soldiers who used its facilities had a very positive view, regardless of political beliefs. Even with this open animosity from the Bolsheviks, the YMCA maintained its office in Vladivostok until 1923.[36]

Conclusion

The intervention ended as each Allied nation evacuated its forces. Some countries would remain in Siberia longer than others. Nonetheless, in the end the Bolsheviks would rise to power. This would affect international relations for years to come even though the intervention itself is generally unknown. A new and Communist country would rise from the ashes of the old czarist regime. The Union of Soviet Socialist Republics would achieve superpower status before finally collapsing because of the failed policies of a totalitarian regime. Different actions during the intervention might have caused a different outcome. The challenges faced by the AEF included a poorly defined mission and conflicts with Allies and within the US government. The lesson to take away from this intervention is a critical need for a clearly defined mission supported by all elements of our government and our allies in the operation.

Poorly Defined Mission

America's participation in the Siberian intervention formally ended with the withdrawal of US troops. But, what happened? Did the United States achieve its objectives? Did the AEF accomplish its mission? Certainly, the American soldiers performed well. The AEF units succeeded on the battlefield in many small-unit actions. Large-unit operations were not conducted because the defeat of a large military force was not the AEF's mission. The factors motivating the Allies to send troops to Siberia included survival on the Western Front, saving an ally, protecting previous military and nonmilitary aid, restraining Japanese ambitions, and assisting the Czech Legion. However, the confused situation in Siberia and the lack of clear military goals made success difficult to define. The lack of a coordinated Allied plan and a single Allied commander increased the confusion and complicated the AEF's tasks.

The Twenty-Seventh Infantry's Ussuri campaign was a violation of the "Aide Memoire." The fault for this breach lays with the War Department, however, not the AEF. Styer was in command before Graves arrived but had received no instructions regarding US policy and the types of actions allowed. His only instructions were that Graves would provide guidance upon his arrival. Consequently, when Otani asked for assistance, Styer provided it. The United States was allied with Japan, and the other Allied units in Siberia were already cooperating with the Japanese. There was no reason for Styer to have refused to help. Army officers are trained to be decisive and show initiative. Japan claimed Central Powers prisoners of war were a threat in the area and had to be defeated. Styer did the same thing that many good officers would have done; he attacked. Fortunately, the American role in the campaign was very limited. After Graves arrived, the AEF would not again take part in a large, cooperative venture with the Japanese.

The Americans gained the upper hand in the majority of their battles. Romanovka was the one major example of the AEF experiencing heavy casualties. However, even there the AEF force did not quit the battlefield. The troops succeeded in fighting off the attackers though suffering severe losses. Viewing this battle from a terrain perspective, this was an American victory. American soldiers still held the field when the fighting stopped. However, the losses make any claim to that characterization difficult to defend.

American combat operations consisted mainly of a fight against partisans. The Bolsheviks and other partisans were poorly equipped. They lacked automotive weapons and artillery when facing the AEF (even though the British did face Bolshevik artillery). The AEF units used patrolling to secure themselves and positions under their control. Patrols to the flanks of moving columns were particularly useful in protecting American units from ambushes and snipers. Individual snipers were often effective due to their pre–civil war occupation—hunting. The partisans, Bolshevik and others, were generally in good physical condition and had high morale. However, poor leadership inhibited their effectiveness. The rough nature of the terrain precluded large-scale American attacks. Partisans often slipped away to fight another day.[1] American small-unit tactics consistently succeeded. US casualties were light. Patrolling kept the rail line open. Possibly the infantry regiments' previous experience in the Philippines helped. Certainly, the situations were similar in that operations consisted of guarding fixed sites with patrolling around these sites to protect them. Even though some accounts are not clear, a review of the AEF-Siberia records shows that the Americans in the end viewed the Bolsheviks and some elements of the White Russian forces such as the Cossacks as the enemy.

Guarding the railroad also required special equipment not usually found in the

American infantry regiment. Graves suggested in his final report that gasoline-powered rail motor carts for patrols and armored trains for reinforcing fires and troops be provided for future rail line guard missions.[2]

Another AEF problem that caused Graves concern was desertion. Apparently, some number of Russian civilians in the United States enlisted in the army for service in Siberia. Graves believed many recruits did this with the sole purpose in mind of obtaining free passage to Siberia. Once "home," they deserted the AEF. Graves recommended that future expeditionary forces exclude natives of the land in which the expeditionary force would serve.[3]

Actions by the AEF in Siberia were much different from the AEF in north Russia. There US troops cooperated with Allied forces and attacked the Bolsheviks. Dreams of linking up with the Czech Legion to reestablish the Eastern Front coupled with an intense hatred of the Bolsheviks spurred these attacks. The American commander, a colonel, bowed to British demands and allowed his troops to be commanded by non-Americans. The degree that this was due to the senior American in north Russia being a colonel versus a major general in Siberia or some other reason is unknown and not the subject of this study. The point made here is that the conduct of the two interventions was drastically different. All elements of the US government were not synchronized in their outlook toward the various factions either. Graves noted that shortly before the armistice in 1918 the State Department officers received guidance to assist local governments. When this occurred, virtually all consular offices were along the railroad and in cities controlled by White Russian factions. This then implied to the Bolsheviks immediately that the Americans were taking the side of the White Russians.[4]

Conflict with Allies and Other Agencies

The relations among the AEF, the Allies, and several US government agencies were not consistent. Initially, all the Allied commanders seemed determined to cooperate. Yet, as time progressed, differences damaged this initial goodwill. Graves was determined to remain neutral in the war even though other Allies and the US State Department wanted to destroy the Bolsheviks. Graves's steadfast loyalty to his orders was commendable. However, this attitude poisoned efforts to achieve Allied unity. The barbarous actions of the Japanese and Cossack soldiers appalled the Americans. When provided the opportunity, American soldiers interfered with Japanese and Cossack brutality, which resulted in Japanese and Cossack resentment toward the AEF. Graves and his men were morally and legally correct in protesting the wanton murder and destruction carried out by the Japanese and Cossack forces. However, being *right* resulted in the AEF having poor relations with the Allies. The conflicts of particular note with the White Russians, the British, the Japanese, and other Allies help to frame the overall problem noted before that the AER faced the continuing challenge of trying to execute a poorly defined mission that the Allies and even all elements of the US government did not support.

White Russian Conflicts

Eichelberger reported to the War Department after the intervention that the AEF labored under orders requiring noninterference in internal Russian affairs. Following this policy in the end resulted in the local people having a higher opinion of the Americans than that held about other Allied forces. This was especially true once the announcement of the planned departure of the AEF became known. The conduct of the Kolchak forces was such that opposition to his government was widespread by the time of his overthrow and execution.[5]

Kolchak's popular support decreased as time progressed. When he first came to power, Kolchak promised to establish a representative government and convene a constituent assembly. However, he failed to carry out this promise. Unfulfilled promises and the cruel actions of some of his followers (such as Semenov) caused the Russian people to turn against him.[6]

Attempts by Graves to stop Cossack atrocities may have improved the AEF's image in the eyes of the Russian civilians, but it did not stop such actions. The Japanese officials promised to talk to Cossack ataman Ivan Kalmikov when Graves protested his actions in Khabarovsk. All this did was force Kalmikov to be more secretive and send people out of Khabarovsk before killing them.[7]

Semenov's armored trains caused problems for the Americans several times even though both groups cooperated during initial operations. One incident occurred when the commander of the Twenty-Seventh Infantry Regiment gave permission for Semenov to repair one of his armored train cars at Verkhne-Udinsk. When the time limit passed for the armored car to be removed, Semenov refused to move the car. The Americans warned him that they would attack to secure the car. A few minutes before the attack occurred, a Japanese force intervened and evacuated the car to their facilities. Another incident occurred when Semenov received permission to travel on a particular sector of the rail line guarded by the AEF. When passing through Posolskaya, the train crew fired on an American platoon killing two American soldiers. The Americans attacked and captured the train including seventy-five members of the train's operational crew.[8]

Atrocities come up time and again in the records of operations in Siberia. Many have already been recounted. Graves reported that atrocities performed by the Cossacks were supported by the Japanese officials, which turned the people against the Americans as well as the perpetrators of the acts. Our being allied with the Japanese resulted in some blame accruing on our soldiers indirectly. Several additional reports will serve to illustrate the depravity of some of America's allies. Mr. M. Lipinski, a transportation agent of the Chinese Eastern Railroad, reported that in September 1919, Cossacks on Semenov's armored train *Terrible* had accused him of being a Bolshevik. After arresting him, they threatened to shoot him in the head but instead settled for whipping him as punishment. After the seventy-eighth lash, Lipinski passed out. He did not know how many times they beat him. After they tired of their recreation, they hit him in the head and shoved him off the train at a station where he received medical attention.[9]

First Lieutenant R. S. Ashby of the Russian Railway Service Corps reported a series of atrocities in the Chita area. One of Semenov's armored trains arrived at Megson on the morning of January 5, 1920. The Cossacks began arresting local civilians and made it clear that they wanted no interference from the Czech soldiers stationed in the area. Words were exchanged but no gunfire between the Russians and the Czechs. Nonetheless, the Cossack train departed with one young woman and eight men, most of whom had been employed by the railroad. The Cossacks jeered at the prisoners' relatives, whose pleas for mercy went unheeded as the train rolled out of town. The following day, the militia of a town approximately twenty miles distant reported finding nine bodies. They maintained a guard over them until the families could reach the site on January 7 to identify the victims. The nine bodies belonged to the young woman and eight men seized in Megson. Two of the young woman's brothers were known to be serving with the Bolsheviks, and she was a friend of the American railway men. The Cossacks apparently took their time killing the nine people. The gunshot wounds did not appear to be fatal. All had several sword and bayonet wounds as well. The young woman was mutilated.[10]

First Lieutenant F. B. Byers of the Russian Railway Service Corps reported several incidents of atrocities including the execution of six men in Sludanka. Czech soldiers brought the bodies to Byers so he could photograph them in order to inform the American people of the horrendous acts of Semenov's Cossacks. These six men had been stripped but apparently tried to fight back as shown by the cuts on their hands and arms. Sword cuts all over their bodies showed a degree of barbarism that would attract attention especially considering the severing of genital organs and limbs. The Czechs retaliated by arresting a number of Russian militia soldiers and officers, many of whom thanked them and then ran away to nearby mountainous area to hide from parties that might be sent to force them back into service with Kolchak's army.[11]

Byers also reported on Semenov's men drowning thirty-one men in Lake Baikal, killing an old woman and her daughter for baking bread that did not taste good, and executing forty people in another town. Russian militiamen ransacked his room and stole personal items when he was not in his room. Byers was in Irkutsk when the Czechs handed over Kolchak to the Bolsheviks.[12]

The most remarkable instance in this string of reports was that reported by 1st Lt. C. I. McNutt, also of the Russian Railway Service Corps. In a report to Colonel Morrow of the Twenty-Seventh Infantry Regiment, McNutt recorded prisoners being transported to an area known as the "slaughter yard" near Adrianovka. He told Morrow of incidents in July 1919 in which a group of thirty-eight men and three women and one of seventeen men and two women were killed. McNutt reported two girls being kidnapped and released after serving as entertainment for Cossack officers. One returned to the train the following day, shot her assailant, and then committed suicide with a revolver. In August 1919, McNutt saw trains with prisoner cars leave the area and later return empty. Trains of forty-one, twenty-nine, twenty-three, and forty-one prisoner cars traveled to the slaughter yard between August 19 and 31 but returned empty. His report contained numerous other examples of beatings and murders by Cossack officers and soldiers with much of the violence directed toward railway employees.[13] This large-scale murder of railway employees and prisoners shows that Cossack brutality was widespread and bound to result in retribution from anyone who could muster the arms to fight.

Semenov and Kalmikov were not the only Cossacks committing atrocities. General Ivanoff-Rinoff sent troops throughout Siberia to maim and torture. At the village of Grodiefka, nine old men were tortured and killed because the village's young men would not respond to Kolchak's mobilization order. The nine men were tortured for two and one-half to three hours before being executed. One man survived the ordeal because the Cossacks thought he was dead. A daughter of one victim reported the incident to Graves, who sent an American officer to investigate. The officer reported the story was true. Inspection of the torture chamber disclosed that the men had been hung by the neck and beaten severely. Blood was splattered all over the room. While the victims were hanging in the room, the Cossacks poured boiling water over their heads. Additional tortures included pencils driven up the nose, cigarette burns, and fingernails pulled out.[14]

Kolchak's representatives in Vladivostok protested Graves's investigation regarding such atrocities. When Graves refused to stop investigating brutality, Kolchak's regional government officials stopped cooperating with the AEF. The majority of the Siberian people looked up to the United States as an example of a representative form of government. But many of Kolchak's supporters (the nobility, large businesses, members of the czar's government, and the wealthy) were opposed to representative government. They were prepared to help the AEF only if the support to the Russian people was funneled through them. American refusal to do so and refusal to commit troops against any faction in the country bred great resentment from Kolchak's government and the privileged elements of society.[15] White Russian disunity precluded their massing sufficient forces to combat the Bolsheviks.

After the World War I armistice, Kolchak's government and Japan conducted a propaganda campaign against the Americans. The intent was to portray the AEF as a Bolshevik supporter in order to force the AEF to fight the Bolsheviks to prove the report untrue. When this failed, the propaganda campaign was used as a way to force the AEF to leave Siberia. One theory was that if Graves attempted to censor the anti-American press, he would be recalled to the United States, given the United States' penchant for freedom of the press. Complaints directly to Kolchak's subordinates, such as General Rozanoff in Vladivostok, were to no avail. However, when Graves reported to the US State Department representative in Omsk that he intended to close the paper in Vladivostok, the propaganda campaign in Vladivostok stopped. Between the overthrow of Rozanoff January 31, 1920, and the departure of the AEF, the tone of the Vladivostok press shifted to a pro-American position.[16]

Conflict with the British

The AEF also experienced problems with the British in Siberia. British general Alfred Knox intended to raise an army and reestablish an Eastern Front. His government promised him arms and equipment for one hundred thousand men. This goal brought the British and Americans into direct conflict. The "Aide Memoire" specified that the United States would not divert any of its military forces from the Western Front as long as the situation there was critical.[17]

Knox caused concern in other ways as well. On October 3, 1918, he announced that the British government claimed most of the supplies at Vladivostok. Therefore, he would be in charge of distributing all military supplies. All the Allies objected to Knox's position, but he refused to consent to the formation of a board with representatives from each of the Allies to govern distribution of the military stores. The Allies never developed a coherent plan to distribute supplies.[18]

The British government was an ardent Kolchak supporter. Winston Churchill announced in the House of Commons that the Kolchak government had been formed "by the British for its own purposes." Knox stayed in Omsk much of the time and tried to show that he was the source of Kolchak's power. This may have backfired in the end, though. Knox disagreed with the AEF neutral position. He even suggested to John Caldwell, the American consul in Vladivostok, that Graves be relieved. In contrast to Knox's position, Graves wrote that a Mr. O'Reilly arrived in Vladivostok to replace the previous British high commissioner and told Graves that he was the only national representative who was carrying out his instructions. Unfortunately a few days later Mr. O'Reilly received notice from London to leave Siberia immediately.[19]

The British support of Kolchak and anti-American attitude apparently resulted mainly due to Knox's opinions. After his departure (December 1919 or January

1920), the British representatives in Siberia criticized Kolchak's regime and previous British policies.[20]

Knox tried to convince all the Allied commanders to place their troops under Otani's command to no avail. When the railway guard mission was being discussed, Knox supported the proposal that the French general Janin command all troops east of Lake Baikal with Otani commanding all forces west of the lake. Had this proposal been accepted by the Americans, the Japanese could have ordered the American guard forces east of Lake Baikal to cease their neutral stance.[21]

Conflict with Japan

Japan announced their goals in Siberia to be the same as those of the United States —noninterference. But Japanese support of the Cossacks was a violation of this neutral pledge. The excuse most often given was that the support to the Cossacks was necessary to "maintain order." Japan supplied money and equipment to the Cossacks and attempted to discredit the United States through propaganda.[22]

The attacks on the AEF by the White Russian leaders ultimately enhanced the AEF's image among many but not all of the common people. They understood the AEF's intentions. This goodwill was further enhanced when the United States was the first Allied power to announce it would withdraw its military forces. Most Russians favored the withdrawal of all the Allied units.[23]

Japanese actions indicated from the beginning that noninterference was not really their policy. The Ussuri campaign was allegedly organized to defeat Austro-Hungarian prisoners of war. However, the Japanese actually fought Bolsheviks. There was no large prisoner of war threat. Japan sought to dominate Siberia for its resources and available land. Economics was the key driver for Japanese actions in Siberia, not helping the Russian people. An American investigation in the Baikal region indicated Semenov killed forty thousand people. One report to Roland B. Morris, ambassador to Japan, by a Russian Railway Service Corps lieutenant McDonald proved Semenov's Cossacks stopped a train loaded with 350 men, women, and children and machine-gunned them. Graves reported that Semenov had "killing stations" in order to satisfy his desire to kill someone every day. This killing of a trainload of prisoners occurred in a time of just under two hours after two Railway Service Corps men were refused their request to accompany the train. The two men the next day traveled to the location of the executions and noted machine-gun shell casings spread over the ground indicating the method used by Semenov's men. The bodies were in two ditches. Arms and legs protruded from one of the ditches.[24]

Japanese collusion with Kolchak's forces was again evidenced when revolutionaries overthrew Rozanoff in Vladivostok on January 31, 1920. Japanese forces attempted to stop the revolutionaries' approach to the city by blocking the railway line from Nikolsk. But the revolutionaries arrived from a different direction and reached Rozanoff's house before the Japanese could interfere. A Japanese general arrived before any shooting and told the revolutionaries to leave because the Allies had decided they would allow no fighting in Vladivostok. However, Eichelberger of the AEF was there and corrected the Japanese officer. The agreement was that Allied troops would only interfere with the revolution to prevent "murder, robbery, and looting." With that, an artillery piece fired one shot at Rozanoff's house. He fled to Oi's house and finally left on a Japanese ship for Japan.[25]

The Japanese, however, did not accept this new government. The Japanese continued to threaten action because the revolutionaries allegedly failed to maintain order, arrested innocent people, and were unfriendly to the Japanese. The Japanese gradually seized the city building by building, street by street until they controlled the entire city.[26]

Even with this ill will between the Japanese and American forces, Graves continued to feel friendly toward the Japanese generals with whom he worked because they always treated him courteously and even awarded him a Japanese decoration. A battalion of Japanese troops was sent to the Vladivostok dock for Graves to inspect before his departure. Generals Oi, Inagaki, and Takayanaga accompanied the battalion.[27]

However, an hour did not pass after Graves's departure on April 1 before the Japanese notified Eichelberger, who had remained in Vladivostok, that they had no intention of immediately departing Siberia. Eichelberger and Graves had noted the Japanese digging fighting positions two days before Graves departed. On April 2, the Japanese raised their flag over fortifications overlooking the city. Then on the night of April 4–5, Japanese units attacked Russian forces throughout the region. Several days later the Japanese claimed that they were acting in self-defense because of having been fired upon. Besides machine-gun fire sweeping the streets, large numbers of Russian civilians were arrested and imprisoned. When Eichelberger departed Vladivostok on April 13, the Japanese were attacking northward along the rail line.[28] Japan elected to retain troops in Siberia until October 1922 when political pressure at home and outside diplomatic pressure forced Japan's withdrawal.[29] The United States left Siberia before Japan because the United States was tired of war. A massive troop deployment would have been necessary to generate sufficient military power to forcibly establish a government for the Russian people. After World War I, there was no general support in the United States for long-term, expensive foreign involvement.

Other Allies

Fortunately for Graves, the Canadians, the Czechs, Chinese, and Italians supported him against the attempts to end his neutrality. Brig. Gen. James H. Elmsley, the Canadian commander, opposed the cruel treatment of the Russian people and repeatedly stood by Graves when under attack by the other Allies. The senior French representative supported the British attempts to end American neutrality. Graves reported that the Italian commander told him that his instructions were to support the American position on all matters. Graves also wrote that Knox referred to Adm. Austin Knight's and his positions on neutrality rather than fighting the Bolsheviks as "being stupid and stubborn." These conflicts with the Allies should have been clear because Graves reported the contradictory motivations early in the intervention.[30]

The Czechs were very friendly to the AEF initially. However, those fighting in the Urals resented the failure of the AEF to join them in establishing a new Eastern Front. This resentment stemmed from broken promises. American consul general De Witt C. Poole at Moscow sent a message to American consul Williams at Samara to tell the Czechs that the Allies supported their holding positions in western Russia. Raymond Teusler, head of the American Red Cross in Siberia, told Gen. Rudolph Gaida, when he was in command of the Czechs, to maintain his position in the Urals. American troops would come to his relief regardless of what other American officials might tell him. US ambassador to Japan, Morris, had just told Gaida that the AEF would not go west of Irkutsk. Teusler's being a cousin of President Wilson's wife seemed to give him the impression that he had the authority to instruct military commanders to take action regardless of the orders that they possessed.[31]

The Czechs in the eastern part of Siberia harbored no resentment toward the Americans. They understood the American position better. Once the Czechs had been helped by the United States to leave Siberia, all were very pro-American.[32]

The Italian troops in Siberia remained in Krasnoyarsk most of the time. Their commander was very critical of Kolchak's officers. The Italians wanted justice for the Russian people and felt Kolchak's supporters were not supplying it. The Chinese played a subordinate role in the intervention. They apparently did not take an active part in debating actions in the country.[33]

Lessons That Should Have Been Learned

The principal lesson to learn from the Siberian intervention is the need for a clear mission that is supported by all elements of the US government and our allies participating in the operation. A failure to provide a clear mission so that soldiers can accomplish something is not only likely to result in failure but also is a moral and leadership failure. Military action always includes the possibility of casualties. No national leader should expect soldiers to die when they cannot define the mission and when other agencies of the government and our allies will interfere with ac-

Table 10. AEF Siberia Casualties

Casualty Type	Number
Killed in action	27
Died of wounds	8
Died of disease and other causes	135
Total dead	170
Wounded	52
Deserted	50

From March, *Nation at War*, p. 132

complishing that very mission. Thankfully, casualties to US units were light considering the number of troops committed and the length of time in-country. A casualty summary is in table 10.[34]

Deaths and injuries were not the only casualties experienced by the AEF. Desertion was a problem. Deserters did not fare well if caught. American soldiers discovered several in Vladivostok at the time of the evacuation and dragged them back to their units for court-martial. Cossack ataman Grigori Semenov captured twelve Americans after the AEF left Vladivostok. One was a lieutenant who had resigned in Vladivostok and tried to go to Verkhne-Udinsk to marry a Russian woman. The other eleven were deserters. The twelve decided to escape rather than face torture and imprisonment at Cossack hands. The ex-lieutenant and one deserter succeeded, walking to China and freedom. The others were killed in the escape attempt.[35]

Support in the United States became a problem over time. The families of draftee soldiers from Illinois petitioned Wilson for their return. This resulted in the replacements mentioned previously, which then caused a training and acclimation problem for the AEF leadership to overcome. The lack of a clear mission, especially after the armistice ending World War I made justifying the presence of the AEF in Siberia difficult. Some feelings back home were supportive of the soldiers in Siberia. AEF soldiers were fortunate that Congresswoman Jeannette Rankin of Montana did not get her way with them. She felt that the AEF soldiers would be too diseased and morally corrupt to be able to live in the United States. Therefore, she suggested that the US government should purchase land in Siberia for the soldiers to settle after discharge. Congress did not agree. Interestingly, Rankin, a pacifist, was the first woman elected to the US Congress. She voted against entry into World War I and against the declaration of war against Japan after the Pearl Harbor attack on December 7, 1941.[36]

The AEF intervention precluded Japanese control of the Trans-Siberian Railroad, which then prevented Japan from controlling the Maritime Provinces. American presence gave the Czechs and Siberians hope that someday their misery would end. Material, medical, and financial aid provided by the AEF elements helped people scattered all over the country.[37]

This intervention was one of the first times in the twentieth century that American military force deployed to a foreign country with an aim to accomplish limited goals. The military did not fully understand what this meant.[38] The State and War Departments did not coordinate their actions. The senior State Department representative, Counsel General Ernest Harris, and Graves viewed each other with mutual contempt. The results were confusion and misunderstanding. One veteran of the expedition recommended that future expeditionary force headquarters have a State Department representative assigned to coordinate political and military activities.[39]

The secretary of war and army chief of staff were pleased with Graves's performance.[40] He was confronted with a confused situation for nineteen months, a poorly defined mission, untrustworthy allies, and no declared enemy (at least initially). Yet he never faltered or turned from the direction his orders provided. He was a remarkable leader.

What about the AEF's mission, its orders? The "Aide Memoire" stated that establishing an Eastern Front against Germany would not serve Russia; it would only make use of Russia.[41] Therefore, establishing such a front was explicitly not a mission of the AEF. Graves complied with this order. He never sent American troops westward to reinforce the Czechs in the Urals, let alone reestablish an Eastern Front.

The "Aide Memoire" stated that intervention was necessary to aid the Czechs who were attempting to leave Siberia.[42] By the time the AEF arrived, the Czechs did not need help. They already controlled the railroad. The Allied intervention delayed the Czech departure because the Czechs stopped moving to Vladivostok in order to prepare to reestablish the Eastern Front. This development was not caused by Graves but resulted from other Allied and American representatives interfering. This original mission, therefore, was not applicable once the AEF landed.

Another AEF mission was to "steady any efforts at self-government or self-defense."[43] There were so many factions vying for power that it was virtually impossible to determine whom to help. White Russians and Bolsheviks abused the local population and promised reforms that were never implemented. The "Aide Memoire" pledged the United States would not interfere with Russian government's activities.[44] Graves's neutrality in the civil war was appropriate based on his instructions. The War Department never ordered Graves to change his policy.

However, as pointed out by Graves, guarding the railroad gave the impression that the AEF was assisting Kolchak. Since Kolchak's forces controlled who could ride trains, the Allied guarding of the rail line benefited Kolchak, not everyone.

Kolchak's brutality turned the Russian people against him. Allied moral and material aid supported Kolchak. Therefore, the Siberian people could not help but conclude that the presence of foreign troops contributed to their abuse. The Russian people experienced horror due to World War I. By the time of the intervention, they were tired of war and tired of suffering at the hands of others. The Soviets promised peace. Therefore, the majority of the Russian people taking an active part in the civil war supported the Soviets rather than Kolchak. The naval blockade of Russia, intended to damage the Bolshevik cause, added to the misery of the Russian civilians.[45] The intervention turned the Communist leaders against the West because the West opposed Soviet rule. Graves commented that most of the atrocities were not committed by the Bolsheviks. In his book about the intervention, Graves wrote that he believed that the "anti-Bolsheviks killed one hundred people in Eastern Siberia, to every one killed by the Bolsheviks." He was convinced that most people believed the wanton murder resulted from Bolshevik actions when in reality the White Russians were at fault for much of this terror through the actions they committed. Other Allies also bore responsibility for actions they sanctioned or ignored.[46]

The "Aide Memoire" also required the AEF to guard military stores, "which may subsequently be needed by Russian forces."[47] Certainly, the AEF guarded those stores under its supervision but lack of Allied cooperation precluded efficient and fair distribution of the supplies. Possession of this military equipment even spurred violence at times.

The soldiers of the AEF also experienced mistrust and poor treatment at the hands of the US government. The lack of coordination between the War and State Departments has been mentioned already. Graves later wrote about apparent communications by individuals in the State Department that he was a weak commander and ill suited for the missions he had. His lack of large-unit command was mentioned as an issue regarding his selection to lead the AEF-Siberia. Negative reports from Russian newspapers were finding their way into the American press and reports within the government. Many of these reports accused the AEF soldiers of actually being Bolsheviks. Graves felt that this was mainly due to his decision not to support Kolchak in his efforts to establish a government.[48]

This concern over Bolshevik influence apparently became so severe that the American government began monitoring the actions of the AEF veterans. Graves reported that about sixty AEF veterans and family members gathered for a dinner in November 1921 at the Commodore Hotel in New York. When an unknown man joined the group, a member of the committee who had organized the dinner inquired as to who he was. This new arrival showed a Department of Justice badge and informed the person questioning his presence that he was there under official orders and that no one should bother him. An inquiry to the hotel assistant manager after the dinner confirmed that the Department of Justice agent had shown the hotel personnel his badge and that they had no choice but to seat him as demanded. Graves was convinced that someone in the government dispatched this agent to observe and report on the actions and comments of the AEF-Siberia veterans. After the Siberian intervention, Graces would command the First Division and the Panama Canal Zone. He provided testimony about the depravity of Semenov before the Senate in 1922. Yet, even with this successful career, he would remain politically suspect until his death in 1940.[49] Imagine the impact today if a federal agent attended a dinner of military veterans in order to spy on them out fear of subversive activities.

Bolshevism, or Communism, remained a force to be confronted. The spread of Communism continued to be a fear of Western democracies and a major factor affecting international relations after both World Wars. Fortunately world domination failed, and the USSR as the successor to Russia eventually collapsed. Looking back to the World War I era, an argument might be made that Western leaders failed to understand the problems within the labor movement in the early twentieth century. The external enemies of opposing states fostered nationalism that prevented an international revolution in Europe.[50]

This review of AEF accomplishments shows that Graves performed his assigned tasks most likely as best anyone could. However, Wilson's intent was unclear. If he wanted the Eastern Front reestablished, he failed. There was no indication that was possible by the time the AEF arrived. If he wanted a democratic government in Russia, he failed. The "Aide Memoire" pledged noninterference in internal affairs. Therefore, Wilson apparently was not prepared to forcibly establish a Russian government. Given that conclusion, the subsequent Communist victory was not a defeat. However, the intervention might have developed differently if the AEF had taken sides. The only clear objective was to help the Czechs, and they did not need help. The other objectives were so nebulous they forced Graves to do nothing. That made the intervention pointless. The sacrifices were for nothing.

The army units that participated in the Siberian intervention had reason to be proud of their service. Given poor instructions, they never shirked their moral and lawful duty to their country. Harsh conditions did not deter them. Unfaithful allies did not stop them. The AEF performed well.

However, political leaders of 1918–20 America had no reason to be proud. They provided a poorly defined mission to the AEF. People died. Equipment was destroyed. Money was wasted. All of this happened for no reason. The United States accomplished nothing in Siberia beyond providing an example of national morality and regard for human life and property (unlike the Cossacks and Japanese). Of course, America's political leaders may have realized the impossibility of the situation in which they placed the AEF. There was little if any benefit from the intervention. Few people today even know it occurred. Learning from any event is difficult when no one discusses it.

The American experience in Siberia provides an example of the problems that can be encountered when military forces are used to achieve limited objectives. The AEF did not deploy to Siberia to destroy the military power of an enemy. Therefore, the lessons from the intervention are useful when examining any military action staged with limited objectives. Political and military goals must be carefully planned and specified. These goals must be coordinated with any allies that will participate. There must be a central authority to lead and coordinate the actions of all forces to avoid conflicts among allies. Sufficient resources must be provided to accomplish the mission. Understanding the situation in the host country before deciding or executing a decision to intervene is important to ensure that resources match the task. Carefully choosing allies is also important. Allies should have complementary political, ideological, and moral objectives. Failure to do these things will doom any intervention to be a waste of time, energy, and resources.

It is unfortunate for the AEF veterans that their efforts served no long-term purpose. They obeyed their country and sacrificed life and limb when necessary. They did not let down America. Whether through lack of experience, knowledge of international realities, or will, the leaders that ordered the AEF to Siberia failed the AEF and this country. They sent American troops to accomplish a mission that was poorly defined. The men of the AEF performed exceptionally well even though faced with an impossible task.

Appendix A: Aide Memoire

The whole heart of the people of the United States is the winning of this war. The controlling purpose of the Government of the United States is to do everything that is necessary and effective to win it. It wishes to cooperate in every practicable way with the allied governments, and to cooperate ungrudgingly; for it has not ends of its own to serve and believes that the war can be won only by common counsel and intimate concert of action. It has sought to study every proposed policy or action in which its cooperation has been asked in this spirit, and states the following conclusions in the confidence that, if it find itself obliged to decline participation in any undertaking or course of action, it will be understood that it does so only because it deems itself precluded from participating by imperative considerations either of policy or of fact.

In full agreement with the allied governments and upon the unanimous advice of the Supreme War Council, the Government of the United States adopted, upon its entrance into the war, a plan for taking part in the fighting on the western front into which all its resources of men and materials were to be put, and put as rapidly as possible, and it has carried out that plan with energy and success, pressing its execution more and more rapidly forward and literally putting into it the entire energy and executive force of the nation. This was its response, its very willing and hearty response, to what was the unhesitating judgment alike of its own military advisers and of the advisers of the allied governments. It is now considering, at the suggestion of the Supreme War Council, the possibility of making very considerable additions even to this immense programme which, if they prove feasible at all, will tax the industrial processes of the United States and the shipping facilities of the whole group of associated nations to the utmost. It has thus concentrated all its plans and all its resources upon this single absolutely necessary object.

In such circumstances it feels it to be its duty to say that it cannot, so long as the military situation on the western front remains critical, consent to break or slacken the force of its present force to other point or objectives. The United States is at a great distance from any other field of action. The instrumentalities by which it is to handle its armies and its stores have at great cost and with great difficulty been created in France. They do not exist elsewhere. It is practicable for her to do a great deal in France; it is not practicable for her to do anything of importance or on a large scale upon any other field. The American Government, therefore, very respectfully requests its Associates to accept its deliberate judgment that it should not dissipate its force by attempting important operations elsewhere.

It regards the Italian front as closely coordinated with the western front, however, and is willing to divert a portion of its military forces from France to Italy if it is the judgment and wish of the Supreme Command that it should do so. It wishes to defer to the decision of the Commander-in-Chief in this matter, as it would wish to defer in all others, particularly because it considers these two fronts so closely related as to be practically but separate parts of a single line and because it would be necessary that any American troops sent to Italy should be subtracted from the number used in France and be actually transported across French territory from the ports now used by the armies of the United States.

It is the clear and fixed judgment of the Government of the United States, arrived at after repeated and very searching reconsiderations of the whole situation in Russia, that military intervention there would add to the present sad confusion in Russia rather than cure it, injure her rather than help her, and that it would be of no advantage in the prosecution of our main design, to win the war against Germany. It cannot, therefore, take part in such intervention or sanction it in principle. Military intervention would, in its judgment, even supposing it to be efficacious in its immediate avowed object of the delivering an attack upon Germany from the east, be merely a method of making use of Russia, not a method of serving her. Her people could not profit by it, if they profited at all, in time to save them from their present distresses, and their substance would be used to maintain foreign armies, not to reconstitute their own. Military action is admissible in Russia, as the Government of the United States sees the circumstances, only to help the Czecho-Slovaks consolidate their forces and get into successful cooperation with their Slavic kinsmen and to steady any efforts at self-government or self-defense in which the Russian themselves may be willing to accept assistance. Whether from Vladivostok or from Murmansk or Archangel, the only legitimate object for which American or allied troops can be employed, it submits, is to guard military stores which may subsequently be needed by Russian forces to render such aid as may be acceptable to the Russians in the organization of their own self-defense. For helping the Czecho-Slovaks there is immediate necessity and sufficient justification. Recent developments have made it evident that that is in the interest of what the Russian people themselves desire, and the Government of the United States is glad to contribute the small force at its disposal for that purpose. It yields, also, to the judgment of the Supreme Command in the matter of establishing a small force at Murmansk, to guard the military stores at Kola and to make it safe for Russian forces to come together in organized bodies in the north. But it owes it to frank counsel to say that it can go no further than these modest and experimental plans. It is not in a position, and has no expectation of being in a position, to take part in organized intervention in adequate force from either Vladivostok or Murmansk and Archangel. It feels that it ought to add, also, that it will feel at liberty to use the few troops it can spare only for the purpose here stated and shall feel obliged to withdraw those forces, in order to add them to the forces at the western front, if the plans in whose execution it is now intended that they shall cooperate should develop into others inconsistent with the policy to which the Government of the United States feels constrained to restrict itself.

At the same time the Government of the United States wishes to say with the utmost cordiality and goodwill that none of the conclusions here stated is meant to wear the least color of criticism of what the other governments associated against Germany may think it wise to undertake. It wishes in no way to embarrass their choices of policy. All that is intended here is a perfectly frank and definite statement of the policy which the United States feels obliged to adopt for herself and in the use of her own military forces. The Government of the United States does not wish it to be understood that in so restricting its own activities it is seeking, even by implication, to set limits to the action or to define the policies of its Associates.

It hopes to carry out the plans for safeguarding the rear of the Czecho-Slovaks operating from Vladivostok in a way that will place it and keep it in close cooperation with a small military force like its own from Japan, and if necessary from other Allies, and that will assure it of the cordial accord of all the allied powers; and it proposes to ask all associated in this course of action to unite in assuring the people of Russia in the most public and solemn manner that none of the governments uniting in action either in Siberia or in northern Russia contemplates any interference of any kind with the political sovereignty of Russia, any intervention of her internal affairs, or any impairment of her territorial integrity either now or hereafter, but that each of the associated powers has the single object of affording such aid as shall be acceptable, and only such aid as shall be acceptable, to the Russian people in their endeavor to regain control of their own affairs, their own territory, and their own destiny.

It is the hope and purpose of the Government of the United States to take advantage of the earliest opportunity to send to Siberia a commission of merchants, agricultural experts, labor advisers, Red Cross representatives, and agents of the Young Men's Christian Association accustomed to organizing the best methods of spreading useful information and rendering education help of a modest sort, in order in some systematic manner to relieve the immediate economic necessities of the people there in every way for which opportunity may open. The execution of this plan will follow and will not be permitted to embarrass the military assistance rendered in the rear of the westward-moving forces of the Czecho-Slovaks.

Department of State,
Washington, July 17, 1918.

Appendix B: AEF Principal Officers

Position	*Date*	*Name*
Commander	August 16, 1918	Col. Henry D. Styer
	September 3, 1918	Maj. Gen. William S. Graves
	July 11, 1919	Col. Frederic H. Sargent
	September 7, 1919	Maj. Gen. William S. Graves
Chief of Staff	September 3, 1918	Lt. Col. Oliver P. Robinson
	September 11, 1918	Maj. Robert L. Eichelberger
	September 17, 1918	Lt. Col. Oliver P. Robinson
	March 30, 1919	Col. Oliver P. Robinson
	September 24, 1919	No Chief of Staff
	September 28, 1919	Col. Joseph D. Leitch
	March 4, 1920	No Chief of Staff
Assistant Chief of Staff	September 3, 1918	Maj. Robert L. Eichelberger
	March 30, 1919	Lt. Col. Robert L. Eichelberger
Intelligence Officer	August 16, 1918	Maj. David P. Barrows
	October 26, 1918	Lt. Col. David P. Barrows
	December 8, 1918	Maj. Robert L. Eichelberger
	January 3, 1919	Lt. Col. David P. Barrows
	March 10, 1919	Maj. Robert L. Eichelberger
	March 30, 1919	Lt. Col. Robert L. Eichelberger
Adjutant General	August 16, 1918	Col. Edwin Landon
	September 15, 1918	Capt. Thomas W. King
	November 8, 1918	Maj. Thomas W. King
	March 30, 1919	Lt. Col. Thomas W. King
Inspector General	August 16, 1918	Lt. Col. Willis V. Morris
	November 11, 1918	Col. Willis V. Morris
	June 5, 1919	Col. Joseph D. Leitch
	March 4, 1920	No Inspector General
Chief Quartermaster	August 16, 1918	Maj. Richard Allen
	August 25, 1918	No Chief Quartermaster
	September 3, 1918	Lt. Col. Gideon H. Williams
	September 29, 1918	Col. Hugh J. Gallagher
	October 8, 1919	Col. William F. Lewis

Chief Surgeon	August 16, 1918	Col. James S. Wilson
	June 5, 1919	Col. William F. Lewis
Chief Engineer Officer	August 16, 1918	Capt. Earle W. Jennings
	March 30, 1919	Maj. Earle W. Jennings
	October 8, 1919	Capt. Harold Van V. Fay
	March 1, 1920	2nd Lt. Robert H. Soule
	March 31, 1920	No Chief Engineer
Judge Advocate	September 3, 1918	Maj. Albert J. Galen
	March 30, 1919	Lt. Col. Albert J. Galen
	June 5, 1919	Maj. George R. McLean
	October 8, 1919	Lt. Col. Philip R. Faymonville.
Chief Ordnance Officer	September 3, 1918	Capt. James A. Lynch
	September 29, 1918	Maj. Philip R. Faymonville
	December 1, 1919	Lt. Col. Philip R. Faymonville
Chief Signal Officer	September 18, 1918	1st Lt. Jones H. Kirk
	March 7, 1919	Capt. Charles Barrett
	September 8, 1919	Capt. William McC. Chapman
	March 31, 1920	No Chief Signal Officer
Commander, Twenty-Seventh Infantry	August 22, 1918	Col. Henry D. Styer
	August 25, 1918	Lt. Col. Charles H. Morrow
	September 7, 1918	Col. Henry D. Styer
	April 11, 1919	Col. Charles H. Morrow
	March 4, 1920	Col. Joseph D. Leitch
Commander, Thirty-First Infantry	August 22, 1918	Col. Frederic H. Sargent
	October 8, 1919	Col. Fred W. Bugbee

(NOTE: The above information was extracted from US Army War College, *Order of Battle of the United States Land Forces in the World War, American Expeditionary Forces* (Washington, DC: Government Printing Officer, 1937), p. 385.

Appendix C: AEF Strength Figures

Date	*Officers*	*Enlisted Men*
August 16, 1918	53	1,537
August 21, 1918	145	4,805
September 2, 1918	188	5,693
September 29, 1918	306	9,257
July 1, 1919	329	8,038
August 29, 1919	326	8,713
October 16, 1919	299	8,643
November 8, 1919	267	7,621
December 31, 1919	264	7,009

(The strength figures above were compiled from information in Packard, "AEF, 1918–1919," and Graves, Report, "Operations 1 July 1919 to 31 March 1920.")

Notes

Chapter 1

1. My early research as a graduate student at the University of Kansas in 1986 provided the foundation for this work. The date of the meeting between Graves and Baker is unclear sometimes in sources about this intervention. Graves, in his book *America's Siberian Adventure 1918–1920* (New York: Jonathan Cape and Harrison Smith, 1931), stated that he received instructions to travel to Kansas City on August 2 (p. 31); however, he also provided an arrival time of 10:00 P.M. with no date (p. 4). In his September 25, 1919, report Graves stated that he received the order to meet with Baker on August 3 and that he arrived in Kansas City on the "following Tuesday." A calendar check shows this Tuesday to be August 6. A memorandum from Graves in 1921 gives August 6 as the date of the meeting (Brigadier William S. Graves, memorandum from Brigadier General Graves to the Adjutant General of the Army, February 14, 1921, National Archives Microfilm Publication M917, Reel 10, National Archives Building, Washington, DC). R. E. Dupuy in *Perish by the Sword* (Harrisburg, PA: Military Service Publishing, 1939) cites Graves's book with August 2 being the date Graves received the order to travel (p. 99). Richard Goldhurst in *The Midnight War* (New York: McGraw-Hill, 1978) provides August 2 as the order receipt day and that Graves faced a two-day trip to Kansas City (p. 76) with no citation reference. Graves's report is in the National Archives Microfilm Publication *Historical Files of the American Expeditionary Forces in Siberia 1918–1920* (Washington, DC: National Archives and Records Service, M017, Reel 10, 1973). Gen. Peyton C. March in *The Nation at War* (Garden City, NY: Doubleday, Doran, 1932) mentioned that Baker explained his need to go to Kansas City as a visit to the "Leavenworth Penitentiary" to meet with conscientious objectors as a way to conceal the meeting with Graves. March stated that Baker met Graves on August 4 (p. 127). When I researched this in 1986, I could find no record of Baker visiting the US Disciplinary Barracks at Fort Leavenworth, Kansas, or the US Federal Penitentiary in Leavenworth, Kansas. In the forward of Graves's book, March wrote that he was visiting the Leavenworth Disciplinary Barracks (p. x).

2. Graves, *America's Siberian Adventure 1918–1920*, pp. 3–4; Clarence A. Manning, *The Siberian Fiasco* (New York: Library Publishers, 1952), p. 80.

3. Virginia C. Westall, "AEF Siberia—The Forgotten Army," *Military Review* 48

(March 1968): 13–15; March, *Nation at War*, p. 127; Robert L. Willett, *Russian Sideshow: America's Undeclared War* (Washington, D.C.: Brassey's), p. 196.

4. US Army Center of Military History, *Lineage and Honors, 27th Infantry* (Fort Lesley J. McNair, Washington, DC: Author), http://www.history.army.mil/html/forcestruc/lineages/ branches/inf/0027in.htm (accessed August 31, 2009); US Army Center of Military History, *Lineage and Honors, 31st Infantry* (Fort Lesley J. McNair, Washington, DC: Author); Lowe, Karl F. *America's Foreign Legion: The 31st Infantry Regiment in War and Peace* (Glen Spey, NY: 31st US Infantry Regiment Association), p. 1, http://www.31stinfantry.org/history.htm (accessed August 31, 2009); James A. Sawicki, *Infantry Regiments of the U.S. Army* (Dumfries, VA: Wyvern Publications, 1981), pp. 10 and 106. The Twenty-Seventh Infantry gained its nickname as the Wolfhounds resulting from a story told by a Russian prisoner. The prisoner insisted that he had outrun a Cossack patrol trying to capture him that also was using wolfhounds as tracking dogs near Spasskoe in August 1919. When he encountered American soldiers, he tried to run away from them initially. An American sentry chased him, caught him, and knocked him down using a rifle butt blow to the head. The prisoner was terrified of soldiers who could outrun wolfhounds after that. A memorandum by Mr. Nick Hochee in a file of papers on the AEF at the US Army Military History Institute provided the story details. The Sawicki regimental histories and the Thirty-First Regiment history relate that regiment nickname to their service in Siberia.

5. "Text of Krushchev Debate with Skouras during the Luncheon at Film Studio," *New York Times*, September 20, 1959, late edition, p. 41.

6. "Transcript of Nixon's Television Address to the Soviet People from the Great Kremlin Palace," *New York Times*, May 29, 1972, late edition, p. 3.

7. Ronald Reagan, *State of the Union Address*, January 25, 1984. http://www.infoplease.com/t/hist/state-of-the-union/198.html (accessed August 23, 2008).

8. David K. Shipler, "How We See Each Other," *New York Times*, November 10, 1985, late edition, p. A33. ProQuest Database (accessed August 20, 2008).

Chapter 2

1. Corelli Barnett, *The Great War* (New York: G. P. Putman's Sons, 1980), pp. 12–15.

2. Ibid., pp. 15–18.

3. Ibid., p. 75.

4. S. L. A. Marshall, *World War I* (New York: American Heritage Press, 1971), pp. 267–68.

5. Ibid., pp. 272–73; Barnett, *The Great War*, p. 112.

6. Marshall, *World War I*, p. 284.

7. Ibid., p. 312.

8. Ibid., pp. 338–39.

9. George F. Kennan, *The Decision to Intervene*, vol. 2 of *Soviet-American Relations, 1917–1920* (Princeton, NJ: Princeton University Press, 1956), p. 5; US Army Center of Military History, *United States Army in the World War 1917–1919: Organization of the American Expeditionary Forces*, vol. 1 (Washington, DC: US Government Printing Office, 1988), p. 341.

10. Marshall, *World War I*, p. 346.

11. Barnett, *The Great War*, pp. 153, 156–57.

12. Ibid., pp. 28–30.

13. Ibid., pp. 110–11.

14. Sophia R. Pelzel, "American Intervention in Siberia, 1918–1920" (PhD dissertation, University of Pennsylvania, 1946), p. 21.

15. Barnett, *The Great War*, p. 108.

16. David R. Francis, *Russia from the American Embassy: April, 1916–November, 1918* (New York: Charles Scribner's Sons, 1921), p. 63.

17. Barnett, *The Great War*, pp. 108–11.

18. Robert J. Maddox, *The Unknown War with Russia: Wilson's Siberian Intervention* (San Rafael, CA: Presidio Press, 1977), p. 15; US Congress, House, *Address of President Wilson to the Congress of the United States, January 8, 1918*, House Doc. 765, 65th Cong., 2d sess., 1918, p. 4; US Congress, Senate, "The Russian Mission," in *Visiting War Missions to the United States from France, Great Britain, Italy, Russia, Belgium, and Japan*, S. Doc. 87, 65th Cong., 1st sess., 1917, pp. 64–65.

19. George F. Kennan, *Russia Leaves the War*, vol. 1 of *Soviet American Relations, 1917–1920* (Princeton, NJ: Princeton University Press, 1956), pp. 16–17.

20. Ibid., p. 10.

21. Richard Luckett, *The White Generals: An Account of the White Movement and the Russian Civil War* (London: Longman Group, 1971), pp. 38–39.

22. Francis, *Russian from the American Embassy*, pp. 94–95.

23. Marshall, *World War I*, pp. 315–18; James L. Stokesbury, *A Short History of World War I* (New York: William Morrow, 1981), p. 209.

24. Barnett, *The Great War*, p. 125.

25. Marshall, *World War I*, p. 320.

26. US Department of State, *Papers Relating to the Foreign Relations of the United States, 1918, Russia*, vol. 1 (Washington, DC: US Government Printing Office, 1931), telegram, Consul at Petrograd to the Secretary of State, 3 July 1917, pp. 99–106.

27. Marshall, *World War I*, p. 320.

28. Elena Varneck and H. H. Fisher, ed., *The Testimony of Kolchak and Other Siberian Materials* (Stanford University, CA: Stanford University Press, 1935), p. 91.

29. William Hard, *Raymond Robins' Own Story* (New York: Harper and Brothers Publishers, 1920), pp. 46, 52.

30. US Department of State, *Papers Relating to the Foreign Relations of the United States, 1918, Russia*, Vol.1, telegram, Ambassador in Russia to the Secretary of State, 6 November 1917, pp. 220–21.

31. Marshall, *World War I*, p. 321.

32. Maddox, *The Unknown War with Russia*, p. 20.

33. Barnett, *The Great War*, p. 127.

34. Maddox, *Unknown War with Russia*, p. 27.

35. Kennan, *Russia Leaves the War*, p. 86.

36. Maddox, *Unknown War with Russia*, p. 32.

37. Francis, *Russia from the American Embassy*, p. 57.

38. Kennan, *Russia Leaves the War*, p. 92.

39. US Department of State, *Papers Relating to the Foreign Relations of the United States, 1917, Supplement 2, The World War*, vol. 1 (Washington, DC: US Government Printing Office, 1932) telegram, Charge in Netherlands to the Secretary of State, 22 August 1917, pp. 169–70.

40. US Department of State, *Papers Relating to the Foreign Relations of the United States, 1918, Russia*, vol. 1, telegram, Consul General at Moscow to the Secretary of State, 18 December 1917, pp. 260–63.

41. US Department of State, *Papers Relating to the Foreign Relations of the United States, 1918, Russia*, vol. 1, telegram, Consul General at Moscow to the Secretary of State, 30 Mar 1918, pp. 442–75.

42. Luckett, *White Generals*, p. 8; Norman Stone, *The Eastern Front 1914–1917* (New York: Charles Scribner's Sons, 1975), pp. 144–53,165, and 223–24.

43. Luckett, *White Generals*, p. 9.

44. Ibid., pp. 9–10.

45. George A. Brinkley, *The Volunteer Army and Allied Intervention in South Russia, 1917–1921* (Notre Dame, IN: University of Notre Dame Press, 1966), p. 14.

46. David McLellan, *Karl Marx: His Life and Thought* (New York: Harper and Row, 1974), pp. 430 and 438–44; Karl Marx, "The Communist Manifesto," in *The World's Great Thinkers, Man and the State: The Political Philosophers*, ed. Saxe Commins and Robert N. Linscott (New York: Random House, 1947), p. 510.

Chapter 3

1. Allen F. Chew, *Fighting the Russians in Winter: Three Case Studies*, Leavenworth Papers, No. 5 (Fort Leavenworth, KS: Combat Studies Institute, US Army Command and General Staff College, December 1981), pp. 1–2; John M. Thompson, *Russia, Bolshevism and the Versailles Peace* (Princeton, NJ: Princeton University Press, 1966) p. 58.

2. Richard Goldhurst, *Midnight War: The American Intervention in Russia, 1918–1920* (New York: McGraw-Hill, 1978), p. 81.

3. US Department of State, *Papers Relating to the Foreign Relations of the United States, 1918, Russia*, vol. 1, telegram, Consul General at Moscow to the Secretary of State, 30 March 1918, p. 444.

4. Major Charles H. Briscoe, "The Prisoner of War Problem in Russia: Justification for Allied Intervention, 1918–1920" (MMAS thesis, US Army Command and General Staff College, Fort Leavenworth, KS, 1977), p. 36; Carl J. Richard, *When the United States Invaded Russia: Woodrow Wilson's Siberian Disaster* (Lanham, MD: Rowman and Littlefield Publishers, 2013), pp. 19–23.

5. Thompson, *Russia, Bolshevism and the Versailles Peace*, p. 10.

6. George Stewart, *White Armies of Russia: A Chronicle of Counter-Revolution and Allied Intervention* (New York: Macmillan, 1933), p. 82.

7. Marx, "The Communist Manifesto," p. 510; Thompson, *Russia, Bolshevism and the Versailles Peace*, pp. 178–79 and 197.

8. Kennan, *The Decision to Intervene*, p. 9.

9. Thompson, *Russia, Bolshevism and the Versailles Peace*, p. 14.

10. Goldhurst, *Midnight War*, p. 22.

11. Ibid., p. 119; Benjamin Isitt, *From Victoria to Vladivostok: Canada's Siberian Expedition, 1917–19* (Vancouver, British Columbia, Canada: UBC Press, 2010), pp. 62 and 65–71; William Appleman Williams, "American Intervention: Strictly Anti-Bolshevik," in *America Intervention in the Russian Civil War*, ed. Betty Miller Unterberger (Lexington, MA: DC Heath, 1969), pp. 83–85.

12. Francis, *Russia from the American Embassy*, pp. 298–301.

13. Major Bruce S. Beals, "Coalition Warfare during the Allied Intervention in North Russia" (MMAS thesis, US Army Command and General Staff College, Fort Leavenworth, KS, 1981), p.11.

14. C. G. Fairfax Channing, *Siberia's Untouched Treasure: Its Future Role in the World* (New York: G. P. Putnam's Sons, 1923), p. 120.

15. Carl W. Ackerman, *Trailing the Bolsheviki: Twelve Thousand Miles with the Allies in Siberia* (New York: Charles Scribner's Sons, 1919), p. 42.

16. Pelzel, "American Intervention in Siberia," p. 29.

17. US Department of State, *Papers Relating to the Foreign Relations of the United States, 1917, Supplement 2, The World War*, vol. 1, message, Acting Secretary of the Treasury to the Secretary of State, 6 July 1917, p. 536.

18. Ibid., message, Assistant Secretary of the Treasury to the Secretary of State, 3 January 1918, p. 592.

19. Kennan, *Russia Leaves the War*, pp. 24–25.

20. US Congress, Senate, *Loans to Foreign Governments*, S. Doc. 86, 67th Cong., 2d sess., 1921, p. 89.

21. Alfred D. Chandler Jr., *The Visible Hand: The Managerial Revolution in American Business* (Cambridge, MA: Belknap Press, 1977), pp. 405, 409.

22. Goldhurst, *Midnight War*, p. 27.

23. Pelzel, "American Intervention in Siberia," pp. 5, 10.

24. Ibid., pp. 8, 10.

25. Goldhurst, *Midnight War*, p. 80.

26. Channing, *Siberia's Untouched Treasure*, p. 75.

27. March, *Nation at War*, p. 124.

28. Pelzel, "American Intervention in Siberia," p. 13.

29. Channing, *Siberia's Untouched Treasure*, p. 75.

30. Pelzel, "American Intervention in Siberia," p. 47.

31. Goldhurst, *Midnight War*, p. 24.

32. Military Attaché, Tokyo, Japan, cablegram to Major D. P. Barrows, Military Intelligence Officer, American Expeditionary Forces, Vladivostok, Siberia, October 26, 1918 (*Japan and America, c1930–1955, The Pacific War and the Occupation of Japan*, series 1, *The Papers of General Robert L. Eichelberger (1886–1971)*, part 4, *Subject Files, Writings, Speeches, Photographs, and Oversize Material*, Rare Book, Manuscript, and Special Collections Library, Duke University, Durham, NC, Adam Matthew Publications Microfilm, M9300, Reel 67.

33. James W. Morley, *The Japanese Thrust into Siberia, 1918* (Freeport, NY: Books for Libraries Press, 1972), pp. 31–37.

34. Dupuy, *Perish by the Sword*, pp. 24–26.

35. US Department of State, *Papers Relating to the Foreign Relations of the United States, 1918*, vol. 1, telegram, Ambassador in Italy to the Secretary of State, 3 May 1918, p. 799.

36. Dupuy, *Perish by the Sword*, p. 30; US, Department of State, *Papers Relating to the Foreign Relations of the United States, 1918*, vol. 1, telegram, Ambassador in Italy to the Secretary of State, 7 May 1918, p. 803.

37. David Brody, *Steelworkers in America: The Nonunion Era* (New York: Harper and Row Publishers, 1960), p. 195.

38. Dupuy, *Perish by the Sword*, pp. 30–31.

39. Ibid., p. 35.

40. Ibid., pp. 39–43.

41. Ibid., pp. 43–46.

42. Ibid., pp. 47–51.

43. Ibid., pp. 51–59.

44. Lieutenant Colonel H. H. Slaughter, "The American Expeditionary Force in Siberia as a Part of Allied Intervention in 1918" (lecture to the Army War College, Washington, DC, March 29, 1934), p. 15.

45. Dupuy, *Perish by the Sword*, pp. 78–79, 82.

46. Maddox, *The Unknown War with Russia*, p. 65.

47. US Department of State, *Papers Relating to the Foreign Relations of the United States, 1918*, vol. 1, telegram, Ambassador in Japan to the Secretary of State, 3 September 1918, pp. 824–25; telegram, Charge in Japan to the Secretary of State, dated 17 September 1918, p. 825; telegram, Ambassador in Paris to the Secretary of State, 16 October 1918, p. 846.

48. Channing, *Siberia's Untouched Treasure*, p. 125.

49. Ackerman, *Trailing the Bolsheviki*, pp. 36–38.

50. Harmon Tupper, *To the Great Ocean: Siberia and the Trans-Siberian Railway* (Boston: Little, Brown, 1965), pp. 235–40.

51. Ibid., pp. 336, 367, 371.

52. Kennan, *Russia Leaves the War*, p. 289.

53. Senate, *American Troops in Siberia*, S. Doc. 60, 66th Cong., 1st sess., 1919, p. 3.

54. Slaughter, "-American Expeditionary Force in Siberia," p. 158.

55. Channing, *Siberia's Untouched Treasure*, p. 158.

56. Bernard Pares, *My Russian Memoirs* (New York: AMS Press, 1969), pp. 507–8.

57. Pelzel, "American Intervention in Siberia," pp. 131–34.

58. Eugene P. Trani, "Woodrow Wilson and the Decision to Intervene in Russia," *Journal of Modern History* 48 (September 1976); 442–43.

59. March, *Nation at War*, pp. 114–15.

60. Trani, "Woodrow Wilson," pp. 449–50; Graves, *America's Siberian Adventure*, pp. 24–26; Richard, *When the United States Invaded Russia*, p. 19; Betty Unterberger, *America's Siberian Expedition, 1918–1920: A Study of National Policy* (New York: Greenwood Press, 1969), p. 46.

61. Keenan, *The Decision to Intervene*, pp. 59, 99–100, 106; Manning, *The Siberian Fiasco*, p. 68.

62. Edwin N. McClellan, "American Marines in Siberia during the World War," *Marine Corps Gazette*, June 1920, pp. 173, 178–80.

63. Ibid., pp. 178–79.

64. Ibid., pp. 179–80.

65. March, *Nation at War*, pp. 116–19.

66. Arthur S. Link, ed., *The Papers of Woodrow Wilson* (Princeton, NJ: Princeton University Press, 1984),vol. 41, letter, Robert Lansing to Woodrow Wilson, 19 March 1917, pp. 425–27; telegram, Lord Reading to David Lloyd George and Others, 2 November 1917, p. 494; memorandum, Woodrow Wilson to Robert Lansing, 3 November 1917, p. 496; vol. 45, telegram, Sir Cecil A. S. Rice to the Foreign Office, 27 December 1917, p. 470; memorandum, Sir Cecil A. S. Rice to Woodrow Wilson, 29 December 1917, pp. 392–93; vol. 46, letter, E. M. House to Woodrow Wilson, 8 March 1918, pp. 576–77; vol. 47, letter, Frank L. Polk to Woodrow Wilson, 14 March 1918, pp. 20–22; Frederick Palmer, *Newton D. Baker: America at War* (New York: Kraus Reprint, 1969), p. 320; Richard, *When the United States Invaded Russia*, pp. 45–47; Graves, *America's Siberian Adventure*, p. 67; Paul Dunscomb, *Japan's Siberian Intervention, 1918–1922: "A Great Disobedience against the People"* (Lanham, MD: Rowman and Littlefield Publishers), p. 66; Unterberger, *America's Siberian Expedition*, p. 67; US Department of State, Telegram from Secretary of State to Russian Embassy in Paris, France, October 5, 1918. Posol'stvo (France) Collection, Box 24, Folder 1, Hoover Institution Archives, Stanford University, Stanford, CA.

67. March, *Nation at War*, pp. 120, 123–24.

68. Ibid., pp. 122, 129.

69. US, Congress, Senate, *American Troops in Siberia*, pp. 4–5.

70. Donald E. Davis and Eugene P. Trani, "The American YMCA and the Russian Revolution," *Slavic Review* 33, no. 3 (1974): 469 and 471–472. Retrieved December 12, 2010, from JSTOR database, http://www.jstor.org/stable/2494734.

71. Clara G. Noyes, "The Red Cross," *American Journal of Nursing* 20, no. 6 (March 1920): 480–81. Retrieved December 12, 2010, from JSTOR database, http://www.jstor.org/stable/3407745.

Chapter 4

1. Stewart, *White Armies of Russia*, pp. 127–28.

2. Ibid., p. 128.

3. Ibid., p. 131.

4. Stewart, *White Armies of Russia*, pp. 131–32; John A. White, *The Siberian Intervention* (New York: Greenwood Press, 1950), pp. 99 and 254; Unterberger, *America's Siberian Expedition*, p. 15.

5. Stewart, *White Armies of Russia*, p. 132.

6. Ibid., pp. 141–43.

7. Stewart, *White Armies of Russia*, pp. 140–41; Graves, *America's Siberian Adventure*, pp. 90–91 and 108.

8. Stewart, *White Armies of Russia*, pp. 144–45.

9. Ibid., p. 145.

10. Ibid., pp. 145–46.

11. Ibid., p. 146.

12. Ibid., pp. 147–50.

13. James Bunyan, *Intervention, Civil War, and Communism in Russia, April–December 1918* (Baltimore: John Hopkins Press, 1936), p. 278.

14. Varneck and Fisher, *Testimony of Kolchak*, pp. 102, 187.

15. Stewart, *White Armies of Russia*, pp. 247, 253.

16. Sylvian G. Kindall, *American Soldiers in Siberia* (New York: Richard R. Smith, 1945), p. 84.

17. Channing, *Siberia's Untouched Treasure*, p. 114.

18. Stewart, *White Armies of Russia*, p. 253; Carol W. Melton, *Between War and Peace: Woodrow Wilson and the American Expeditionary Forces in Siberia, 1918–1920* (Macon, GA: Mercer University Press, 2001), p. 95; N. G. O. Pereira, *White Siberia: The Politics of Civil War* (Montreal: McGill-Queen's University Press, 1996), p. 130.

19. Thompson, *Russia, Bolshevism and the Versailles Peace*, pp. 105–8, 114.

20. Ibid., pp. 119–22.

21. Ibid., pp. 281–82.

22. Seth P. Tillman, *Anglo-American Relations of the Paris Peace Conference of 1919* (Princeton, NJ: Princeton University Press, 1961), 147–48.

23. Goldhurst, *Midnight War*, p. 22.

24. Colonel John Ward, *With the "Die-Hards" in Siberia* (New York: George H. Doran Company, 1920), pp. 17–19.

25.Ibid., p. 22; Miles Hudson, *Intervention in Russia 1918–1920: A Cautionary Tale* (Barnsley, South Yorkshire, Great Britain: Leo Cooper, 2004), pp. 92–95.

26. Ward, *With the "Die-Hards,"* pp. 23, 32.

27. Ibid., p. 41.

28. Goldhurst, *Midnight War*, p. 81.

29. Stewart, *White Armies of Russia*, p. 153.

30. W. P. Coates and Zelda K. Coates, *Armed Intervention in Russia: 1918–1922* (London: Victor Gollancz, 1935), p. 207.

31. Lieutenant Colonel Vladimir Klecanda, "Operations of the Czechoslovak Army in Russia during the Period 1917–1920," trans. Captain Jerry V. Matejka, *Journal of Military Science* (1921): 13.

32. Kennan, *Russia Leaves the War*, p. 305.

33. Headquarters, AEF Siberia, Intelligence Section, newspaper summary, October 28, 1918, p. 3, National Archives Microfilm Publication M917, Reel 3, National Archives Building, Washington, DC.

34. Alfred Knox, "General Janin's Siberian Diary," *Slavonic Review* 3, no. 9 (1925): 724.

35. Ackerman, *Trailing the Bolsheviki*, pp. 175–76.

36. Headquarters, Japanese Army at Vladivostok, letter to the Commanders of the Allied Armies, August 18, 1918, National Archives Microfilm Publication M917, Reel 2, National Archives Building, Washington, DC.; Unterberger, *America's Siberian Expedition*, p. 89.

37. Headquarters, AEF Siberia, memorandum, January 18, 1919, National Archives Microfilm Publication M917, Reel 2, National Archives Building, Washington, DC.; Graves, *America's Siberian Adventure*, pp. 57–59.

38. Stewart, *White Armies of Russia*, p. 35.

39. Bunyan, *Intervention, Civil War, and Communism in Russia*, pp. 226–27, 236–39.

40. Ibid., pp. 266–67.

41. Goldhurst, *Midnight War*, pp. 114–15.

42. L. B. Packard, "The American Expeditionary Forces in Siberia, 1918–1919," Vladivostok, April 1919, National Archives Microfilm Publication M917, Reel 10, National Archives Building, Washington, DC, p. 19.

43. Orlando Figes, "The Red Army and Mass Mobilization during the Russian Civil War 1918–1920," *Past & Present* 129 (November 1990): 168–211. Retrieved December 12, 2009, from JSTOR database, http://www.jstor.org/stable/650938; Major General William S. Graves, Report to the Adjutant General of the Army, "Conditions in Siberia," p. 1, June 4, 1919, William S. Graves Papers, Box 2, Folder GW12, Hoover Institution Archives, Stanford University, Stanford, CA.

44. Figes, "The Red Army," pp. 174–75, 177–80, 184, and 199.

45. Channing, *Siberia's Untouched Treasure*, pp. 189–90.

46. William H. Chamberlin, *1918–1921: From the Civil War to the Consolidation of Power*, vol. 2 of *The Russian Revolution 1917–1921* (New York: Grossett and Dunlap, 1965), pp. 30–32.

47. Ibid., pp. 32–34 and 64–67.

48. Ibid., pp. 72–73.

49. US Department of State, *Papers Relating to the Foreign Relations of the United States, 1918, Russia*, vol. 3, telegram, Ambassador in Russia to the Secretary of State, 12 February 1918, p. 32.

50. Pereira, *White Siberia*, pp. 138–39 and 144; White, *Siberian Intervention*, p. 269; For a personal recollection of a partisan who fought with the Czechs, then for Kolchak, and finally as part of the Bolshevik partisans, see Anton Z. Ovchinnikov's account in "Memoirs of the Red Partisan Movement in the Russian Far East, 1918–1920" in Varneck and Fisher, *Testimony of Kolchak*, pp. 265–328.

51. Pereira, *White Siberia*, pp. 145, 156–59, and 168.

52. Ibid., pp. 274–75 and 278–84.

53. Arthur Banks, *A Military Atlas of the First World War* (New York: Taplinger Publishing, 1975), pp. 34–35.

54. Ibid.

55. US Army Center of Military History, *United States Army in the World War*, pp. 162 and 341.

56. Ibid., pp. 343–44.

Chapter 5

1. Channing, *Siberia's Untouched Treasure*, p. 164.

2. Ibid., p. 325.

3. Ward, *With the "Die-Hards,"* pp. 201–2.

4. US War Department, *Military Monograph on Siberia Containing Information and Route Notes from Vladivostok to Irkutsk* (Washington, DC: Military Intelligence Branch, Executive Division, General Staff, 5 August 1918; Carlisle Barracks, PA: US Army Military History Institute, 17013–5008, Shelf No. 50894, 1974), p. 8.

5. Ibid., p. 9.

6. Ibid.

7. Ibid., p. 10.

8. Kindall, *American Soldiers in Siberia*, p. 53.

9. Ward, *With the "Die-Hards,"* pp. 201–2.

10. Channing, *Siberia's Untouched Treasure*, p. 143.

11. Lieutenant Colonel Fred W. Bugbee, "The AEF in Siberia," in *Monographs of the World War* (Fort Benning, GA: US Army Infantry School, n.d.), p. 634.

12. Major Jewett C. Baker, "A Study of the Supply of the 31st Infantry, A.E.F., Siberia, from August 10, 1918 to April 1, 1920" (Fort Leavenworth, KS: US Army Command and General Staff School, Individual Research Paper No. 87, 1931), pp. 2–4.

13. Major O. R. Rhoads, "A Study of the Operations and Supply of the American Forces in the Suchan Mine Area Siberia, September 1918–January 1020" (Fort Leavenworth, KS: US Army Command and General Staff School, Individual Research Paper No. 90, 1932), pp. 2, 24–25.

14. Channing, *Siberia's Untouched Treasure*, pp. 320–21, 358–59, 441.

15. Ibid., pp. 326, 328–29.

16. Ackerman, *Trailing the Bolsheviki*, p. 43.

17. Baker, "A Study of the Supply of the 31st Infantry," p. 2.

18. Lieutenant Frank L. Hughes, personal letter, 7 November 1984, Knights of Columbus Archives File SC-16–1–169, p. 1.

19. Bugbee, "The AEF in Siberia," p. 633.

20. Ibid.

21. US War Department, *Military Monograph on Siberia*, p. 72.

22. Ibid.

23. Ibid.

24. Ibid., p. 73.

25. Bugbee, "The AEF in Siberia," p. 633.

26. Ibid.

27. Ibid., p. 634

28. Ibid.

29. US War Department, *Military Monograph on Siberia*, p. 6.

30. Ibid.

31. Ibid.

32. Rhoads, "Study of the Operations and Supply," pp. 24–25.

33. Ibid., pp. 25–26.

34. Ackerman, *Trailing the Bolsheviki*, pp. 45–46.

35. Ibid., p. 47.

36. Ibid., pp. 47–48; Richard, *When the United States Invaded Russia*, pp. 112–13 and 121–23; Melton, *Between War and Peace*, p. 153.

37. Ackerman, *Trailing the Bolsheviki*, pp. 48–49.

38. Ibid., pp. 52–53.

39. Ibid., pp. 59–60.

40. US War Department, *Military Monograph on Siberia*, pp. 1–4.

41. Ibid., p. 4.

42. Michael R. Kamiske, letter to the author, February 4, 1986. In the letter, Mr. Kamiske provided a newspaper clipping with a handwritten annotation indicating publication in the *Spokane Daily Chronicle* on February 18, 1974. In his interview for the article Mr. Kamiske stated that he had received a letter in December 1973 indicating that the Russian Railway Service Corps veterans were now considered military veterans. Also see Joe Michael Feist's article "Theirs Not to Reason Why: The Case of the Russian Railway Service Corps," *Military Affairs* 42 (February 1978): 1–6. Feist reported that the issue of the Russian Railway Service Corps men being veterans was not resolved until a lawsuit was won in 1971 (*Hoskin vs. Resor*). The government appealed but lost again before the US Court of Appeals in 1973. Feist also noted that only thirty-three of the Russian Railway Service Corps veterans were alive when finally awarded army veteran status for their World War I service.

Chapter 6

1. US Congress, House, Hearing, Committee on Military Affairs. Russian Railway Service Corps, House S. 28, 67th Cong., 2d sess., January 17, 1922, p. 26. Retrieved November 8, 2009, from Google Books.

2. US Congress, House, Hearing, Committee on Military Affairs, Russian Railway Service Corps, House S. 28, 67th Cong., 2d sess., Part 3, February, 9, 1923, p. 9. Retrieved November 8, 2009, from Google Books.

3. Ibid.

4. US Congress, House, Hearing, Committee on Military Affairs,, January 17, 1922, p. 49, and February, 9, 1923, p. 10.

5. US Congress, House, Hearing, Committee on Military Affairs, February, 9, 1923, pp. 10–11.

6. US Congress, House, Hearing, Committee on Military Affairs, January 17, 1922, pp. 26–27; Willett, *Russian Sideshow*, pp. 154–55.

7. US Congress, House, Hearing, Committee on Military Affairs, January 17, 1922, p. 25.

8. Ibid. p. 29.

9. Ibid.

10. US Congress, House, Hearing, Committee on Military Affairs, February, 9, 1923, pp. 2–3.

11. US Congress, House, Hearing, Committee on Military Affairs, January 17, 1922, p. 29.

12. Ibid., pp. 35–36.

13. US Congress, House, Hearing, Committee on Military Affairs, January 17, 1922, pp. 41, 54; Second Lieutenant William C. Jones, diary, November 26 and December 14, 1917. Retrieved November 10, 2009, from http://nortvoods.net/rrs/japan/journal-1.htm.

14. US Congress, House, Hearing, Committee on Military Affairs, January 17, 1922, pp. 53–59.

15. US Congress, House, Hearing, Committee on Military Affairs, January 17, 1922, pp. 41, 54, and February, 9, 1923, pp. 2–3.

16. Lane R. Earns, *Where Do We Go from Here: The Russian Railway Service Corps in Nagasaki*. Retrieved November 26, 2009, from www.uwosh.edu/faculty_staff/earns/rrsc.html.

17. Ibid.

18. Ibid.

19. Jones, diary, December 19, 1917.

20. US Congress. House. Hearing. Committee on Military Affairs. Russian Railway Service Corps. House S. 28, 67th Cong., 2d sess., January 17, 1922, pp. 41, 54; US Congress. House. Hearing. Committee on Military Affairs. Russian Railway Service Corps. House S. 28, 67th Cong., 2d sess., Part 3, February, 9, 1923, pp. 2–3; Lane R. Earns, *Where Do We Go from Here: The Russian Railway Service Corps in Nagasaki.*

21. US Congress, House, Hearing, Committee on Military Affairs, February, 9, 1923, pp. 2–3.

22. Ibid., p. 3.

23. Ibid.

24. Ibid.

25. Ibid.

26. Ibid., p. 4.

27. Ibid.

28. Ibid.

29. Ibid.

30. Ibid.

31. Ibid., pp. 4 and 22.

32. Jones, diary, October 15, 1918.

Chapter 7

1. US War Department, memorandum for the Chief of Staff, Office of the Chief of Staff, Washington, DC, July 6, 1918, p. 1, National Archives Microfilm Publication M917, Reel 1, National Archives Building, Washington, DC.

2. Ibid., p. 2.

3. Ibid., pp. 2–3.

4. Admiral A. M. Knight, Vice Admiral Hirogan Kato, Captain Payne, Colonel Paris, Captain K. L. Lin, and Captain Badyovea, "The Allies' Proclamation," Vladivostok, July 6,

1918, National Archives Microfilm Publication M917, Reel 1, National Archives Building, Washington, DC.

5. US War Department, telegram, War Department to Commanding General, 8th Division, Camp Fremont, August 3, 1918, p. 1, National Archives Microfilm Publication M917, Reel 1, National Archives Building, Washington, DC.

6. Ibid., pp. 1–2.

7. US War Department, memorandum for the Adjutant General, War Department, Washington, DC, August 5, 1918, National Archives Microfilm Publication M917, Reel 1, National Archives Building, Washington, DC.

8. Headquarters, Philippine Department, General Order Number 48, Manila, PI, August 6, 1918, National Archives Microfilm Publication M917, Reel 2, National Archives Building, Washington, DC.

9. Headquarters, Philippine Department, General Order Number 50, Manila, PI, August 12, 1918, National Archives Microfilm Publication M917, Reel 2, National Archives Building, Washington, DC.

10. Packard, "AEF, 1918–1919," p. 7.

11. Headquarters, AEF Siberia, AEF War Diary, August 14, 1918, National Archives Microfilm Publication M917, Reel 2, National Archives Building, Washington, DC.

12. Packard, "AEF, 1918–1919," p. 8.

13. Headquarters, AEF Siberia, AEF War Diary, August 16, 1918, National Archives Microfilm Publication M917, Reel 2, National Archives Building, Washington, DC.

14. Kindall, *American Soldiers*, p. 17.

15. Headquarters, Japanese Army in Vladivostok.

16. Headquarters, AEF Siberia, telegram from Colonel Henry Styer to Adjutant General of the Army, August 24, 1918, National Archives Microfilm Publication M917, Reel 2, National Archives Building, Washington, DC.

17. Headquarters, AEF Siberia, AEF War Diary, August 16, 1918.

18. Headquarters, AEF Siberia, AEF War Diary, August 17, 1918, National Archives Microfilm Publication M917, Reel 2, National Archives Building, Washington, DC.

19. Headquarters, AEF Siberia, telegram from Major General Graves to Adjutant General of the Army, September 2, 1918, National Archives Microfilm Publication M917, Reel 2, National Archives Building, Washington, DC.

20. Packard, "AEF, 1918–1919," pp. 63–64.

21. Ibid., pp. 62–63.

22. US Army Center of Military History, *United States Army in the World War*, pp. 343–44.

23. Packard, "AEF, 1918–1919," pp. 63–64.

24. Ibid., pp. 64–65; Lieutenant Colonel Robert L. Eichelberger, "Final Report on the Operations of the Intelligence Section of the A.E.F. Siberia," October 20, 1920, in *Japan and America, c1930–1955, The Pacific War and the Occupation of Japan*, series 1, *The Papers of General Robert L. Eichelberger (1886–1971)*, part 4, *Subject Files, Writings, Speeches, Photographs, and Oversize Material*, from the Rare Book, Manuscript, and Special Collections Library, Duke University, Durham, NC, Adam Matthew Publications Microfilm, M9300, Reel 71, p. 3.

25. Packard, "AEF, 1918–1919," pp. 65–66.

26. Ibid., pp. 66–67.

27. Captain Howard P. Kingmore, Signal Corps Photographic Unit attached to AEF Siberia, report, Vladivostok, February 7, 1919, National Archives Microfilm Publication M917, Reel 11, National Archives Building, Washington, DC.

28. Packard, "AEF, 1918–1919," pp. 68–70.

29. Colonel James S. Wilson, "Medical History of the Siberian Expedition," undated, pp. 16–17, National Archives Microfilm Publication M917, Reel 11, National Archives Building, Washington, DC.

30. Chief Quartermaster, AEF Siberia, "Report of Operations," January 30, 1919, p. 2, National Archives Microfilm Publication M917, Reel 11, National Archives Building, Washington, DC.

31. Wilson D. Keenan, personal letter concerning his brother, Homer Keenan in the AEF Siberia, January 20, 1986.

32. Chief Quartermaster, AEF Siberia, "Report of Operations," January 30, 1919, p. 2.

33. Baker, "A Study of the Supply of the 31st Infantry," p. 7.

34. Supply Company, 31st Infantry, memorandum to Adjutant, 31st Infantry, February 1, 1919 (National Archives Microfilm Publication M917, Reel 10), National Archives Building, Washington, DC.

35. Major General William S. Graves, Report to the Adjutant General of the Army, "Operations to June 30, 1919," Vladivostok, September 25, 1919, p. 21 (National Archives Microfilm Publication M917, Reel 10), National Archives Building, Washington, D.C.

36. Chief Quartermaster, AEF Siberia, "Report of Operations," January 30, 1919, pp. 2–3.

37. Ibid., pp. 6–10.

38. Packard, "AEF, 1918–1919," p. 72.

39. US War Department, telegram, War Department to Commanding General, 8th Division, Camp Fremont, August 6, 1918, National Archives Microfilm Publication M917, Reel 1, National Archives Building, Washington, DC.

40. Ordnance Department, AEF Siberia, "Report of Operations of the Ordnance Department, AEF Siberia, July 1, 1919 to December 31, 1919," p. 2, National Archives Microfilm Publication M917, Reel 11, National Archives Building, Washington, DC.

41. Ordnance Department, AEF Siberia, "Report of Operations," December 31, 1918, pp. 2–3, National Archives Microfilm Publication M917, Reel 11, National Archives Building, Washington, DC.

42. Ordnance Department, AEF Siberia, "Report of Operations, January 1, 1919–June 30, 1919," February 25, 1920, p. 2, National Archives Microfilm Publication M917, Reel 11, National Archives Building, Washington, DC.

43. US War Department, *Handbook of the Browning Rifle, Model of 1918 (Air Cooled)* (Washington, DC: Government Printing Office, 1918), pp. 11, 38.

44. US War Department, *Technical Training Handbook of the Browning Automatic Rifle Model of 1918 (Air Cooled)* (Washington, DC: Government Printing Office, 1918), pp. 13, 49.

45. US War Department, *Handbook on Machine Gun Cart Model 1917* (Washington, DC: Government Printing Office, 1918), pp. 7–8.

46. Ibid., pp. 8–11.

47. Ibid., pp. 11–12.

48. US War Department, *Provisional Instruction for the 37mm Gun Model 1916 R.F.* (Washington, DC: Government Printing Office, 1918), pp. 3, 7, 21–22, 91.

49. Channing, *Siberia's Untouched Treasure*, pp. 205–6.

50. US War Department, *Basic Weapons, Part One, Rifle Company, Rifle Marksmanship*, vol. 3 of *Basic Field Manuel* (Washington, DC: Government Printing Office, 1932), p.1.

51. Kindall, *American Soldiers*, p. 118.

52. US War Department, *Manual of the Automatic Pistol Caliber .45* (Washington, DC: Government Printing Office, 1918), p. 13.

53. Major General William S. Graves, Report to the Adjutant General of the Army, "Operations July 1, 1919 to March 31, 1920," Fort McKinley, Philippine Islands, May 26, 1920, p. 6, National Archives Microfilm Publication M917, Reel 10, National Archives Building, Washington, DC.

54. Baker, "A Study of the Supply of the 31st Infantry," p. 11.

55. Packard, "AEF 1918–1919," p. 72.

56. Kindall, *American Soldiers*, p. 56.

57. Graves, "Operations July 1, 1919 to March 31, 1920," p. 6.

58. Hard, *Raymond Robins' Own Story*, pp. 10, 60–61.

59. Goldhurst, *Midnight War*, p. 84.

60. Channing, *Siberia's Untouched Treasure*, p. 122.

61. Foster R. Dulles, *The American Red Cross* (New York: Harper and Brothers, 1950) pp. 210–11.

62. Virginia C. Westall, "AEF Siberia—The Forgotten Army," *Military Review* 48 (March 1968): 15.

63. Emerson, memorandum to Graves and American Red Cross, December 5, 1918.

64. Channing, *Siberia's Untouched Treasure*, p. 135.

65. US Army, TV 612, *The American Expeditionary Forces in Siberia*, motion picture, Big Picture series, 1964.

66. John J. Noll, " Wolfhounds Pick a Winner," *American Legion Monthly*, September 1934, p. 34.

67. Kindall, *American Soldiers*, pp. 231–32.

68. American Library Association, Library War Service, letter to Commanding General, AEF Siberia, Vladivostok, May 6, 1919, National Archives Microfilm Publication M917, Reel 1, National Archives Building, Washington, DC.; Davis and Trani, "The American YMCA," 476–85.

69. Graves, *America's Siberian Adventure*, p. 141.

70. Knights of Columbus, "Report of the Supreme Board of Directors, Knights of Columbus, for Fiscal Year Ending June 30, 1920," New Haven, CT, Knights of Columbus Archives File SC-16-1, August 3, 1920, pp. 36–37.

71. John Raymond, "Christmas Ship for Siberia," *Columbiad*, December 1919, p. 10.

72. Graves, "Operations July 1, 1919 to March 31, 1920," pp. 6–7.

73. US Army, TV 612, *AEF in Siberia.*

74. Ward, *With the "Die-Hards,"* pp. 58–65.

75. Headquarters, AEF Siberia, Intelligence Section, newspaper summary, October 21, 1918, p. 3, National Archives Microfilm Publication M917, Reel 3, National Archives Building, Washington, DC.

76. Tupper, *To the Great Ocean*, p. 388.

77. Ibid., p. 374.

78. Ward, *With the "Die-Hards,"* p.54.

79. Kindall, *American Soldiers*, pp. 112–13.

80. Headquarters, AEF Siberia, AEF War Diary, March 8, 1919, "Notes on Armored Trains in Use in Siberia," p. 1, National Archives Microfilm Publication M917, Reel 5, National Archives Building, Washington, DC.

81. Ibid.

82. Headquarters, AEF Siberia, "Memorandum of Conversation with General Nicolas Kholovof," p. 1, National Archives Microfilm Publication M917, Reel 5, National Archives Building, Washington, DC.

83. Ibid.

84. Ibid, p. 2.

85. Ibid., pp. 2–3.

86. Kindall, *American Soldiers*, pp. 105–6.

87. Ibid., pp. 118–20.

88. Ibid., pp. 163–64; Channing, *Siberia's Untouched Treasure*, pp. 207, 266–68.

89. Ward, *With the "Die-Hards,"* p. 215.

90. Channing, *Siberia's Untouched Treasure*, pp. 123, 169.

91. Kindall, *American Soldiers*, p. 85.

92. Channing, *Siberia's Untouched Treasure*, p. 229.

93. Ibid., pp. 230–32.

94. Ibid., pp. 134–37.

95. Kindall, *American Soldiers*, pp. 153–60.

96. Ibid., pp. 199–200, 219, 225.

97. Ibid., p. 199.

98. Channing, *Siberia's Untouched Treasure*, p. 156.

99. William H. Chamberlin, *1918–1921: From the Civil War to the Consolidation of Power*, vol. 2 of *The Russian Revolution 1917–1921* (New York: Grossett and Dunlap, 1965), pp. 84–87.

100. Ibid., pp. 87–88.

101. Ibid., pp. 88–90.

102. Ibid., pp. 90–93.

103. Luckett, *White Generals*, p. 165.

104. Ibid., pp. 167–69.

105. Ibid., pp. 169–70.

106. Luckett, *White Generals*, p. 173; Paul Dotsenko, *The Struggle for a Democracy in*

Siberia, 1919–1920 (Stanford University, Stanford, CA: Hoover Institution Press, 1983), p. 122.

Chapter 8

1. Captain George A. Hunt, *The History of the Twenty-Seventh Infantry* (Honolulu: Honolulu Star-Bulletin, 1931), pp. 49–50.

2. Captain Frank Brezina, Headquarters, AEF Siberia, Intelligence Office, *Intelligence Diary August 7 to 17, 1918*, August 17, 1918 (*Japan and America, c1930–1955, The Pacific War and the Occupation of Japan*, series 1, *The Papers of General Robert L. Eichelberger (1886–1971)*, part 4, *Subject Files, Writings, Speeches, Photographs, and Oversize Material.* Rare Book, Manuscript, and Special Collections Library, Duke University, Durham, NC, Adam Matthew Publications Microfilm, M9300, Reel 67, p. 1.

3. Ibid., pp. 1–2.

4. Hunt, *The History of the Twenty-Seventh Infantry*, p. 50; Packard, "AEF, 1918–1919," p. 27.

5. 27th Infantry Regiment, "History of the Twenty-Seventh US Infantry" (Schofield Barracks, HI: 27th Infantry Regiment, 1922), p. 10; Eichelberger, "Final Report," pp. 1–2.

6. Hunt, *The History of the Twenty-Seventh Infantry*, p. 51; Eichelberger, "Final Report," pp. 1–2.

7. Headquarters, AEF Siberia, report for General Otani, Imperial Japanese Army, August 23, 1918, National Archives Microfilm Publication M917, Reel 2, National Archives Building, Washington, DC; Graves, *America's Siberian Adventure*, pp. 52 and 60–61.

8. Headquarters, AEF Siberia, Vladivostok, Field Order No. 1, August 24, 1918, National Archives Microfilm Publication M917, Reel 2, National Archives Building, Washington, DC; Packard, "AEF, 1918–1919," pp. 22–23.

9. Kindall, *American Soldiers*, pp. 62–63.

10. Hunt, *The History of the Twenty-Seventh Infantry*, p. 51.

11. Captain Ira C. Nicholas, "A Critical Analysis of the AEF, Siberia, Including Relations with Other Allies" (Fort Leavenworth, KS: US Army Command and General Staff School, Individual Research Paper, 1932), p. 12; Packard, "AEF, 1918–1919," pp. 34–38.

12. Captain Frank Brezina, Headquarters, AEF Siberia, Intelligence Office, *Weekly Summary August 25–31, 1918*, August 31, 1918 (*Japan and America, c1930–1955, The Pacific War and the Occupation of Japan*, series 1, *The Papers of General Robert L. Eichelberger (1886–1971)*, part 4, *Subject Files, Writings, Speeches, Photographs, and Oversize Material.* Rare Book, Manuscript, and Special Collections Library, Duke University, Durham, NC, Adam Matthew Publications Microfilm, M9300, Reel 67), pp. 4–5.

13. 27th Infantry, "History of the Twenty-Seventh US Infantry," p. 11.

14. 27th Infantry, "History of the Twenty-Seventh US Infantry," p. 11; Headquarters, AEF Siberia, AEF War Diary, September 3, 1918, General Headquarters, Bureau of Information, Communiqué Number 16, dated September 3, 1918, National Archives Microfilm Publication M917, Reel 2, National Archives Building, Washington, DC.

15. Ibid.

16. Ibid., p. 12.

17. Ibid.

18. Ibid.

19. Headquarters, Japanese Army, Vladivostok, letter from General Otani to Major General Graves, September 28, 1918, National Archives Microfilm Publication M917, Reel 1, National Archives Building, Washington, DC; Headquarters, 27th Infantry Regiment, letter from Colonel Henry Styer to General Uehara, Japanese Army chief of staff, September 26, 1918, (National Archives Microfilm Publication M917, Reel 1), National Archives Building, Washington, DC.

20. 27th Infantry, "History of the Twenty-Seventh Infantry," p. 12; Hunt, *The History of the Twenty-Seventh Infantry*, pp. 55–56.

21. 27th Infantry, "History of the Twenty-Seventh Infantry," p. 12; Hunt, *The History of the Twenty-Seventh Infantry*, p. 55.

22. Headquarters, AEF Siberia, Intelligence Section, Intelligence Summary Number 15, September 27, 1918, pp. 1–2 (National Archives Microfilm Publication M917, Reel 2), National Archives Building, Washington, D.C.

23. 27th Infantry, "History of the Twenty-Seventh Infantry," p. 12; Hunt, *The History of the Twenty-Seventh Infantry*, p. 55.

24. William D. Leipold, "America's Siberian Expedition 1918–1920" (Fort Leavenworth, KS: US Army Command and General Staff College, student paper, 1981), p. 6.

25. Dorothea York, *The Romance of Company A, 339th Infantry* (Detroit, MI: McIntrye Printing Company, 1923), p. 23.

26. Bugbee, "The AEF in Siberia," p. 637.

27. 31st Infantry Regiment, "Twenty-Third Anniversary Organization Day, 1916–1939 Program" (Manila, PI: 31st Infantry Regiment, 1939), p. 7.

28. Headquarters, AEF Siberia, Vladivostok, note, August 22, 1918, National Archives Microfilm Publication M917, Reel 2, National Archives Building, Washington, DC.

29. Frank A. Paul, *Regimental History, Thirty-First US Infantry, July 1916—July 1920* (Manila, PI: 31st Infantry Regiment, 1920), p. 15.

30. 31st Infantry, "Twenty-Third Anniversary Program," p. 7.

31. Paul, *Regimental History, Thirty-First US Infantry*, p. 15.

32. Rhoads, "Study of the Operations and Supply," pp. 1–2.

33. Ibid., p. 2.

34. Packard, "AEF, 1918–1919," pp. 73–74.

35. Ibid., pp. 74–75; A slightly different listing of guard details was provided by Rhoads in his "Study of the Operations and Supply." Rhoads states one squad from M Company was left at Kanguaz, forty M Company soldiers were stationed at Tigrovia, a Chinese company was at Fanza, a Japanese company was at Mine No. 2, and the American headquarters element with the remainder of M Company was at Mine No. 1.

36. Packard, "AEF, 1918–1919," p. 75.

37. Ibid., pp. 75–76.

38. Ibid., pp. 76–77.

39. Ibid., pp. 77–78.

40. Ibid., p. 78.

41. Rhoads, "Study of the Operations and Supply," p. 3.

42. Headquarters, AEF Siberia, Intelligence Section, memorandum for Major Barrows, October 20, 1919, National Archives Microfilm Publication M917, Reel 2, National Archives Building, Washington, DC.

43. Goldhurst, *Midnight War*, pp. 33, 60.

44. Graves, Report, "Operations to June 30, 1919," p. 5.

45. Headquarters, AEF Siberia, memorandum, January 18, 1919.

46. Graves, Report, "Operations to June 30, 1919," pp. 7–8.

47. Headquarters, AEF Siberia, letter from Major General Graves to General Otani, September 9, 1918, National Archives Microfilm Publication M917, Reel 1, National Archives Building, Washington, DC.

48. Graves, Report, "Operations to June 30, 1919," p. 6; Manning, *The Siberian Fiasco*, pp. 94–95.

49. Packard, "AEF, 1918–1919," p. 68.

50. Ibid., p. 69.

51. Ibid., p. 91.

52. Ibid.

53. Ibid., pp. 95–96.

54. Ibid., pp. 88–89.

55. Ibid., pp. 22–24.

56. Headquarters, AEF Siberia, Intelligence Section, Memorandum, Strategic Situation, October 17, 1918, pp. 1–2, National Archives Microfilm Publication M917, Reel 2, National Archives Building, Washington, DC.

57. Headquarters, AEF Siberia, Intelligence Section, Memorandum, Friendly Russian Forces in Eastern European Russia, October 11, 1918, pp. 1–4, National Archives Microfilm Publication M917, Reel 2, National Archives Building, Washington, DC.

58. Headquarters, AEF Siberia, Vladivostok, letter, September 6, 1918, National Archives Microfilm Publication M917, Reel 1, National Archives Building, Washington, DC.

59. Headquarters, AEF Siberia, Vladivostok, memorandum, September 18, 1918, National Archives Microfilm Publication M917, Reel 1, National Archives Building, Washington, DC.

60. Chamberlin, *1918–1921*, pp.15–19.

61. Ibid., pp. 20–23.

62. Luckett, *White Generals*, pp. 198–99; Chew, *Fighting the Russians*, p. 1.

63. E. M. Halliday, *The Ignorant Armies* (New York: Harper and Brothers, 1958), pp. 26–27; Luckett, *White Generals*, p. 201.

64. Halliday, *Ignorant Armies*, pp. 28–29; Chew, *Fighting the Russians*, p. 2.

65. Jones, diary, August 16, August 26 to September 16, and October 13, 1918.

66. Ibid., October 30, 1918.

67. Ibid.

68. Headquarters, AEF Siberia, Intelligence Section. Weekly Intelligence Summary, September 15–21, 1918, dated September 21, 1918 (National Archives Microfilm Publication M917, Reel 2), National Archives Building, Washington, D.C., p. 1.

69. Headquarters, AEF Siberia, Intelligence Section. Memorandum, October 6, 1918 (National Archives Microfilm Publication M917, Reel 2), National Archives Building, Washington, D.C., pp. 1–2.

Chapter 9

1. Headquarters, AEF Siberia, letter from Major General Graves to the Commanding General and the Adjutant General, October 31, 1918, National Archives Microfilm Publication M917, Reel 1, National Archives Building, Washington, DC.

2. Channing, *Siberia's Untouched Treasure*, pp. 225–26; Richard, *When the United States Invaded Russia*, p. 171.

3. Thompson, *Russia, Bolshevism, and the Versailles Peace*, pp. 12–13.

4. Brody, *Steelworkers in America*, p. 247.

5. Lieutenant Colonel David P. Barrows, telegram to Major Eichelberger, December 21, 1918, National Archives Microfilm Publication M917, Reel 4, National Archives Building, Washington, DC.

6. Ibid.

7. Lieutenant Colonel David P. Barrows, letter to Director of Military Intelligence, Washington, D.C., February 5, 1919, National Archives Microfilm Publication M917, Reel 4, National Archives Building, Washington, DC.

8. Nicholas, "Critical Analysis of the AEF," p. 13.

9. Hunt, *The History of the Twenty-Seventh Infantry*, pp. 56–58; 27th Infantry, "History of the Twenty-Seventh US Infantry," pp. 15, 18.

10. 27th Infantry, "History of the Twenty-Seventh Infantry," p. 13.

11. Ibid.

12. Ibid.

13. Ibid., p. 14.

14. Ibid.

15. Ibid., p. 15.

16. Ibid., p. 16.

17. Ibid., p. 17.

18. Ibid.

19. Ibid., p. 18.

20. Hunt, *The History of the Twenty-Seventh Infantry*, p. 58.

21. Ibid.

22. Kindall, *American Soldiers*, pp. 20, 23–25.

23. Ibid., p. 26

24. Ibid., p. 27

25. Ibid., pp. 30–31.

26. 27th Infantry, "History of the Twenty-Seventh US Infantry," p. 19.

27. Packard, "AEF, 1918–1919," pp. 103–4.

28. Ibid., p. 104.

29. Ibid., p. 105.

30. Ibid., p. 105; Headquarters, AEF Siberia, AEF War Diary, December 21, 1918, report from the Intelligence Officer at Khabarovsk to Intelligence Officer, AEF, Khabarovsk, December 6, 1918, National Archives Microfilm Publication M917, Reel 4, National Archives Building, Washington, DC.

31. Packard, "AEF, 1918–1919," p. 106.

32. Ibid., p. 106; Headquarters, AEF Siberia, AEF War Diary, multiple telegrams in AEF War Diary, February 8, 1919, p. 108, National Archives Microfilm Publication M917, Reel 4, National Archives Building, Washington, DC.

33. Packard, "AEF, 1918–1919"; Headquarters, AEF Siberia, AEF War Diary, February 8, 1919, letter from Major General Graves to Major General Inagaki, January 30, 1919, p. 109, National Archives Microfilm Publication M917, Reel 4, National Archives Building, Washington, DC.

34. Packard, "AEF, 1918–1919," pp. 110–11.

35. 27th Infantry, "History of the Twenty-Seventh US Infantry," pp. 16, 20.

36. Packard, "AEF, 1918–1919," p. 112; Headquarters, AEF Siberia, AEF War Diary, February 8, 1919, telegram, Styer to Amex.

37. Packard, "AEF, 1918–1919," p. 113.

38. Ibid., pp. 106, 113.

39. Ibid., pp. 114–16.

40. Ibid., pp. 117–18.

41. Headquarters, AEF Siberia, Intelligence Section, Memorandum, Currency Conditions—Khabarovsk to Ushumun, October 20, 1918, p. 1, National Archives Microfilm Publication M917, Reel 2, National Archives Building, Washington, DC.

42. Ibid.

43. Ibid.

44. Headquarters, AEF Siberia, Intelligence Section. Memorandum, Economic Conditions as Far North as Ushumun, October 20, 1918, National Archives Microfilm Publication M917, Reel 2, National Archives Building, Washington, DC.

45. Paul, *Regimental History*, p. 16; Headquarters, Allied Mine Guard, AEFS, Suchan Mines. January 7, 1919. Report in Compliance with Memorandum No. 48, AEFS, dated November 25, 1918, p. 5, National Archives Microfilm Publication M917, Reel 10, National Archives Building, Washington, DC.

46. Paul, *Regimental History*, p. 16; Headquarters, Allied Mine Guard, AEFS, Suchan Mines. January, 7, 1919.

47. Paul, *Regimental History*, p. 16.

48. Baker, "A Study of the Supply of the 31st Infantry," p. 9.

49. Rhoads, "A Study of the Operations and Supply," p. 3.

50. Ibid., pp. 3–4.

51. Ibid., p. 4.

52. Brinkley, *Volunteer Army*, pp. 22–32 and 134.

53. Chamberlin, *1918–1921*, p. 165.

54. Chew, *Fighting the Russians*, p. 2.

55. Halliday, *Ignorant Armies*, pp. 1–2.

56. Ibid., p. 4.

57. Ibid., pp. 5–8.

58. Ibid., pp. 7–12.

59. Jones, diary, October 30, 1918.

60. Ibid., January.

61. Ibid.

62. Dunscomb, *Japan's Siberian Intervention*, p. 89

Chapter 10

1. Graves, Report, "Operations to June 30, 1919," pp. 13–14.

2. Ibid., p. 14.

3. Ibid., pp. 15–18.

4. Albert W. Palmer, "A Summer in Russia," diary, June 28, 1919, Kautz Family YMCA Archives. University of Minnesota Libraries.

5. Palmer, "A Summer in Russia," diary, June 29 and July 1, 1919; Willett, *Russian Sideshow*, p. 197; Major Sydney C. Graves, "Report on Operations of HMS Kent and Interallied Committee," pp. 1–2, May 17, 1919, Vladivostok, William S. Graves Papers, Box 2, Folder GW12, Hoover Institution Archives, Stanford University, Stanford, CA.

6. Palmer, "A Summer in Russia," diary, July 4, 1919.

7. 27th Infantry, "History of the Twenty-Seventh US Infantry," p. 21.

8. Allderdice (officer at Spasskoe, no first name provided), telegram to Chief of Staff AEF, May 21, 1919, National Archives Microfilm Publication M917, Reel 6, National Archives Building, Washington, DC. (This may be the Maj. F. B. Alderdice mentioned in the text covered by note 31 in chapter 8. The two sources disagree by one letter in the spelling. The locations imply this is the same person.)

9. Headquarters, 27th Infantry Regiment, Report, "Operations of the 27th Infantry, and incidents connected therewith, in the guarding of the railroad from Verkhne-Udinsk, Siberia, inclusive, from May 2nd, 1919, to January 29th, 1920," dated January 29, 1920, National Archives Building, Washington, DC, pp. 14, 16–17.

10. Ibid., pp. 14–15, 21–23.

11. Kindall, *American Soldiers*, pp. 75–77.

12. Ibid., p. 77; 27th Infantry, "History of the Twenty-Seventh US Infantry," p. 21.

13. Kindall, *American Soldiers*, p. 79; 27th Infantry, "History of the Twenty-Seventh US Infantry," p. 21.

14. Kindall, *American Soldiers*; 27th Infantry, "History of the Twenty-Seventh US Infantry," p. 21.

15. Kindall, *American Soldiers*, p. 79

16. Ibid., p. 80.

17. Ibid., p. 81; Hunt, *The History of the Twenty-Seventh Infantry*, p. 66; 27th Infantry, "History of the Twenty-Seventh US Infantry," p. 21.

18. Hunt, *The History of the Twenty-Seventh Infantry*, pp. 67–68; 27th Infantry, "History of the Twenty-Seventh US Infantry," p. 21

19. Kindall, *American Soldiers*, p. 82; Hunt, *The History of the Twenty-Seventh Infantry*, p. 68.

20. Channing, *Siberia's Untouched Treasure*, pp. 169, 171.

21. Hunt, *The History of the Twenty-Seventh Infantry*, p. 68.

22. Ibid., pp. 68–69; Channing, *Siberia's Untouched Treasure*, pp. 169, 172.

23. Hunt, *The History of the Twenty-Seventh Infantry*, p. 69.

24. Ibid.

25. Ibid., p. 70; Channing, *Siberia's Untouched Treasure*, pp. 175–77; Kindall, *American Soldiers*, pp. 95–96.

26. Hunt, *The History of the Twenty-Seventh Infantry*; Channing, *Siberia's Untouched Treasure*, pp. 180–81, 188. The identity of the lieutenant leading the advance guard posed a challenge and a bit of a mystery to resolve. In *Siberia's Untouched Treasure*, C. G. Fairfax Channing provides a firsthand account of the battle near Uspenka. However, other sources such as Sylvian G. Kindall in *American Soldiers in Siberia* refer to a Lt. Christian Channing Gross. Hunt's *The History of the Twenty-Seventh Infantry* lists two lieutenants, Channing and Gross, receiving the Distinguished Service Cross for the same actions on the same day in the same place—the battle near Uspenka. When searching for Channing's book to review it a second time, I discovered a copy at the University of Georgia library. The book catalog record listed Channing as a pseudonym with Christian Gross being the actual name of the author. Caroline Barratt, a University of Georgia librarian, researched their catalog entry but could not confirm anything other than that when the book was cataloged by the librarian at that time, it was determined that the actual author was Christian Channing Gross, 1895–1933. Additional research at the genealogy section of the Columbus Public Library in Columbus, Georgia, produced a 1930 US census report through Ancestry.com listing Christian Gross with daughter Barbara from Illinois living in Berne, Switzerland, in the employ of the US Foreign Service. No record of a C. G. Fairfax Channing was available. Christian Gross did not appear in the 1940 census, which was logical if he died in 1933. Therefore, I concluded that the University of Georgia librarian was most likely correct in listing Channing as the pseudonym for Gross. This then means that the lieutenant leading the advance guard at Uspenka was Christian Gross and not Fairfax Channing.

27. Hunt, *The History of the Twenty-Seventh Infantry*, p. 71; Channing, *Siberia's Untouched Treasure*, pp. 180–87.

28. Hunt, *The History of the Twenty-Seventh Infantry*, p. 71; Channing, *Siberia's Untouched Treasure*, pp. 180–87.

29. Hunt, *The History of the Twenty-Seventh Infantry*, p. 71; Channing, *Siberia's Untouched Treasure*, pp. 180–87.

30. Hunt, *The History of the Twenty-Seventh Infantry*, p. 71; Channing, *Siberia's Untouched Treasure*, pp. 190–95.

31. Hunt, *The History of the Twenty-Seventh Infantry*, p. 71; 27th Infantry, "History of the Twenty-Seventh US Infantry," p. 21.

32. Hunt, *The History of the Twenty-Seventh Infantry*, pp. 72–73.

33. Ibid., pp. 71, 73; 27th Infantry, "History of the Twenty-Seventh US Infantry," p. 22.

34. Hunt, *The History of the Twenty-Seventh Infantry*, pp. 71, 73; 27th Infantry, "History of the Twenty-Seventh US Infantry," p. 22.

35. Hunt, *The History of the Twenty-Seventh US Infantry*, p. 73

36. Hunt, *The History of the Twenty-Seventh US Infantry*, p. 74; Kindall, *American Soldiers*, pp. 203–4.

37. Hunt, *The History of the Twenty-Seventh US Infantry*, p. 74; Kindall, *American Soldiers*, p. 204.

38. Hunt, *The History of the Twenty-Seventh US Infantry*, p. 74; Kindall, *American Soldiers*, p. 205; Channing, *Siberia's Untouched Treasure*, pp. 250–54; 27th Infantry, "History of the Twenty-Seventh US Infantry," p. 22.

39. Hunt, *The History of the Twenty-Seventh Infantry*, p. 74.

40. Hunt, *The History of the Twenty-Seventh Infantry*, p. 75; Stewart's *The White Armies of Russia* (pp. 276–77) records that the Allied Supreme Council agreed in May 1919 to provide Kolchak munitions, supplies, and food. The council demanded a freely elected assembly, no revival of a privileged class, an independent Poland, an independent Finland, that the Peace Conference assist the settling of boundary disputes, acceptance of liability for the Russian national debt, and that Russia would join the Peace Conference in exchange for their support. Kolchak's June 4 reply was accepted June 12. Kolchak's government received de facto recognition from the United States and the Allies through this agreement but the United States remained opposed to official recognition.

41. Hunt, *The History of the Twenty-Seventh Infantry*, p. 75.

42. Richard, *When the United States Invaded Russia*, p. 79; First Lieutenant Albert E. Ryan, Headquarters, 31st Infantry Regiment, report, November 16, 1919, pp. 1–2, National Archives Microfilm Publication M917, Reel 1, National Archives Building, Washington, DC.

43. Ryan, report, November 16, 1919, p. 2.

44. Headquarters, 27th Infantry Regiment, report, November 3, 1919, National Archives Microfilm Publication M917, Reel 1, National Archives Building, Washington, DC.

45. Ryan, report, November 16, 1919, p. 3.

46. Ibid., pp. 3–4.

47. Graves, *America's Siberian Adventure*, pp. 263–65; Richard, *When the United States Invaded Russia*, p. 157.

48. Jones, diary, May 25 and June 4, 1919.

49. Ibid., June 8 and 10, 1919.

50. Ibid., June 11, 1919.

51. Ibid., June 15 and 17, 1919.

52. Ibid., July 14 and 15, 1919.

53. Ibid., July 20, 1919.

54. Fred M. Roberts, diary, August 6 through September 14, 1919. In *Assignment Siberia 1917–1919: Russian Railway Service Corp World War I.* CD-ROM. Dana Point, CA: FM Roberts, 2000.

55. Jones, diary, August 27, 1919.

56. Ibid., October 16 through November 5, 1919.

57. Ibid., November 5 through November 19, 1919.

58. Ibid., December 10 through February 5, 1919.

Chapter 11

1. Paul, *Regimental History, Thirty-First US Infantry*, pp. 19–20; Rhoads, "A Study of the Operations and Supply," pp. 4–5.

2. Headquarters, AEF Siberia, Intelligence Section, Intelligence Summary, April 21, 1919, National Archives Microfilm Publication M917, Reel 5, National Archives Building, Washington, DC.

3. Headquarters, 31st Infantry Regiment, "Report of Operations, January 1—June 30, 1919," July 20, 1919, p. 3, National Archives Microfilm Publication M917, Reel 10, National Archives Building, Washington, DC.

4. Lieutenant Colonel Robert Eichelberger, *Report of Visit to Suchan Mine*, April 26, 1919 *Japan and America, c1930–1955, The Pacific War and the Occupation of Japan*, series 1, *The Papers of General Robert L. Eichelberger (1886–1971)*, part 4, *Subject Files, Writings, Speeches, Photographs, and Oversize Material* Rare Book, Manuscript, and Special Collections Library, Duke University, Durham, NC, Adam Matthew Publications Microfilm, M9300, Reel 68, pp. 1–3.

5. Rhoads, "A Study of the Operations and Supply," p. 5; Headquarters, AEF Siberia, Intelligence Section, Intelligence Summary, June 24, 1920, p. 1 and enclosure 1, National Archives Microfilm Publication M917, Reel 6, National Archives Building, Washington, DC.

6. Rhoads, "A Study of the Operations and Supply," p. 5; Headquarters, AEF Siberia, Intelligence Section, Intelligence Summary, June 24, 1920, p. 1 and enclosure 1.

7. Rhoads, "A Study of the Operations and Supply," pp. 5–6; Headquarters, AEF Siberia, Intelligence Section, Intelligence Summary, June 24, 1920, p. 1 and enclosure 1.

8. Rhoads, "A Study of the Operations and Supply," p. 6; Headquarters Allied Mine Guard, AEFS, Suchan, report, July 10, 1919, p. 3, National Archives Microfilm Publication M917, Reel 3, National Archives Building, Washington, DC.; Headquarters, AEF Siberia, Intelligence Section, Intelligence Summary, June 24, 1919, p. 1 and enclosure 4.

9. Estimates vary on the number of men in the detachment: Channing, *Siberia's Untouched Treasure*, p. 213—approximately one hundred; Maddox, *The Unknown War with Russia*, p. 101—seventy-five; Rhoads, "A Study of the Operations and Supply," p. 6—platoon.

10. Channing, *Siberia's Untouched Treasure*, pp. 211–12; Joseph B. Longuevan, letter to Siberia veterans, n.d., Military History Institute, Carlisle Barracks, PA.

11. Channing, *Siberia's Untouched Treasure*, p. 213; Headquarters, Allied Mine Guard,

AEFS, Suchan Mines, War Diary, phone message, June 26, 1919, National Archives Microfilm Publication M917, Reel 9, National Archives Building, Washington, DC.; Kindall, *American Soldiers*, p. 57; Willett, *Russian Sideshow*, p. 225.

12. Channing, *Siberia's Untouched Treasure*, p. 213; Headquarters, Allied Mine Guard, AEFS, Suchan Mines, War Diary, phone message, June 26, 1919.

13. Channing, *Siberia's Untouched Treasure*, pp. 214–15; Paul, *Regimental History, Thirty-First US Infantry*, p. 20; Longuevan, letter to Siberia veterans; Headquarters, Allied Mine Guard, AEFS, Suchan Mines, War Diary, phone message, June 26, 1919; Kindall, *American Soldiers*, p. 58.

14. Maddox, *The Unknown War with Russia*, p. 102; Headquarters, 31st Infantry Regiment, "Report of Operations, January 1—June 30, 1919," July 20, 1919, p. 4; Longuevan, letter to Siberia veterans; Headquarters, Allied Mine Guard, AEFS, Suchan Mines, War Diary, phone message, June 26, 1919; Kindall, *American Soldiers*, p. 59.

15. Rhoads, "A Study of the Operations and Supply," p. 6.

16. Ibid.

17. Ibid., pp. 6–7.

18. Ibid., pp. 7–8.

19. Ibid., p. 8.

20. Headquarters Allied Mine Guard, AEFS, Suchan, report, July 10, 1919, Appendix: Report of Operations in Suchan Valley, p. 1.

21. Rhoads, "A Study of the Operations and Supply," pp. 8–9; Captain William J. Kunzman, "Operations of the Fourth Platoon Company C, 31st Infantry, Kazanka, Siberia, July 3, 1919." Student research paper, Advanced Course 1933–1934 (Fort Benning, GA: US Army Infantry School, undated), pp. 2–5.

22. Rhoads, "A Study of the Operations and Supply," p. 9; Kunzman, "Operations of the Fourth Platoon Company C," pp. 5–8.

23. Kunzman, "Operations of the Fourth Platoon Company C," pp. 8–11.

24. Rhoads, "A Study of the Operations and Supply," p. 9; Kunzman, "Operations of the Fourth Platoon Company C," pp. 11–13.

25. Rhoads, "A Study of the Operations and Supply," p. 9; Kunzman, "Operations of the Fourth Platoon Company C," pp. 13–20.

26. Rhoads, "A Study of the Operations and Supply," pp. 9–10; Headquarters Allied Mine Guard, AEFS, Suchan, report, July 10, 1919, Appendix: Report of Operations in Suchan Valley, p. 5.

27. Rhoads, "A Study of the Operations and Supply," p. 10.

28. Ibid., pp. 10–11.

29. Ibid., p. 11.

30. Rhoads, "A Study of the Operations and Supply," pp. 11–12; Colonel O. P. Robinson, memorandum Operation to Olga, July 28, 1919, National Archives Microfilm Publication M917, Reel 7, National Archives Building, Washington, DC; Headquarters, AEF Siberia, Intelligence Section, Intelligence Summary, July 30, 1919, p. 1, National Archives Microfilm Publication M917, Reel 7, National Archives Building, Washington, DC.

31. Robinson, memorandum Operation to Olga, July 28, 1919; Headquarters, AEF Siberia, Intelligence Section, Intelligence Summary, July 30, 1919, p. 1.

32. Headquarters, AEF Siberia, Intelligence Section, Intelligence Summary, August 8, 1919, Appendix: Memorandum for Captain Larimer, pp. 1–2, National Archives Microfilm Publication M917, Reel 7, National Archives Building, Washington, DC.

33. Headquarters, AEF Siberia, Intelligence Section, Intelligence Summary, August 8, 1919, Appendix: Memorandum for Captain Larimer, pp. 2–7.

34. Headquarters, AEF Siberia, Intelligence Section, Intelligence Summary, August 8, 1919, Appendix: Memorandum for Captain Larimer, pp. 2–7.

35. Headquarters, AEF Siberia, Intelligence Section, Intelligence Summary, August 8, 1919, Appendix: Memorandum for Captain Larimer, pp. 2–7.

36. Rhoads, "A Study of the Operations and Supply," p. 12.

37. Ibid., p. 28.

38. Ibid., pp. 28–29

39. Ibid., pp. 29–30.

40. Ibid., p. 30.

41. Ibid., pp. 30–34.

42. Ibid., pp. 12–13.

43. Ibid., p. 13; Lowe, *America's Foreign Legion*, ch. 2, p. 14; Graves, Report to the Adjutant General of the Army, "Operations July 1, 1919 to March 31, 1920," p. 4.

44. Rhoads, "A Study of the Operations and Supply," pp. 13–14.

45. Ibid., p. 14

46. Ibid., p. 15.

47. Ibid., p. 16.

48. Ibid., pp. 16–17.

49. Headquarters, 31st Infantry, "Report of Operations, January 1—June 30, 1919," pp. 1–6.

50. Ibid., pp. 2–3.

51. Ibid., p. 3.

52. Ibid., pp. 3–4.

53. Major W. H. Joiner, Report to Commander of US Troops, Suchan, June 29, 1919, National Archives Microfilm Publication M917, Reel 9, National Archives Building, Washington, DC.

54. Headquarters, AEF Siberia, Intelligence Section, Conditions in the Suchan Mine district from June 27th until July 7th, July 10, 1919, p. 1, National Archives Microfilm Publication M917, Reel 7, National Archives Building, Washington, DC.

55. Headquarters, AEF Siberia, Intelligence Section, Conditions in the Suchan Mine district from June 27th until July 7th, July 10, 1919, p. 2.

56. Headquarters, AEF Siberia, Intelligence Section, Conditions in the Suchan Mine district from June 27th until July 7th, July 10, 1919, p. 3.

57. Graves, Report to the Adjutant General of the Army, "Operations July 1, 1919 to March 31, 1920," p. 4.

58. Arms, "Siberian Expedition," p. 4.

59. Ibid., pp. 5–7.

60. Ibid., p. 8.

61. Ibid., p. 9.

62. Ibid.

63. Ibid., pp. 10–11.

64. Ibid., pp. 11–12.

65. Ibid., pp. 12–13.

66. Kindall, *American Soldiers*, p. 237.

67. Arms, "Siberian Expedition," pp. 12–15.

68. Headquarters, 31st Infantry, "Report of Operations, January 1—June 30, 1919," July 20, 1919, pp. 1–3.

69. Paul, *Regimental History, Thirty-First US Infantry*, p. 27.

70. Ibid.

71. Goldhurst, *Midnight War*, pp. 216–19.

72. Headquarters, AEF Siberia, AEF War Diary, November 18, 1919, Intelligence Summary dated November 18, 1919, p. 1, National Archives Microfilm Publication M917, Reel 8, National Archives Building, Washington, DC.

Chapter 12

1. Palmer, "A Summer in Russia," diary, July 12, 1919.

2. Ibid., July 12 and 13, 1919.

3. Ibid., July 17, 1919.

4. Ibid., July 19 and 20.

5. Ibid., August 18–21.

6. Ibid., August 24 and 26.

7. Ibid., August 27–31.

8. Ibid., September 10.

9. Corporal Jesse A. Anderson, *A Doughboy in the American Expeditionary Forces Siberia: The Diary of Corporal Jesse A. Anderson, 1918–1919* (Berkley, CA: William A. Anderson, 1983, Kautz Family YMCA Archives, University of Minnesota Libraries), pp. xii–xiii.

10. Ibid., pp. 30–31.

11. Ibid., pp. 24, 37, 39, 42, 52–53, and 60.

12. Headquarters, AEF Siberia, cablegram to War Department, September 13, 1919 (*Japan and America, c1930–1955, The Pacific War and the Occupation of Japan*, series 1, *The Papers of General Robert L. Eichelberger (1886–1971)*, part 4, *Subject Files, Writings, Speeches, Photographs, and Oversize Material* Rare Book, Manuscript, and Special Collections Library, Duke University, Durham, NC, Adam Matthew Publications Microfilm, M9300, Reel 68), p. 1; Major General William S. Graves, Report to the Adjutant General of the Army, "Conditions in Siberia," p. 6, September 26, 1919, William S. Graves Papers, Box 2, Folder GW12, Hoover Institution Archives, Stanford University, Stanford, CA; Lieutenant Colonel Robert L. Eichelberger, Report to Director, Military Intelligence Division, Washington, "Conditions in Siberia," p. 1, October 16, 1919, William S. Graves Papers, Box 1, Folder GW7, Hoover Institution Archives, Stanford University, Stanford, CA.

13. Chamberlin, *1918–1921*, pp. 166–67.

14. Ibid., p. 167.

15. Ibid., pp. 168–69.

16. Ibid.

17. Ibid., pp. 230–31.

18. Ibid., pp. 196–97.

19. Chew, *Fighting the Russians*, pp. 4–6.

20. Ibid., pp. 6–8.

21. Ibid., p. 8.

22. Halliday, *Ignorant Armies*, pp. 194–96.

23. Ibid., pp. 197–207.

24. Ibid., p. 209.

25. [L. C.] Convis, "From Omsk to Darien: A Trans-Siberian Odyssey," February 26, 1920, transcribed by Paul H. Hopwood, 1997, Kautz Family YMCA Archives, University of Minnesota Libraries, pp. 2–3.

26. Ibid., p. 4.

27. Ibid., p. 5.

28. Ibid., pp. 5–6.

29. Ibid., p. 6.

30. Ibid., pp. 7–10.

31. Ibid., pp. 11–17.

32. Headquarters, AEF Siberia, Intelligence Section, Intelligence Summary Number 28, Enclosure II, report of radio-telegraph message from the Polish Intelligence Officer, January 28, 1920 (*Japan and America, c1930–1955, The Pacific War and the Occupation of Japan*, series 1, *The Papers of General Robert L. Eichelberger (1886–1971)*, part 4, *Subject Files, Writings, Speeches, Photographs, and Oversize Material*, Rare Book, Manuscript, and Special Collections Library, Duke University, Durham, NC, Adam Matthew Publications Microfilm, M9300, Reel 70), p. 5.

33. Lieutenant Colonel Robert L. Eichelberger, Report to the Director of Military Intelligence, War Department, Washington, D.C., "Conditions in Siberia" (*Japan and America, c1930–1955, The Pacific War and the Occupation of Japan*, series 1, *The Papers of General Robert L. Eichelberger (1886–1971)*, part 4, *Subject Files, Writings, Speeches, Photographs, and Oversize Material*, Rare Book, Manuscript, and Special Collections Library, Duke University, Durham, NC, Adam Matthew Publications Microfilm, M9300, Reel 71), p. 2.

Chapter 13

1. Robert H. Ferrell, *Woodrow Wilson and World War I 1917–1921* (New York: Harper and Row Publishers, 1985), pp. 156–70.

2. Graves, Report, "Operations July 1, 1919 to March 31, 1920," p. 2

3. Chamberlin, *1918–1921*, pp. 200–202; John Bradley, *Allied Intervention in Russia* (New York: Basic Books, 1968), p. 128.

4. Varneck and Fisher, *The Testimony of Kolchak*, p. 338; Channing, *Siberia's Untouched Treasure*, p. 270; Goldhurst, *Midnight War*, pp. 228–30; Chamberlin, *1918–1921*, pp. 202–3; Bradley, *Allied Intervention*, pp. 128–29; Luckett, *White Generals*, pp. 346–47.

5. Hunt, *The History of the Twenty-Seventh Infantry*, p. 75.

6. Ibid., p. 76.

7. 27th Infantry, "History of the Twenty-Seventh US Infantry," p. 24; "Two Trophies of Company M," *Bark* vol. 4, no. 6 (February 21, 1930): p. 5.

8. Graves, Report, "Operations July 1, 1919 to March 31, 1920," p. 5; "Two Trophies of Company M," p. 4.

9. 27th Infantry, "History of the Twenty-Seventh US Infantry," p. 24; "Two Trophies of Company M," p. 4.

10. Graves, Report, "Operations July 1, 1919 to March 31, 1920," p. 5; "Two Trophies of Company M," p. 4.

11. Graves, Report, "Operations July 1, 1919 to March 31, 1920," p. 5; "Two Trophies of Company M," p. 4.

12. Graves, Report, "Operations July 1, 1919 to March 31, 1920," p. 5; "Two Trophies of Company M," p. 4.

13. Graves, Report, "Operations July 1, 1919 to March 31, 1920," p. 5; "Two Trophies of Company M," p. 4.

14. Graves, Report, "Operations July 1, 1919 to March 31, 1920," p. 5; "Two Trophies of Company M," p. 5.

15. Leipold, "America's Siberian Expedition," p. 11.

16. 27th Infantry, "History of the Twenty-Seventh US Infantry," p. 24.

17. Ibid.

18. Ibid.

19. Ibid., p. 24; Headquarters, 27th Infantry Regiment, Report, "Operations of the 27th Infantry," pp. 117–19.

20. Channing, *Siberia's Untouched Treasure*, pp. 306–7.

21. Arms, "Siberian Expedition," p. 15.

22. Ibid., pp. 15–16.

23. Paul, *Regimental History Thirty-First US Infantry*, p. 30.

24. Ibid.

25. Ibid., p. 31.

26. Eichelberger, Report to the Director of Military Intelligence, War Department, Washington, D.C., "Conditions in Siberia," p. 4.

27. Paul, *Regimental History Thirty-First US Infantry*, pp. 33–35.

28. Chamberlin, *1918–1921*, pp. 319–21.

29. Ibid., pp. 323–24.

30. Ibid., pp. 324–27.

31. Ibid., pp. 328–33.

32.Ibid., p. 164; Bradley, *Allied Intervention*, p. 130; Luckett, *White Generals*, pp. 388–89; Unterberger, *America's Siberian Expedition*, pp. 171 and 234; Manning, *The Siberian Fiasco*, pp. 182–83.

33. Luckett, *White Generals*, pp. 389–90.

34. Ibid., pp. 390–91.

35. Luckett, *White Generals*, p. 391; Major Robert. L. Eichelberger, "Interview with Ataman Semenoff at the New Willard Hotel," April 4, 1922, (*Japan and America, c1930–*

1955, The Pacific War and the Occupation of Japan, series 1, *The Papers of General Robert L. Eichelberger (1886–1971)*, part 4, *Subject Files, Writings, Speeches, Photographs, and Oversize Material*, Rare Book, Manuscript, and Special Collections Library, Duke University, Durham, NC, Adam Matthew Publications Microfilm, M9300, Reel 71), pp. 1–2.

36. Davis and Trani, "The American YMCA," 488–90.

Conclusion

1. Graves, Report, "Operations July 1, 1919 to March 31, 1920," pp. 6–7.

2. Ibid., p. 8.

3. Ibid.

4. Graves, *America's Siberian Adventure*, p. 97; Goldhurst, *Midnight War*, pp. 86–110.

5. Eichelberger, Report to the Director of Military Intelligence, War Department, Washington, DC, "Conditions in Siberia," March 18, 1920, pp. 6–7.

6. Graves, Report, "Operations July 1, 1918 to March 31, 1920," p. 9.

7. Ibid., pp. 9–10.

8. Nicholas, "Critical Analysis of the AEF," p. 14.

9. M. Lipinski, report, February 18, 1920 (*Japan and America, c1930–1955, The Pacific War and the Occupation of Japan*, series 1, *The Papers of General Robert L. Eichelberger (1886–1971)*, part 4, *Subject Files, Writings, Speeches, Photographs, and Oversize Material*, Rare Book, Manuscript, and Special Collections Library, Duke University, Durham, NC, Adam Matthew Publications Microfilm, M9300, Reel 70), p. 1; William S. Graves, Report to the Adjutant General of the Army, "Conditions in Siberia," p. 1, March 21, 1919, William S. Graves Papers, Box 2, Folder GW12, Hoover Institution Archives, Stanford University, Stanford, CA.

10. First Lieutenant R. S. Ashby, Report, Armored Car Atrocities, February 7, 1920 (*Japan and America, c1930–1955, The Pacific War and the Occupation of Japan*, series 1, *The Papers of General Robert L. Eichelberger (1886–1971)*, part 4, *Subject Files, Writings, Speeches, Photographs, and Oversize Material*, Rare Book, Manuscript, and Special Collections Library, Duke University, Durham, NC, Adam Matthew Publications Microfilm, M9300, Reel 70), pp. 1–4.

11. First Lieutenant F. B. Byers, "Report of the Activities in and around Sludanka, during the Recent Uprising along the Trans-Baikal Railway," January 24, 1920 (*Japan and America, c1930–1955, The Pacific War and the Occupation of Japan*, series 1, *The Papers of General Robert L. Eichelberger (1886–1971)*, part 4, *Subject Files, Writings, Speeches, Photographs, and Oversize Material*, Rare Book, Manuscript, and Special Collections Library, Duke University, Durham, NC, Adam Matthew Publications Microfilm, M9300, Reel 70), pp. 5–7.

12. Ibid., pp. 7–8.

13. First Lieutenant C.I. McNutt, "Various Observations, Olevenaya-Milek District," February 10, 1920 (*Japan and America, c1930–1955, The Pacific War and the Occupation of Japan*, series 1, *The Papers of General Robert L. Eichelberger (1886–1971)*, part 4, *Subject Files, Writings, Speeches, Photographs, and Oversize Material*, Rare Book, Manuscript, and

Special Collections Library, Duke University, Durham, NC, Adam Matthew Publications Microfilm, M9300, Reel 70), pp. 9–12.

14. Graves, Report, "Operations July 1, 1918 to March 31, 1920," p. 10.

15. Ibid., p. 11.

16. Ibid., pp. 12–13.

17. Ibid., p. 13.

18. Ibid., p. 14.

19.Ibid., pp. 14–15; Graves, *America's Siberian Adventure*, pp. 269–70.

20. Graves, Report, "Operations July 1, 1918 to March 31, 1920," p. 15.

21. Ibid.

22. Ibid., pp. 19–20; David F. Trask, *The United States in the Supreme War Council: American War Aims and Inter-Allied Strategy 1917–1918* (Middletown, CT: Wesleyan University Press), p. 127.

23. Ibid., p. 21.

24. Graves, Report, "Operations July 1, 1918 to March 31, 1920," pp. 23–25; Graves, *America's Siberian Adventure*, pp. 241–42.

25. Graves, Report, "Operations July 1, 1918 to March 31, 1920," p. 28,

26. Ibid., p. 29.

27. Ibid.

28. Lieutenant Colonel Robert L. Eichelberger, Report to the Director of Military Intelligence, War Department, Washington, D.C., "Conditions in Eastern Siberia," April 21, 1920 (*Japan and America, c1930–1955, The Pacific War and the Occupation of Japan*, series 1, *The Papers of General Robert L. Eichelberger (1886–1971)*, part 4, *Subject Files, Writings, Speeches, Photographs, and Oversize Material*, Rare Book, Manuscript, and Special Collections Library, Duke University, Durham, NC, Adam Matthew Publications Microfilm, M9300, Reel 71), pp. 1–4; Edward M. Coffman, *The Hilt of the Sword* (Madison: University of Wisconsin Press), p. 218.

29. Captain Mark G. Brislawn, "Allied Intervention in Russia" (US Command and General Staff School, Individual Research Paper No. 17, Fort Leavenworth, KS, 1932), p. 19.

30. Graves, *America's Siberian Adventure*, p. 84; Graves, Report, "Operations July 1, 1918 to March 31, 1920," pp. 15–16; Major General William S. Graves. Report to the Adjutant General of the Army, "Conditions in Siberia," October 6, 1918, William S. Graves Papers, Box 2, Folder GW12, Hoover Institution Archives, Stanford University, Stanford, CA.

31. Graves, *America's Siberian Adventure*, pp. 85–86; Graves, Report, "Operations July 1, 1918 to March 31, 1920," pp. 17–18.

32. Graves, Report, "Operations July 1, 1918 to March 31, 1920," p. 17.

33. Ibid., p. 18.

34. Channing, *Siberia's Untouched Treasure*, p. 302.

35. Kindall, *American Soldiers*, pp. 250–51.

36. Kindall, *American Soldiers*, p. 229; Richard, *When the United States Invaded Russia*, p. 171; *World Book Encyclopedia*, 1994, s.v. "Rankin, Jeanette."

37. Pelzel, "American Intervention in Siberia," p. 82.

38. Captain Judith A. Luckett, "The Siberian Intervention: Military Support of Foreign Policy," *Military Review* 64 (April 1984): 62.

39. Slaughter, "The American Expeditionary Force in Siberia," pp. 23–24.

40. March, *Nation at War*, p. 131.

41. US Department of State, "Aide Memoire," July 17, 1918, p. 3, National Archives Microfilm Publication M917, Reel 10, National Archives Building, Washington, DC.

42. Ibid.

43. Ibid.

44. Ibid., p. 5.

45. Ibid., p. 5; Graves, Report, "Operations July 1, 1919 to March 31, 1920," pp. 32–34; Richard, *When the United States Invaded Russia*, p. 117 and 121–26.

46. Graves, *America's Siberian Adventure*, p. 108; Goldhurst, *Midnight War*, p. 240.

47. US Department of State, "Aide Memoire," July 17, 1918, p. 4.

48. Graves, *America's Siberian Adventure*, p. 122

49. Graves, *America's Siberian Adventure*, pp. 122–24; Melton, *Between War and Peace*, p. 207.

50. David Kirby, *War, Peace and Revolution: International Socialism at the Crossroads 1914–1918* (New York: St. Martin's Press, 1986), p. 25.

Bibliography

Ackerman, Carl W. *Trailing the Bolsheviki: Twelve Thousand Miles with the Allies in Siberia*. New York: Charles Scribner's Sons, 1919.

Allerdice (officer at Spasskoe, no first name). Telegram to Chief of Staff AEF, May 21, 1919. National Archives Microfilm Publication M917, Reel 6. National Archives Building, Washington, DC.

American Library Association, Library War Service. Letter to Commanding General, AEF Siberia, Vladivostok, May 6, 1919. National Archives Microfilm Publication M917, Reel 1. National Archives Building, Washington, DC.

Anderson, Jesse A., Corporal. *A Doughboy in the American Expeditionary Forces Siberia: The Diary of Corporal Jesse A. Anderson, 1918–1919*. Berkley, CA: William A. Anderson, 1983. Kautz Family YMCA Archives. University of Minnesota Libraries.

Arms, Thomas S., Major. "Siberian Expedition—The Shkotovo Sector, 31st Infantry, From September 1919 until the Withdrawal of the Expedition." Individual Research Paper No. 84. US Army Command and General Staff School, Fort Leavenworth, KS, 1931.

Ashby, R. S. First Lieutenant. Report, Armored Car Atrocities, February 7, 1920. *Japan and America, c1930–1955, The Pacific War and the Occupation of Japan*. Series 1, *The Papers of General Robert L. Eichelberger (1886–1971)*. Part 4, *Subject Files, Writings, Speeches, Photographs, and Oversize Material*. Rare Book, Manuscript, and Special Collections Library, Duke University, Durham, NC, Adam Matthew Publications Microfilm, M9300, Reel 70.

Baker, Jewett C., Major. "A Study of the Supply of the 31st Infantry, A.E.F. Siberia, from August 10, 1918 to April 1, 1920." Individual Research Paper No. 87. US Army Command and General Staff School, Fort Leavenworth, KS, 1931.

Banks, Arthur. *A Military Atlas of the First World War*. New York: Taplinger Publishing, 1975.

Barnett, Corelli. *The Great War*. New York: G. P. Putnam's Sons, 1980.

Barrows, David P., Lieutenant Colonel. Letter to Director of Military Intelligence, Washington, DC, February 5, 1919. National Archives Microfilm Publication M917, Reel 4. National Archives Building, Washington, DC.

———. Telegram to Major Eichelberger, December 21, 1918. National Archives Microfilm Publication M917, Reel 4. National Archives Building, Washington, DC.

Beals, Bruce S., Major. "Coalition Warfare during the Allied Intervention in North Russia, 1918–1919." MMAS thesis, US Army Command and General Staff College, Fort Leavenworth, KS, 1981.

Bradley, John. *Allied Intervention in Russia*. New York: Basic Books, 1968.

Brezina, Frank, Captain. Headquarters, AEF Siberia, Intelligence Office. *Intelligence Diary August 7 to 17, 1918*, August 17, 1918. *Japan and America, c1930–1955, The Pacific War and the Occupation of Japan*. Series 1, *The Papers of General Robert L. Eichelberger (1886–1971)*. Part 4, *Subject Files, Writings, Speeches, Photographs, and Oversize Material*. Rare Book, Manuscript, and Special Collections Library, Duke University, Durham, NC, Adam Matthew Publications Microfilm, M9300, Reel 67.

———. *Weekly Summary August 25–31, 1918*, August 31, 1918. *Japan and America, c1930–1955, The Pacific War and the Occupation of Japan*. Series 1, *The Papers of General Robert L. Eichelberger (1886–1971)*. Part 4, *Subject Files, Writings, Speeches, Photographs, and Oversize Material*. Rare Book, Manuscript, and Special Collections Library, Duke University, Durham, NC, Adam Matthew Publications Microfilm, M9300, Reel 67.

Brinkley, George A. *The Volunteer Army and Allied Intervention in South Russia, 1917–1921*. Notre Dame, IN: University of Notre Dame Press, 1966.

Briscoe, Charles H., Major. "The Prisoner of War Problem in Russia: Justification for Allied Intervention, 1918–1920." MMAS thesis, US Army Command and General Staff College, Fort Leavenworth, KS, 1977.

Brislawn, Mark G., Captain. "Allied Intervention in Russia." Individual Research Paper No. 17. US Army Command and General Staff School, Fort Leavenworth, KS, 1932.

Brody, David. *Steelworkers in America: The Nonunion Era*. New York: Harper and Row Publishers, 1960.

Bugbee, Fred W., Lieutenant Colonel. "The AEF in Siberia." In *Monographs of the World War*, 631–42. Fort Benning, GA: US Army Infantry School, n.d.

Bunyan, James. *Intervention, Civil War, and Communism in Russia, April–December 1918*. Baltimore: Johns Hopkins Press, 1936.

Byers, F. B., First Lieutenant. "Report of the Activities in and around Sludanka, during the Recent Uprising along the Trans-Baikal Railway." In *Japan and America, c1930–1955, The Pacific War and the Occupation of Japan*. Series 1, *The Papers of General Robert L. Eichelberger (1886–1971)*. Part 4, *Subject Files, Writings, Speeches, Photographs, and Oversize Material*. Rare Book, Manuscript, and Special Collections Library, Duke University, Durham, NC, Adam Matthew Publications Microfilm, M9300, Reel 70.

Chamberlin, William H. *1918–1921: From the Civil War to the Consolidation of Power*. Vol. 2 of *The Russian Revolution 1917–1921*. New York: Grossett and Dunlap, 1965.

Chandler, Alfred D., Jr. *The Visible Hand: The Managerial Revolution in American Business*. Cambridge, MA: Belknap Press, 1977.

Channing, C. G. Fairfax. *Siberia's Untouched Treasure: Its Future Role in the World*. New York: G. P. Putnam's Sons, 1923.

Chew, Allen F., Dr. *Fighting the Russians in Winter: Three Case Studies*. Leavenworth Papers No. 5. Combat Studies Institute, US Army Command and General Staff College, Fort Leavenworth, KS, 1981.

Chief Quartermaster, AEF Siberia. "Report of Operations," January 30, 1919, p. 2. National Archives Microfilm Publication M917, Reel 11. National Archives Building, Washington, DC.

Coates, W. P., and Zelda K. Coates. *Armed Intervention in Russia: 1918–1922*. London: Victor Gollancz, 1935.

Coffman, Edward M. *The Hilt of the Sword*. Madison: University of Wisconsin Press.

Convis, [L. C.?]. "From Omsk to Darien: A Trans-Siberian Odyssey." February 26, 1920. Transcribed by Paul H. Hopwood, 1997. Kautz Family YMCA Archives, University of Minnesota Libraries.

Davis, Donald E., and Eugene P. Trani. "The American YMCA and the Russian Revolution." *Slavic Review* 33, no. 3 (1974): 469–91. Retrieved December 12, 2010, from JSTOR database, http://www.jstor.org/stable/2494734.

Dotsenko, Paul. *The Struggle for a Democracy in Siberia, 1919–1920*. Stanford, CA: Hoover Institution Press, 1983.

Dulles, Foster R. *The American Red Cross*. New York: Harper and Brothers, 1950.

Dunscomb, Paul E. *Japan's Siberian Intervention, 1918–1922: "A Great Disobedience against the People."* Lanham, MD: Rowman and Littlefield Publishers, 2011.

Dupuy, R. Ernest. *Perish by the Sword*. Harrisburg, PA: Military Service Publishing, 1939.

Dupuy, R. Ernest, and Trevor N. Dupuy. *The Encyclopedia of Military History: From 3500 B.C. to the Present*. Rev. ed. New York: Harper and Row Publishers, 1977.

Earns, Lane R. *Where Do We Go from Here: The Russian Railway Service Corps in Nagasaki*. Retrieved November 26, 2009, from http://www.uwosh.edu/faculty_staff/earns/rrsc.html.

Eichelberger, Robert L., Lieutenant Colonel. "Final Report on the Operations of the Intelligence Section of the A.E.F. Siberia," October 20, 1920. *Japan and America, c1930–1955, The Pacific War and the Occupation of Japan*. Series 1, *The Papers of General Robert L. Eichelberger (1886–1971)*. Part 4, *Subject Files, Writings, Speeches, Photographs, and Oversize Material*. Rare Book, Manuscript, and Special Collections Library, Duke University, Durham, NC, Adam Matthew Publications Microfilm, M9300, Reel 71.

———. "Report of Visit to Suchan Mine," April 26, 1919. *Japan and America, c1930–1955, The Pacific War and the Occupation of Japan*. Series 1, *The Papers of General Robert L. Eichelberger (1886–1971)*. Part 4, *Subject Files, Writings, Speeches, Photographs, and Oversize Material*. Rare Book, Manuscript, and Special Collections Library, Duke University, Durham, NC, Adam Matthew Publications Microfilm, M9300, Reel 68.

———. Report to Director, Military Intelligence Division, Washington, "Conditions in Siberia," 1, October 16, 1919. William S. Graves Papers, Box 1, Folder GW7, Hoover Institution Archives, Stanford University, Stanford, CA.

———. Report to the Director of Military Intelligence, War Department, Washington, DC, "Conditions in Eastern Siberia," April 21, 1920. *Japan and America, c1930–1955, The Pacific War and the Occupation of Japan*. Series 1, *The Papers of General Robert L.*

Eichelberger (1886–1971). Part 4, *Subject Files, Writings, Speeches, Photographs, and Oversize Material*. Rare Book, Manuscript, and Special Collections Library, Duke University, Durham, NC, Adam Matthew Publications Microfilm, M9300, Reel 71.

———. Report to the Director of Military Intelligence, War Department, Washington, DC, "Conditions in Siberia," March 18, 1920. *Japan and America, c1930–1955, The Pacific War and the Occupation of Japan*. Series 1, *The Papers of General Robert L. Eichelberger (1886–1971)*. Part 4, *Subject Files, Writings, Speeches, Photographs, and Oversize Material*. Rare Book, Manuscript, and Special Collections Library, Duke University, Durham, NC, Adam Matthew Publications Microfilm, M9300, Reel 71.

Eichelberger, Robert L., Major. "Interview with Ataman Semenoff at the New Willard Hotel," April 4, 1922. *Japan and America, c1930–1955, The Pacific War and the Occupation of Japan*. Series 1, *The Papers of General Robert L. Eichelberger (1886–1971)*. Part 4, *Subject Files, Writings, Speeches, Photographs, and Oversize Material*. Rare Book, Manuscript, and Special Collections Library, Duke University, Durham, NC, Adam Matthew Publications Microfilm, M9300, Reel 71.

Emerson, George H., Colonel. Memorandum to Major General Graves and American Red Cross in Vladivostok, December 5, 1918. National Archives Microfilm Publication M917, Reel 3. National Archives Building, Washington, DC.

Feist, Joe Michael. "Theirs Not to Reason Why: The Case of the Russian Railway Service Corps." *Military Affairs* 42 (February 1978): 1–6.

Ferrell, Robert H. *Woodrow Wilson and World War I 1917–1921*. New York: Harper and Row Publishers, 1985.

Figes, Orlando. "The Red Army and Mass Mobilization during the Russian Civil War 1918–1920." *Past & Present*, no. 129 (November 1990): 168–211. Retrieved December 12, 2009, from JSTOR database, http://www.jstor.org/stable/650938.

Francis, David R. *Russia from the American Embassy: April, 1916–November, 1918*. New York: Charles Scribner's Sons, 1921.

Goldhurst, Richard. *The Midnight War: The American Intervention in Russia, 1918–1920*. New York: McGraw-Hill, 1978.

Graves, Sydney C., Major. "Report on Operations of HMS Kent and Interallied Committee," May 17, 1919, Vladivostok. William S. Graves Papers, Box 2, Folder GW12, Hoover Institution Archives, Stanford University, Stanford, CA.

Graves, William S., Brigadier General. Memorandum from Brigadier General Graves to the Adjutant General of the Army, February 14, 1921. National Archives Microfilm Publication M917, Reel 10. National Archives Building, Washington, DC.

Graves, Williams S., Major General. *America's Siberian Adventure 1918–1920*. New York: Jonathan Cape and Harrison Smith, 1931.

———. Report to the Adjutant General of the Army, "Conditions in Siberia," October 6, 1918. William S. Graves Papers, Box 2, Folder GW12, Hoover Institution Archives, Stanford University, Stanford, CA.

———. Report to the Adjutant General of the Army, "Conditions in Siberia," March 21, 1919. William S. Graves Papers, Box 2, Folder GW12, Hoover Institution Archives, Stanford University, Stanford, CA.

———. Report to the Adjutant General of the Army, "Conditions in Siberia," June 4, 1919. William S. Graves Papers, Box 2, Folder GW12, Hoover Institution Archives, Stanford University, Stanford, CA.

———. Report to the Adjutant General of the Army, "Conditions in Siberia," September 26, 1919. William S. Graves Papers, Box 2, Folder GW12, Hoover Institution Archives, Stanford University, Stanford, CA.

———. Report to the Adjutant General of the Army, "Operations to June 30, 1919," Vladivostok, September 25, 1919. National Archives Microfilm Publication M917, Reel 10, National Archives Building, Washington, DC.

———. Report to the Adjutant General of the Army, "Operations July 1, 1919 to March 31, 1920," Fort McKinley, Philippine Islands, May 26, 1920. National Archives Microfilm Publication M917, Reel 10. National Archives Building, Washington, DC.

Halliday, E. M. *The Ignorant Armies*. New York: Harper and Brothers, 1958.

Hard, William. *Raymond Robins' Own Story*. New York: Harper and Brothers Publishers, 1920.

Headquarters, AEF Siberia. AEF War Diary, August 14, 1918. National Archives Microfilm Publication M917, Reel 2. National Archives Building, Washington, DC.

———. AEF War Diary, August 16, 1918. National Archives Microfilm Publication M917, Reel 2. National Archives Building, Washington, DC.

———. AEF War Diary, August 17, 1918. National Archives Microfilm Publication M917, Reel 2. National Archives Building, Washington, DC.

———. AEF War Diary, September 3, 1918. General Headquarters, Bureau of Information, Communiqué Number 16, dated September 3, 1918. National Archives Microfilm Publication M917, Reel 2. National Archives Building, Washington, DC.

———. AEF War Diary, December 21, 1918. Report from the Intelligence Officer at Khabarovsk to Intelligence Officer, AEF, Khabarovsk, December 6, 1918. National Archives Microfilm Publication M917, Reel 4. National Archives Building, Washington, DC.

———. AEF War Diary, February 8, 1919. Letter from Major General Graves to Major General Inagaki, January 30, 1919. National Archives Microfilm Publication M917, Reel 4. National Archives Building, Washington, DC.

———. AEF War Diary, February 8, 1919. Multiple Telegrams. National Archives Microfilm Publication M917, Reel 4. National Archives Building, Washington, DC.

———. AEF War Diary, February 8, 1919. Telegram from Colonel Styer to Amex dated January 31, 1919. National Archives Microfilm Publication M917, Reel 4. National Archives Building, Washington, DC.

———. AEF War Diary, March 8, 1919. "Notes on Armored Trains in Use in Siberia." National Archives Microfilm Publication M917, Reel 5. National Archives Building, Washington, DC.

———. AEF War Diary, November 18, 1919. Intelligence Summary. National Archives Microfilm Publication M917, Reel 8. National Archives Building, Washington, DC.

———. Cablegram to War Department, September 13, 1919. *Japan and America, c1930–1955, The Pacific War and the Occupation of Japan*. Series 1, *The Papers of General Robert L. Eichelberger (1886–1971)*. Part 4, *Subject Files, Writings, Speeches, Photographs, and*

Oversize Material. Rare Book, Manuscript, and Special Collections Library, Duke University, Durham, NC, Adam Matthew Publications Microfilm, M9300, Reel 68.

———. Field Order No. 1, August 24, 1918. National Archives Microfilm Publication M917, Reel 2. National Archives Building, Washington, DC.

———. Letter from Major General Graves to the Commanding General and the Adjutant General, October 31, 1918. National Archives Microfilm Publication M917, Reel 1. National Archives Building, Washington, DC.

———. Letter from Major General Graves to General Otani, September 9, 1918. National Archives Microfilm Publication M917, Reel 1. National Archives Building, Washington, DC.

———. Letter, September 6, 1918. National Archives Microfilm Publication M917, Reel 1. National Archives Building, Washington, DC.

———. "Memorandum of Conversation with General Nicolas Kholovof." National Archives Microfilm Publication M917, Reel 5. National Archives Building, Washington, DC.

———. Memorandum, September 18, 1918. National Archives Microfilm Publication M917, Reel 1. National Archives Building, Washington, DC.

———. Memorandum, January 18, 1919. National Archives Microfilm Publication M917, Reel 2. National Archives Building, Washington, DC.

———. Note, August 22, 1918. National Archives Microfilm Publication M917, Reel 2. National Archives Building, Washington, DC.

———. Report for General Otani, Imperial Japanese Army, August 23, 1918. National Archives Microfilm Publication M917, Reel 2. National Archives Building, Washington, DC.

———. Telegram from Colonel Henry Styer to Adjutant General of the Army, August 24, 1918. National Archives Microfilm Publication M917, Reel 2. National Archives Building, Washington, DC.

———. Telegram from Major General Graves to Adjutant General of the Army, September 2, 1918. National Archives Microfilm Publication M917, Reel 2. National Archives Building, Washington, DC.

Headquarters, AEF Siberia, Intelligence Section. Conditions in the Suchan Mine District from June 27th until July 7th, July 10, 1919. National Archives Microfilm Publication M917, Reel 7. National Archives Building, Washington, DC.

———. Intelligence Summary Number 15, September 27, 1918. National Archives Microfilm Publication M917, Reel 2. National Archives Building, Washington, DC.

———. Intelligence Summary, April 21, 1919. National Archives Microfilm Publication M917, Reel 5. National Archives Building, Washington, DC.

———. Intelligence Summary, July 30, 1919. National Archives Microfilm Publication M917, Reel 7. National Archives Building, Washington, DC.

———. Intelligence Summary, August 8, 1919, Appendix: Memorandum for Captain Larimer. National Archives Microfilm Publication M917, Reel 7. National Archives Building, Washington, DC.

———. Intelligence Summary, June 24, 1920. National Archives Microfilm Publication M917, Reel 6. National Archives Building, Washington, DC.

———. Intelligence Summary Number 28, Enclosure 2, Report of Radio-telegraph Message from the Polish Intelligence Officer, January 28, 1920. *Japan and America, c1930–1955, The Pacific War and the Occupation of Japan.* Series 1, *The Papers of General Robert L. Eichelberger (1886–1971).* Part 4, *Subject Files, Writings, Speeches, Photographs, and Oversize Material* from the Rare Book, Manuscript, and Special Collections Library, Duke University, Durham, North Carolina, Adam Matthew Publications Microfilm, M9300, Reel 70.

———. Memorandum, Currency Conditions—Khabarovsk to Ushumun, October 20, 1918. National Archives Microfilm Publication M917, Reel 2. National Archives Building, Washington, DC.

———. Memorandum, Economic Conditions as Far North as Ushumun, October 20, 1918. National Archives Microfilm Publication M917, Reel 2. National Archives Building, Washington, DC.

———. Memorandum for Major Barrows, October 20, 1919. National Archives Microfilm Publication M917, Reel 2. National Archives Building, Washington, DC.

———. Memorandum, Friendly Russian Forces in Eastern European Russia, October 11, 1918. National Archives Microfilm Publication M917, Reel 2. National Archives Building, Washington, DC.

———. Memorandum, October 6, 1918. National Archives Microfilm Publication M917, Reel 2. National Archives Building, Washington, DC.

———. Memorandum, Strategic Situation, October 17, 1918. National Archives Microfilm Publication M917, Reel 2. National Archives Building, Washington, DC.

———. Newspaper summary, October 21, 1918. National Archives Microfilm Publication M917, Reel 3. National Archives Building, Washington, DC.

———. Newspaper summary, October 28, 1918. National Archives Microfilm Publication M917, Reel 3. National Archives Building, Washington, DC.

———. Weekly Intelligence Summary, September 15–21, 1918, dated September 21, 1918. National Archives Microfilm Publication M917, Reel 2. National Archives Building, Washington, DC.

Headquarters, Allied Mine Guard, AEFS, Suchan. Report, July 10, 1919, National Archives Microfilm Publication M917, Reel 3. National Archives Building, Washington, DC.

Headquarters, Allied Mine Guard, AEFS, Suchan Mines. January, 7, 1919. Report in Compliance with Memorandum No. 48, AEFS, dated November 25, 1918. National Archives Microfilm Publication M917, Reel 10. National Archives Building, Washington, DC.

———. War Diary, Phone Message, June 26, 1919. National Archives Microfilm Publication M917, Reel 9. National Archives Building, Washington, DC.

Headquarters, Japanese Army in Vladivostok. Letter from General Otani to Major General Graves, September 28, 1918. National Archives Microfilm Publication M917, Reel 1. National Archives Building, Washington, DC.

———. Letter to the Commanders of the Allied Armies, August 18, 1918. National Archives Microfilm Publication M917, Reel 2. National Archives Building, Washington, DC.

Headquarters, Philippine Department. General Order Number 48, Manila, PI, August

6, 1918. National Archives Microfilm Publication M917, Reel 1. National Archives Building, Washington, DC.

———. General Order Number 50, Manila, PI, August 12, 1918. National Archives Microfilm Publication M917, Reel 1. National Archives Building, Washington, DC.

Headquarters, 31st Infantry Regiment. "Report of Operations, January 1—June 30, 1919," July 20, 1919. National Archives Microfilm Publication M917, Reel 10. National Archives Building, Washington, DC.

Headquarters, 27th Infantry Regiment. Letter from Colonel Henry Styer to General Uehara, Japanese Army Chief of Staff, September 26, 1918. National Archives Microfilm Publication M917, Reel 1. National Archives Building, Washington, DC.

———. Report, November 3, 1919. National Archives Microfilm Publication M917, Reel 1. National Archives Building, Washington, DC.

———. Report, "Operations of the Twenty-Seventh Infantry, and incidents connected therewith, in the guarding of the railroad from Verkhne-Udinsk, Siberia, inclusive, from May 2nd, 1919, to January 29th, 1920," dated January 29, 1920. National Archives. National Archives Building, Washington, DC.

Hochee, Nick. "Some Highlights of Doings and Moves of the 27th Infantry Regiment While I Served in It, 1914–1920." Memorandum on file with US Army Military History Institute papers on the AEF Siberia, undated.

Hudson, Miles. *Intervention in Russia 1918–1920: A Cautionary Tale*. Barnsley, South Yorkshire, UK: Leo Cooper, 2004.

Hughes, Frank L., Lieutenant. Personal letter to "Joe." Knights of Columbus Archives File, SC-16-1-169, concerning the AEF Siberia, November 7, 1918.

Hunt, George A., Captain. *The History of the Twenty-Seventh Infantry*. Honolulu: Honolulu Star-Bulletin, 1931.

Isitt, Benjamin. *From Victoria to Vladivostok: Canada's Siberian Expedition, 1917–19*.Vancouver, British Columbia, Can.: UBC Press, 2010.

Joiner, W. H., Major. Report to Commander of US Troops, Suchan, June 29, 1919. National Archives Microfilm Publication M917, Reel 9. National Archives Building, Washington, DC.

Jones, William C., Second Lieutenant. Diary. Retrieved November 10, 2009, from http://nortvoods.net/rrs/japan/journal-1.htm.

Kennan, George F. *The Decision to Intervene*. Vol. 2 of *Soviet-American Relations, 1917–1920*. Princeton, NJ: Princeton University Press, 1958.

———. *Russian Leaves the War*. Vol. 1 of *Soviet-American Relations, 1917–1920*. Princeton, NJ: Princeton University Press, 1956.

Kindall, Sylvian G. *American Soldiers in Siberia*. New York: Richard R. Smith, 1945.

Kingmore, Howard P., Captain. Signal Corps Photographic Unit attached to AEF Siberia, Vladivostok, Report, February 7, 1919. National Archives Microfilm Publication M917, Reel 11. National Archives Building, Washington, DC.

Kirby, David Kirby. *War, Peace and Revolution: International Socialism at the Crossroads 1914–1918*. New York: St. Martin's Press, 1986.

Klecanda, Vladimir, Lieutenant Colonel. "Operation of the Czechoslovak Army in Russia During the Period 1917–1920." Translated by Captain Jerry V. Matejka. *Journal of Military Science* (1921).

Knight, A. M., Admiral, Vice Admiral Hirogan Kato, Captain Payne, Colonel Paris, Captain K. L. Lin, and Captain Badyovea. "The Allies' Proclamation," Vladivostok, July 6, 1918. National Archives Microfilm Publication M917, Reel 1. National Archives Building, Washington, DC.

Knights of Columbus. "Report of the Supreme Board of Directors, Knights of Columbus for Fiscal Year Ending June 30, 1920." Knights of Columbus Archives File SC-16–1 3, August 3, 1920, New Haven, CT.

Knox, Alfred. "General Janin's Siberian Diary." *Slavonic Review* 3, no. 9 (1925): 724.

Kunzman, William J., Captain. "Operations of the Fourth Platoon Company C, 31st Infantry, Kazanka, Siberia, July 3, 1919." Student research paper, Advanced Course 1933–1934. US Army Infantry School, Fort Benning, GA, n.d.

Leipold, William D. "America's Siberian Expedition 1918–1920." Student paper. US Army Command and General Staff College, Fort Leavenworth, KS, April 24, 1981.

Link, Arthur S., ed. *The Papers of Woodrow Wilson*. Vols. 41, 44–47. Princeton, NJ: Princeton University Press, 1983–84.

Lipinski, M. Report, February 18, 1920. *Japan and America, c1930–1955, The Pacific War and the Occupation of Japan*. Series 1, *The Papers of General Robert L. Eichelberger (1886–1971)*. Part 4, *Subject Files, Writings, Speeches, Photographs, and Oversize Material*. Rare Book, Manuscript, and Special Collections Library, Duke University, Durham, NC, Adam Matthew Publications Microfilm, M9300, Reel 70.

Longuevan, Joseph B. Letter to Siberia Veterans. Military History Institute, Carlisle Barracks, PA, n.d.

Lowe, Karl F. *America's Foreign Legion: The 31st Infantry Regiment in War and Peace*. Glen Spey, NY: 31st US Infantry Regiment Association. http://www.31stinfantry.org/history.htm (accessed August 31, 2009).

Luckett, Judith A., Captain. "The Siberian Intervention: Military Support of Foreign Policy." *Military Review* 64 (April 1984): 54–63.

Luckett, Richard. *The White Generals: An Account of the White Movement and the Russian Civil War*. London: Longman Group, 1971.

Maddox, Robert J. *The Unknown War with Russia: Wilson's Siberian Intervention*. San Rafael, CA: Presidio Press, 1977.

Manning, Clarence A. *The Siberian Fiasco*. New York: Library Publishers, 1952

March, Peyton C., General. *The Nation at War*. Garden City, NY: Doubleday, Doran, 1932.

Marshall, S. L. A. *World War I*. New York: American Heritage Press, 1971.

Marx, Karl. "The Communist Manifesto." In *The World's Great Thinkers, Man and the State: The Political Philosopher*, pp. 487–523. Edited by Saxe Commins and Robert N. Linscott. New York: Random House, 1947.

McClellan, Edwin N., Major. "American Marines in Siberia during the World War." *Marine Corps Gazette*, June 1920, 173–81.

McLellan, David. *Karl Marx: His Life and Thought*. New York: Harper and Row, 1974.

McNutt, C. I., First Lieutenant. "Various Observations, Olevenaya—Milek District," February 10, 1920. *Japan and America, c1930–1955, The Pacific War and the Occupation of Japan*. Series 1, *The Papers of General Robert L. Eichelberger (1886–1971)*. Part 4, *Subject Files, Writings, Speeches, Photographs, and Oversize Material*. Rare Book, Manuscript, and Special Collections Library, Duke University, Durham, NC, Adam Matthew Publications Microfilm, M9300, Reel 70.

Melton, Carol W. *Between War and Peace: Woodrow Wilson and the American Expeditionary Forces in Siberia, 1918–1920*. Macon, GA: Mercer University Press, 2001.

Military Attaché, Tokyo, Japan. Cablegram to Major D. P. Barrows, Military Intelligence Officer, American Expeditionary Forces, Vladivostok, Siberia, October 26, 1918. In *Japan and America, c1930–1955, The Pacific War and the Occupation of Japan*. Series 1, *The Papers of General Robert L. Eichelberger (1886–1971)*. Part 4, *Subject Files, Writings, Speeches, Photographs, and Oversize Material*. Rare Book, Manuscript, and Special Collections Library, Duke University, Durham, NC, Adam Matthew Publications. Microfilm, M9300, Reel 67.

Morley, James W. *The Japanese Thrust into Siberia, 1918*. Freeport, NY: Books for Libraries Press, 1972.

Nicholas, I. C., Captain. "A Critical Analysis of the AEF, Siberia, Including Relations with Other Allies." Individual Research Paper. US Army Command and General Staff School, Fort Leavenworth, KS, 1932.

Noll, John J. "Wolfhounds Pick a Winner." *American Legion Monthly*, September 1934, 34–37, 62–63.

Noyes, Clara G. "The Red Cross." *American Journal of Nursing* 20, no. 6 (March 1920): 480–84. Retrieved December 12, 2010, from JSTOR database, http://www.jstor.org/stable/3407745.

Ordnance Department, AEF Siberia. "Report of Operations of the Ordnance Department, AEF Siberia, for the period July 1, 1919 to December 31, 1919," p. 2. National Archives Microfilm Publication M917, Reel 11. National Archives Building, Washington, DC.

———. "Report of Operations, December 31, 1918," pp. 2–3. National Archives Microfilm Publication M917, Reel 11. National Archives Building, Washington, DC.

———. "Report of Operations, January 1, 1919–June 30, 1919," February 25, 1920, p. 2. National Archives Microfilm Publication M917, Reel 11. National Archives Building, Washington, DC.

Packard, L. B., Captain. "The American Expeditionary Forces in Siberia, 1918–1919," Vladivostok, April 1919. National Archives Microfilm Publication M917, Reel 10. National Archives Building, Washington, DC.

Packer, George. *The Assassins' Gate*. New York: Farrar, Straus, and Giroux, 2005.

Palmer, Albert W. "A Summer in Russia." Diary. Kautz Family YMCA Archives, University of Minnesota Libraries.

Palmer, Frederick. *Newton D. Baker: America at War*. New York: Kraus Reprint Company, 1969.

Pares, Bernard. *My Russian Memoirs*. New York: AMS Press, 1969.

Paul, Frank A. *Regimental History, Thirty-First US Infantry July 1916–July 1920*. Manila, PI: 31st Infantry Regiment, 1920.

Pelzel, Sophia R. "American Intervention in Siberia, 1918–1920." PhD dissertation, University of Pennsylvania, Philadelphia, PA, 1946.

Pereira, N. G. O. *White Siberia: The Politics of Civil War*. Montreal: McGill-Queen's University Press, 1996.

Raymond, John. "Christmas Ship for Siberia." *Columbiad*, December 1919, 10.

Reagan, Ronald. *State of the Union Address*, January 25, 1984. Accessed August 23, 2008, http://www.infoplease.com/t/hist/state-of-the-union/198.html.

Rhoads, O. R., Major. "A Study of the Operations and Supply of the American Forces in the Suchan Mine Area Siberia, September 1918–January 1920." Individual Research Paper No. 90. US Army Command and General Staff School, Fort Leavenworth, KS, 1932.

Richard, Carl J. *When the United States Invaded Russia: Woodrow Wilson's Siberian Disaster*. Lanham, MD: Rowman and Littlefield Publishers, 2013.

Roberts, Fred M. Diary, August 6 through September 14, 1919. In *Assignment Siberia 1917–1919: Russian Railway Service Corp World War I*. CD-ROM. Dana Point, CA: FM Roberts, 2000.

Robinson, O. P., Colonel. Memorandum Operation to Olga, July 28, 1919. National Archives Microfilm Publication M917, Reel 7. National Archives Building, Washington, DC.

Ryan, Albert E., First Lieutenant. Headquarters, 31st Infantry Regiment, report, November 16, 1919, pp. 1–2. National Archives Microfilm Publication M917, Reel 1. National Archives Building, Washington, DC.

Sawicki, James A. *Infantry Regiments of the U.S. Army*. Dumfries, VA: Wyvern Publications, 1981.

Shipler, David K. "How We See Each Other." *New York Times*, November 10, 1985, late edition, p. A33. Accessed August 20, 2008, http://www.nytimes.com/1985/11/10/magazine/how-we-see-each-other-the-view-from-america.html.

Slaughter, H. H., Lieutenant Colonel. "The American Expeditionary Force in Siberia as a Part of Allied Intervention in 1918." Lecture delivered at the Army War College, Washington, DC, March 29, 1934. Combined Arms Research Library, Ft. Leavenworth, KS.

Stewart, George. *The White Armies of Russia: A Chronicle of Counter-Revolution and Allied Intervention*. New York: MacMillan, 1933.

Stokesbury, James, L. *A Short History of World War I*. New York: William Morrow, 1981.

Stone, Norman. *The Eastern Front 1914–1917*. New York: Charles Scribner's Sons, 1975.

Supply Company, 31st Infantry. Memorandum to Adjutant, 31st Infantry, February 1, 1919. National Archives Microfilm Publication M917, Reel 10. National Archives Building, Washington, DC.

"Text of Krushchev Debate with Skouras during the Luncheon at Film Studio." *New York Times*, September 20, 1959, late edition, 41.

31st Infantry Regiment. "Twenty-Third Anniversary Organization Day, 1916–1939, Program." Manila, P.I.: 31st Infantry Regiment, August 13, 1939.

Thompson, John M. *Russia, Bolshevism and the Versailles Peace*. Princeton, NJ: Princeton University Press, 1966.

Tillman, Seth P. *Anglo-American Relations at the Paris Peace Conference of 1919*. Princeton, NJ: Princeton University Press, 1961.

Trani, Eugene P. "Woodrow Wilson and the Decision to Intervene in Russia." *Journal of Modern History* 48 (September 1976): 440–61.

"Transcript of Nixon's Television Address to the Soviet People from the Great Kremlin Palace." *New York Times*, May 29, 1972, late edition, 3.

Trask, David F. *The United States in the Supreme War Council: American War Aims and Inter-Allied Strategy1917–1918*. Middletown, CT: Wesleyan University Press.

Tupper, Harmon. *To the Great Ocean: Siberia and the Trans-Siberian Railway*. Boston: Little, Brown, 1965.

27th Infantry Regiment. "History of the Twenty-Seventh US Infantry." Schofield Barracks, HI: 27th Infantry Regiment, 1922.

"Two Trophies of Company M." *Bark* vol. 4, no. 6 (February 21, 1930): 5–6.

Unterberger, Betty M. ed. *American Intervention in the Russian Civil War*. Lexington, MA: D. C. Heath, 1969.

———. *America's Siberian Expedition, 1918–1920: A Study of National Policy*. New York: Greenwood, 1969.

US Army. Field Manual 3–07: *Stability Operations*. Washington, DC: US Government Printing Office, 2008.

———. Field Manual 3–24: *Counterinsurgency*. Washington, DC: US Government Printing Office, 2006.

———. TV 612: *The American Expeditionary Forces in Siberia*. Motion picture, Big Picture series, 1964.

US Army Center of Military History. *Lineage and Honors, 31st Infantry*. Fort Lesley J. McNair, Washington, DC.

———. *Lineage and Honors, 27th Infantry*. Fort Lesley J. McNair, Washington, DC. Accessed August 31, 2009, http://www.history.army.mil/html/forcestruc/lineages/branches / inf/0027in.htm.

——. *United States Army in the World War 1917–1919: Organization of the American Expeditionary Forces*. Vol. 1. Washington, DC: US Government Printing Office, 1988.

US Army War College. *Order of Battle of the United States Land Forces in the World War, American Expeditionary Forces*. Washington, DC: US Government Printing Office, 1937.

US Congress, House. Address of President Wilson to the Congress of the United States. House Doc. 765, 65th Cong., 2d sess., January 8, 1918.

———. Hearing. Committee on Military Affairs. Russian Railway Service Corps. House S. 28, 67th Cong., 2d sess., January 17, 1922, p. 26. Retrieved November 8, 2009, from Google Books.

———. Hearing. Committee on Military Affairs. Russian Railway Service Corps. House S. 28, 67th Cong., 2d sess., part 3, February, 9, 1923. Retrieved November 8, 2009, from Google Books.

US Congress, Senate. *American Troops in Siberia*. S. Doc. 60, 66th Cong., 1st sess., 1919.

———. *Loans to Foreign Governments*. S. Doc. 86, 67th Cong., 2d sess., 1921.

———. "The Russian War Mission." In *Visiting War Missions to the United States from*

France, Great Britain, Italy, Russia, Belgium, and Japan. S. Doc. 87, 65th Cong., 1st sess., 1917.

US Department of State. "Aide Memoire," July 17, 1918. National Archives Microfilm Publication M917, Reel 10. National Archives Building, Washington, DC.

———. *Papers Relating to the Foreign Relations of the United States, 1917, Supplement 2, The World War*. Vol. 1. Washington, DC: US Government Printing Office, 1932.

———. *Papers Relating to the Foreign Relations of the United States, 1918, Russia*. Vol. 1. Washington, DC: US Government Printing Office, 1931.

———. *Papers Relating to the Foreign Relations of the United States, 1918, Russia*. Vol. 3. Washington, DC: US Government Printing Office, 1932.

———. *Papers Relating to the Foreign Relations of the United States, 1918, Supplement 1, The World War*. Vol. 1. Washington, DC: US Government Printing Office, 1933.

———. Telegram from Secretary of State to Russian Embassy in Paris, France, October 5, 1918. Posol'stvo (France) Collection, Box 24, Folder 1, Hoover Institution Archives, Stanford University, Stanford, CA.

US War Department. *Basic Weapons, Part One, Rifle Company, Rifle Marksmanship*. Volume 3 of *Basic Field Manual*. Washington, DC: US Government Printing Office, 1932.

———. *Handbook of the Browning Machine Rifle, Model of 1918 (Air Cooled)*. Washington, DC: US Government Printing Office, 1918.

———. *Handbook on Machine Gun Cart Model 1917*. Washington, DC: US Government Printing Office, 1918.

———. *Manual of the Automatic Pistol Caliber .45*. Washington, DC: Government Printing Office, 1918.

———. Memorandum for the Adjutant General, War Department, Washington, DC, August 5, 1918. National Archives Microfilm Publication M917, Reel 1. National Archives Building, Washington, DC.

———. Memorandum for the Chief of Staff, Office of the Chief of Staff, Washington, DC, July 6, 1918, p. 1. National Archives Microfilm Publication M917, Reel 1. National Archives Building, Washington, DC.

———. *Military Monograph on Siberia Containing Information and Route Notes from Vladivostok to Irkutsk*. Washington, DC: Military Intelligence Branch, Executive Division, General Staff, 5 August 1918; Carlisle Barracks, PA: US Army Military History Institute, 17013–5008, Shelf No. 50894, 1974.

———. *Provisional Instruction for the 37mm Gun Model 1916 R.F.* Washington, DC: US Government Printing Office, 1918.

———. *Technical Training Handbook of the Browning Automatic Rifle Model of 1918 (Air Cooled)*. Washington, DC: US Government Printing Office, 1918.

———. Telegram from War Department to Commanding General, 8th Division, Camp Fremont, August 3, 1918, p. 1. National Archives Microfilm Publication M917, Reel 1. National Archives Building, Washington, DC.

———. Telegram from War Department to Commanding General, 8th Division, Camp Fremont, August 6, 1918. National Archives Microfilm Publication M917, Reel 1. National Archives Building, Washington, DC.

Varneck, Elena, and H. H. Fisher, eds. and trans. *The Testimony of Kolchak and Other Siberian Materials*. Stanford, CA: Stanford University Press, 1935.

Ward, John, Colonel. *With the "Die-Hards" in Siberia*. New York: George H. Doran, 1920.

Westall, Virginia C. "AEF Siberia—The Forgotten Army." *Military Review* 48 (March 1968): 11–18.

White, John A. *The Siberian Intervention*. New York: Greenwood Press, 1950.

Willett, Robert L. *Russian Sideshow: America's Undeclared War, 1918–1920*. Washington, DC: Brassey's, 2003.

Williams, William Appleman. "American Intervention: Strictly Anti-Bolshevik." In *America Intervention in the Russian Civil War*, 83–85. Edited by Betty Miller Unterberger. Lexington, MA: DC Heath, 1969.

Wilson, James S., Colonel. "Medical History of the Siberian Expedition," undated, pp. 16–17. National Archives Microfilm Publication M917, Reel 11. National Archives Building, Washington, DC.

York, Dorothea. *The Romance of Company A, 339th Infantry*. Detroit, MI: McIntyre Publishing, 1923.

Index